THE LIFE AND CAREER OF DAVID BECKHAM

THE LIFE AND CAREER OF DAVID BECKHAM

FOOTBALL LEGEND, CULTURAL ICON

Tracey Savell Reavis

**Cuyahoga Falls
Library**
Cuyahoga Falls, Ohio

ROWMAN & LITTLEFIELD
Lanham • Boulder • New York • Toronto • Plymouth, UK

Published by Rowman & Littlefield
4501 Forbes Boulevard, Suite 200, Lanham, Maryland 20706
www.rowman.com

10 Thornbury Road, Plymouth PL6 7PP, United Kingdom

British Library Cataloguing in Publication Information Available

Library of Congress Cataloging-in-Publication Data
Reavis, Tracey Savell.
  The life and career of David Beckham : football legend, cultural icon / Tracey Savell Reavis.
    pages cm
  Includes bibliographical references and index.
  ISBN 978-1-4422-2992-1 (cloth : alk. paper) — ISBN 978-1-4422-2993-8 (ebook)
  1. Beckham, David, 1975– 2. Soccer players—England—Biography. I. Title.
  GV942.7.B432R43 2014
  796.334092—dc23
  [B]   2014006799

♾TM The paper used in this publication meets the minimum requirements of American National Standard for Information Sciences—Permanence of Paper for Printed Library Materials, ANSI/NISO Z39.48-1992. Printed in the United States of America

To my dear mother, Audrey Corina,
to Chris, Cory, and Jordyn, my three loves . . .
and to anyone who struggles with
what seems impossible—keep kicking.

CONTENTS

CONTENTS

ACKNOWLEDGMENTS

I'd like to thank the following folks for their contribution to making this book possible:

Thank you to the staff at Rowman & Littlefield for your dedication to moving this project from idea to published book.

Thank you to my immediate family—Audrey, Lloyd, Tabitha—for being so supportive, not just the past year, but always.

Thank you to my extended family—you know who you are—I know you are in my corner.

Thank you to my treasured friends—Keri, Lily, Lisa, Marcia, Maxine, Milagros, and Shelley—for being my cheerleaders and for taking my late-night phone calls.

Thank you to my savvy research team—Kim Howard, Vicky Ndukwe, Deborah Tague, and Candace Young—the details matter.

Thank you to my NY, DC, and BCN circle of friends—for helping me find community with new faces and in new places.

Thank you to all of my colleagues in the sports and writing communities for your advice and guidance—the lessons have been invaluable.

Thank you to all of my former colleagues at Communities In Schools—for encouraging me and putting up with my daily, David updates.

Thank you to the helpful staff at all of the coffee shops that I worked from in DC, Maryland, and Virginia, and especially the folks at Whole Foods Friendship Heights, Maryland. I am truly, forever grateful for the Wi-Fi and a space to write.

INTRODUCTION

Somewhere in London, there's a young boy practicing kicking a football who hopes to one day grow up to be just like his hero, David Beckham.

The first time I'd ever heard of David Beckham I was sitting with a friend in a pub in Barcelona, Spain. A commercial had come on the TV and I asked, "*Who is that handsome man?*" In my defense, it was 2001, and Beckham's career and celebrity had not reached otherworldly magnitude yet. Plus, as an American, I was caught up in another kind of football, and I had not yet discovered the wonders of the beautiful game.

When I was young, I followed baseball and was a huge New York Yankees fan. I'd watch the games past my bedtime, wear Yankee T-shirts and caps and could recite the lineup and the pitching rotation. I started watching and enjoying other sports shortly after and found my passion. I wasn't interested in becoming an athlete, but I knew sports would be a big part of my life. Having grown up idolizing athletes, it was easy to fall under the spell of footballer David Beckham.

What's not to like? He's handsome, talented on the field, and by all accounts genuinely likeable. He's every kid's, woman's, mother's, athlete's, man's idea of perfection and that adds to the fascination factor that the entire planet seems to have with him.

Now I know all about Beckhamania and the footballer's ginormous global appeal. I was reminded how wide- and far-ranging is his reach with the comments I got from my family when I told them about the book assignment.

My sixty-eight-year-old mother literally stopped mid-sentence to comment on his looks: "Oh, I walked into the living room and this book is lying on the coffee table, and I'm looking right at David. He's just so handsome!"

My twenty-five-year-old gay nephew, after a not-so-subtle swoon: "Of course I know who he is—he's married to Posh Spice. He's gorgeous!"

My sixteen-year-old cousin, who plays girls softball: "That's cool. I always see him on the entertainment shows with his wife. He's really good-looking."

Not one of them follows Beckham's soccer career.

To start the work on the book I thought I'd first get myself on the level of a hard-core fan, and began absorbing all things Beckham. And as there was no shortage of material on the most photographed athlete on the planet, I'd have my fill of material. Then I got down to the research and found "no shortage of material" meant I would have the challenge of a great deal of information to sort through.

What I learned I've shared in the pages that follow. Yes, we all know about what makes headlines: the comings and goings with his wife, Victoria, the former Posh Spice and über-celebrity; the jaw-dropping Beckham-in-only-his-briefs posters; the records and titles the footballer has won with every team he's played for. But there is more to the man. He is a devoted family man, husband, and father. He's proven to be a smart and savvy businessman. And he's taken on the role of global ambassador with diplomacy and compassion. Super sleuthing uncovered little-known tidbits such as Beckham has played his entire career as an asthmatic, he wears glasses, and is a big fan of playing snooker.

As impressive as Beckham's success and wealth are, I also found his values admirable. His never-say-never attitude, his hard work ethic, his commitment to practice. He used his powers for good. Beckham's endless determination, focus, and ability to deal with adversity, major cornerstones that shaped his lengthy career, are life lessons anyone can follow to achieve success.

This book tells the story of David Beckham's singular dedication to becoming a great football player, spanning the life and career of the legendary footballer, from his early years in Leytonstone, London, through his rise to stratospheric fame.

I can't point to one specific reason why everyone seems to love the man, but I sure had fun trying to find out. An athlete and icon like David Beckham comes around only once in a lifetime, and I am overjoyed to be able to write about him.

1

BORN TO BEND IT

I was proud to get the 100th cap and it was also a proud moment to receive something like that from Sir Bobby Charlton.

—David Beckham, May 28, 2008, Wembley Stadium,
London, England.[1]

If England is the birthplace of modern football, its heartbeat for the past ninety years has been booming loudest from Wembley Stadium. It is an iconic symbol of English pride and tradition. A crown jewel in the magnificent London landscape, the original arena was an architectural marvel when it opened in 1923.

The Wembley suburb northwest of London housed the stadium as part of the British Empire Exhibition after the end of World War I. Stepping out from the city's underground rail station on the Jubilee Line, the looming white twin towers immediately caught the eye. The walk along Olympic Way, a path constructed and opened just before the 1948 Olympic Games, was tree lined and bursting with football fans. It carried you directly to the North entrance. On a terrace between the towers was the cauldron that held the flame from the Summer Games, and alongside it was a four-ton bust of Sir Arthur Elvin, the entrepreneur who purchased the stadium and saved it from demise back in 1927. Just below the balcony, were the famous, timber-red gates that led up to the Wembley tunnel and directly onto the hallowed ground.[2]

And inside is where memories and moments enrapture with the rich history of the stadium.

Moments lovingly recalled, like the White Horse final, a Football Association Cup matchup that saw the Bolton Wanderers FC beat West Ham United, 2–0.[3] Or when England, the host nation and national team, captured the country's only World Cup title with a stunning extra-time win in 1966. And when legends Bobby Charlton and George Best powered Manchester United past Benfica of Portugal to win England's first-ever European Cup in 1968.[4] The thrill of Wembley is standing on the sacred pitch, climbing thirty-nine steps from the field to the Royal Box to collect a trophy, listening to the roar of the chants and cheers of a crowd of nearly a hundred thousand.[5]

Wembley Stadium, synonymous with the history of the game itself, is where millions of young boys dared to dream of playing football. Spending countless hours imagining what it would be like to walk where their heroes have walked and to stand on the pitch where champions once stood. And for those living in London and nearby towns, the dream can seem deceptively close enough to achieve. But it is a long way to the gravel and cinder that covered the pitch at Wadham Lodge, not fifteen minutes from where David Beckham, one of those young dreamers, grew up in Chingford, London, England.

David Robert Joseph Beckham was born on May 2, 1975, at Whipps Cross University Hospital in Leytonstone, London, a rural suburb east of London.[6] Tracing David's ancestry back to 1870 finds his paternal great-great-grandfather, William John Beckham, born in St. Saviour, Surrey, England.[7] One hundred years ago, William John's son Edward Charles "Ted" Beckham, made a now historic journey, along a stretch of the Thames River, with a pass under the Tower Bridge. It is thanks to his survival from that ill-fated trip that we have David Beckham today.

THE BOY SCOUTS IN ENGLAND, 1910s

On Saturday, August 3, 1912, the Walworth Boy Scout Troop, from the South East section of London, set sail in a thirty-two-foot cutter from Waterloo Bridge along the Thames, heading east toward the Isle of Sheppey. Three of William John and Harriet Beckham's sons were among the crew of five adults and twenty-four young scouts.[8]

At 4 AM the next day, the troop set off on the final leg of its journey. Two miles away from where they had planned to set up camp, a sudden violent gust of wind hit the mainsail and the boat capsized.

Most of the occupants were thrown into the sea and some of them were washed seaward. The cutter righted itself, but then capsized again. Some of the boys were able to cling to the upturned boat, but a number of them were washed clear. Most of the lads were able to swim, and the men in the party did their best to keep them afloat, but the cutter had capsized in six fathoms of water, and before help could reach them from the shore, a number of them had perished.[9]

Chief Petty Officer Streeter of the Coastguard arrived to a horrific scene. Boys were in the icy cold water crying out for help and Scoutmaster Marsh was on the point of drowning. Marsh was rescued, but immediately plunged back in again to save a drowning boy, then another. The lifeboat rescued twenty, including Marsh, but they were not able to recover any others or bodies not visible at this time, for there was a strong tide. Due to several acts of selfless heroism, especially by their Scoutmaster Sydney Marsh, many lives were saved. But eight scouts and Frank Masters from the training ship *Arethusa* had drowned. Had the lifeboat been ten minutes later, the loss of life would have been much greater.[10]

The news from London left the country grieving with a huge national outpouring. Winston Churchill, then first lord of the admiralty, ordered the boys' bodies to be brought back by naval warship. A mass funeral followed, with the eight coffins draped in the Union Flag, and an estimated one million mourners present. Scout patrol leader William Beckham, one of the eight boys who drowned in the accident, had two brothers in the boat whose lives had been saved. William's mother told a reporter that she owed their lives to Scoutmaster Marsh to whom she would be eternally grateful. David Beckham's great-great-grandmother Harriet said: "No blame should be attached to Scoutmaster Marsh who did all that was humanly possible."[11] The younger Beckham brothers, John and Ted, survived. Ted, who went on to join the Royal Navy, eventually rising to become Chief Petty Officer, is believed to be the football legend's great-grandfather.

Edward Charles "Ted" Beckham and Queenie Violet Eldridge were parents to Aubrey Edward Jack "Ted," who was also a seaman like his father.[12] While many football clubs in England had been founded by the mid- to late 1800s—Manchester United started in 1878—there is no known record of what team David's great-grandparents supported. His maternal grandparents, porter Joseph West and dressmaker Margaret Jean Wiggins, leaned decidedly toward Tottenham. When their daughter, Sandra Georgina, married David's dad, David Edward Alan 'Ted' Beckham, theirs was a Man United household.

Is this the evidence that young David was destined for football?

YOU ARE HERE: CHINGFORD, LONDON, ENGLAND

Ted and Sandra's only son, David, was the middle child, born between first daughter Lynne, and Joanne, the youngest. For a while the Beckhams lived in a Victorian three-bedroom terraced house at 155 Norman Road, Leytonstone, in East London.[13] But the family moved when David was still young to the even leafier suburb of Chingford, ten miles from downtown London.[14] The town was already known in the modern era from the murals painted in the rail stations that honored the city's most famous native, filmmaker Alfred Hitchcock.

Excavated tin pots and coins provide evidence that, as with many parts of this country, the Romans had once occupied Chingford. In 1086, settlers had oxen plowing the fields and sheep grazing the acres of pasture in the district. The clay soil in the area also accounted for pottery, tile, and brick manufacturing, as these industries were recorded in historic documents around the fourteenth and fifteenth centuries. By the late 1800s, farmsteaders turned to dairy farming.[15]

But the landscape of Chingford was about to change dramatically, and usher in the modern version that is known today.

David Young, president of the Chingford Historical Society:

> Chingford was quite a small village in 1086, and it remained fairly small for several hundred years and did not really expand till the railway was built in 1882 from London, Liverpool Street station to Chingford. Then many folks living in the crowded East End of London came to live in new estates built around the railway terminus and were given cheap "workman's" fares to commute to their jobs in the City. Chingford offered a pleasant place to live bordering on Epping Forest, which had been bought and maintained by the City to give free open access to the people of London.[16]

From 1800 to 1860 there were less than 20,000 people in Chingford. Thanks to the railroad, by 1950 that number had rocketed to 50,000. The Epping Forest Act of 1878 not only assisted in preserving the forest but also helped develop the towns around it: Chingford, Walthamstow, and Leyton. The location between the city of London and Epping Forest encouraged the large-scale urban development of much of the borough.[17]

Chingford is also known for a number of historic landmarks. Queen Elizabeth's Hunting Lodge, built in 1543 for King Henry VIII, was used as a grandstand for watching royal hunts. The Tudor-style property, which sits on the southern edge of Epping Forest, was fully restored in 1899–1900 and is open to the public today. There's the All Saints Church, on Old Church Road, which dates back to the twelfth century. Chingford is also famous for being on the Meridian line. The Royal Observatory in Greenwich erected the Pole Hill Obelisk in 1824 to mark the 0 degree line of longitude that passes through the city.[18]

In 1975, the year David Beckham was born, the town was largely considered a residential favorite for families, with its wide-open green spaces. David Bowie, the Bee Gees, and Rod Stewart occupied the top of the pop charts that year, and West Germany had just won the country's first World Cup trophy in 1974.[19] Housing prices hovered around $60,000. Everyone was playing Pac-Man, which is why the video game eventually earned a place in the Smithsonian. *Looking for Mr. Goodbar* was on the *New York Times* bestseller list.[20]

Within five years, England would be pitched into a recession. Unemployment levels rose steadily, while wages remained stagnant.[21] A liter of gas cost 16p, a loaf of bread 9½ and a pint of beer 11.[22] The mood of the nation was slightly less than optimistic. Great Britain lost filmmaker Alfred Hitchcock and the Beatles' John Lennon. In the sports world, future English football players John Terry, Steve Gerrard, and Ashley Cole were all born in 1980.

This is the era in which the early years of David Beckham's life were molded.

ABOUT A BOY

Beckham's Chingford childhood was filled with family and school events, but football seemed to always be at the center. By the time he was seven years old, David Beckham already had years of football under his belt. David first attended the Chase Lane Primary School. He played football at this school. He remembers his coach, Mr. McGhee, as being a disciplinarian but had fond memories. Beckham moved on to the Chingford Foundation School and continued playing football.[23]

In a 2007 interview, Beckham said, "At school whenever the teachers asked, 'What do you want to do when you're older?' I'd say, 'I want to be a footballer.' And they'd say, 'No, what do you really want to do, for a job?' But that was the only thing I ever wanted to do."[24] He also attended his first soccer academy about this time, the Roger Morgan Soccer School, started by the former Tottenham Spurs winger.

When he finally arrived at Chingford High, Beckham found himself at a school without a football team. He recalls that the rugby coach, Mr. John Bullock, was amiable and he and his schoolmates were able to talk the coach into creating a football team. The new squad played well together, earning wins in cups and leagues. At school Beckham enjoyed art, drawing cartoon characters when he could. He was on the school's swimming and cross-country teams, and won a championship in the latter.

While at Chingford High, Beckham played on teams that represented the Waltham Forest district and Essex County. And when he was thirteen he went with his Essex team to play in a tournament in Texas, his first trip to the United States.[25]

School took up Beckham's days, passing time until he could get back to football.

Like many boys born into football-obsessed England, Beckham was introduced to the game at an early age. On many different occasions he has remarked on spending time in his family's back garden, kicking a soccer ball with his father. While Chingford owes its existence in large part to Epping Forest, it is ironically several neighboring parks and green spaces where David Beckham practiced while he was young.

He regularly played football in Ridgeway Park, a public park not far from the Chingford Foundation School on Nevin Drive. Ridgeway was home to a miniature railway, and hosted the annual Chingford Day celebration. Cartoonist Walt Disney attended the 1954 event and took a ride on the famous railway. On weekends, Beckham would often be found playing in London's Victoria Park.

Beckham has always credited the support he got from his family growing up. His mother was a true "Soccer Mom," scheduling time to drive him to practices and weekend matches, and making football a family activity. It helped that his parents were big fans of the sport and that making time for the game was something they equally enjoyed.

David revealed that his parents were devoted Manchester United fans, and his grandfather was a huge supporter of Tottenham Hotspur. In personal photos found in books and online, Beckham is often pictured wearing a Manchester United outfit. When he was young, his Christmas present every year was a football uniform from both Tottenham and Manchester. And when he wasn't playing football in the park or in school, there were trips to the stadium to watch live matches.

Beckham's grandfather was a huge follower of Tottenham Hotspur and took David to see the team at the club's ground in the northwest of London. White Hart Lane, which opened in 1899, has hosted the England national team as well as the Football Association's Cup matches. Beckham wasn't just a fan in the stands at the Lane. He actually played games on the pitch as a youth.

Perhaps the ultimate way to experience a live football game in England is a visit to Wembley Stadium. Beckham and his father made many trips during the late '80s and the football star fondly recalled how exciting it was to take in the venue's football atmosphere. Though the famed facility had a historic pedigree, young David was likely only aware that he was spending a day with his Dad at a cool stadium and getting to imagine himself one day playing football out on that field.

But even as spectacular as those memories of visits to Wembley were, David also treasured the frequent trips he made with his parents north of London to see the Manchester United Red Devils. The team played their home matches on the grounds of Old Trafford, a compound that seated well over seventy thousand, the second-largest football stadium in the United Kingdom after Wembley.

David's father was part of the United faithful, supporters who proudly backed their team. This passion, obsession, lifestyle, was passed on to his son, who became equally impressed with the Reds. Beckham was enraptured with all things Manchester United. And perhaps it was on one of the trips to see a game where the idea of actually growing up to play for them first occurred to him. With the players the club had, and the history, how could he *not*? David Beckham loved football the sport, but was equally in love with the notion of one day playing for the Red Devils. It became his life's dream.

CHASE LANE PARK

There were days when the young Beckham would cut through an alley near his house and head toward nearby Chase Lane Park to play with other neighborhood boys.

But it was David's father who had the most influence in his early football development. The elder Beckham nurtured this talent by working with David and honing his skills hour after hour, night after night at Chase Lane Park. Ted Beckham:

> I can't say how much is down to me. I'm just part of a big cog that's helped him to get where he is today. I was probably the big cog at the beginning but there's been other cogs since.
>
> We'd go over to the park all the time for a kick-around. I'd get one side of the goal and David the other and we'd try to chip the ball and hit the crossbar. I'd probably get it once in about 20 shots but he would hit it about 12 or 14 times. That's how good he was as a boy.[26]

BENDING IT LIKE BECKHAM

Beckham's time in the parks as a youngster helped him learn, practice, and master a crucial element in the offensive arsenal of playmakers of soccer—the free kick.

A significant scoring tactic in football, and an excellent skill to possess, free kicks are defined as such: An unobstructed kick of a stationary ball awarded for an infringement by an opposing player. Free kicks are most commonly awarded for fouls, handballs, or off-sides.

For decades, free-kick specialists have entertained with their talent for out-foxing both the wall and goalkeepers. Historically there has been the king, Pelé, the all-time leader in goals scored, his fellow Brazilian Zico, and France's Michel Platini. Add to this group today's free-kick artists, Cristiano Ronaldo and Lionel Messi.[27]

And then there is David Beckham, and his infamous bend. Chipping in the park with his father helped him learn the technique. His admirable work ethic meant he was willing to put in the time needed to develop what would be the most effective method. He practiced it, day after day, session after session, year after year. And he perfected it.

In 2012, students from the University of Leicester, England, Department of Physics and Astronomy, published a paper outlining a formula they devised that explained the Beckham bend. And their formula was based on Magnus force; that is, when a football spins in the air, it is subjected to a force called the Magnus force. This makes it curl sideways from the direction it was originally kicked.[28] Matt Carré, director of the sports engineering research group at the University of Sheffield, England:

> What we found is that [Beckham] kicks to one side of the ball to give it some sidespin and make it curve, but he's able to effectively wrap his foot around it to also give it some topspin to go up and down. He's very unique in the way he's able to caress the ball with his foot. It's almost like he's stroking the ball in the way a tennis player would.[29]

Today, thanks to science and math, and formulas that involve the physics of velocity and wind and gravity, a football player can use his body and foot to create the kick and curve that will leave his team's fans screaming with joy. Beckham would entertain a generation of football fans for years with the spectacular goals he scored with his signature free-kick, which he first learned in the parks and pitches of his youth in Chingford, London, England.

GET UP AND GET ON WITH IT

In 1982, a skinny seven-year-old David Beckham took his first steps toward training for a career as a professional football player. His father's semipro club team, Kingfisher, in the Forest and District League, played and trained at nearby Wadham Lodge, and the son began accompanying him to the team's games during the week. When Kingfisher held practice, David would sometimes join them for five-a-sides.

Here, on the gravel and cinder pitch, Beckham ran and passed and kicked it with adult players three times his age and twice his size. The kid took his hits then, and later acknowledged the importance of the experience. He attributes his time going up against bigger and stronger athletes, and his father's words, "Get up and get on with it,"[30] whenever he was knocked down, as keys that helped him eventually develop into a better player.

Wadham is also where Beckham practiced taking free kicks. He stayed after the older players were done and took shot after shot, kicking a dead ball into the box. He was after accuracy. As an added incentive, he got a reward from his father whenever he hit the bar. Beckham's first steps at perfecting what would ultimately become the signature move of his career were first taken on a practice pitch in Chingford. And it was enough to impress.

The world did not know him yet, but the father recognized the talent in his son. He ended his own playing career to focus on coaching David into greatness. An advertisement announcing that a youth club team was starting provided the perfect launching ground.

EDUCATING DAVID

The man many came to affectionately call "Sarge," because of his no-nonsense approach to football training and discipline, is largely credited for helping a young David Beckham develop the skills that would form the foundation of his football career. Stuart Underwood, who by day worked as a manufacturing manager, decided to place an advertisement in the *Walthamstow Guardian* newspaper announcing a tryout for players for an under-eight youth team. Forty-three reportedly showed up, and the final, eighteen-member squad included the eight-year-old David Beckham.[31]

The Ridgeway Rovers, managed by Underwood and assistant coaches Steve Kirby and David's father Ted, learned football skills as well as teamwork and sportsmanship. On weekdays the kids practiced basic skills that are typically taught to youngsters—footwork; dribbling, passing, shooting. They learned offensive strategies and defensive tactics and the fundamentals of the game. According to Beckham, each coach brought something different to the team, making sure each of the kids learned both technical and tactical skills.

Underwood as the team manager is credited with teaching the boys discipline and was the drillmaster of the three coaches. Beckham himself recalls that the coach encouraged the youngsters to dress smartly for important games. But Underwood was also the coach that made sure the boys had fun and got to enjoy the experience of playing the game.

The three-pronged coaching program worked for developing the youths, and the Ridgeway Rovers F.C. represented the Enfield and District League, as well as Middlesex County honorably. They club won several titles and cups and a buzz began to build about the talented squad.

A 1987 program states the club won the Middlesex County F.A. Cup Under-10 and Under-11 titles.[32]

News articles, perhaps fueled by local lore, or vice versa, have credited the team with such accolades as winning seventy-eight consecutive games. And it has been reported in numerous places that Beckham himself had scored 100 goals by the time he was eight years old.[33]

There is a photo of David Beckham at eleven years old holding an Under-12 Cup trophy the Rovers won in the 1986 season.

Legend or embellished tale, fact or fiction, it didn't take long to separate the talent from those who were just playing games.

In 1998 Underwood remarked on what he saw as something special early on in Beckham:

> David looked a professional from day one. Even at eight he could hit the ball from every corner of the pitch. His timing was incredible. He could strike the ball like a rocket—from any distance. He was a slight boy and I feared he wasn't going to be strong enough—but his skills won through. I knew David would make it. He was always out there training. He was so dedicated even then.[34]

Underwood's coaching prowess propelled more than just the career of David Beckham. On that same Rovers team of thirty years ago were four additional athletes who would turn pro: Watford's Chris Day and Micah Hyde, and Bournemouth's Jason Brisset and Ryan Kirby, formerly of Northampton.

The Ridgeway Rovers football club still fields youth teams today, at the Parmiters Sports Ground in Chingford. David Beckham has since been named an honorary life president of the club. Ian Marshall, Ridgeway Rovers chairman:

David would always be welcome to visit us at Ridgeway Rovers. We're very proud that he started here. We're honored. His legacy is that we still get kids saying they want to play for us because of Beckham. He still inspires kids to want to play so it's very positive. We're very grateful for that association and his history is our history.[35]

IN THE ACADEMY NOW

David Beckham's foundation in football would include enrolling in the Bobby Charlton Soccer and Sports Academy, a residential training facility started by its namesake in Manchester.

Bobby Charlton, known for his graceful movement, range of passing, and strong goal attempts, is one of a handful who survived a plane disaster in 1958 that killed eight Manchester United players. Physically injured and emotionally bruised, Charlton returned to the game he loved the season following the tragedy. He helped the Red Devils win the league title in 1965 and 1967, and was a critical part of the offense in England's first, and only, 4–2 World Cup victory over West Germany in 1966. The United great, who ended his illustrious career with 109 caps and forty-nine goals for England, was knighted in 1994.[36]

The Bobby Charlton Soccer Schools and Academy website proudly reports about Beckham's success at the school. Bryn Cooper, a UEFA "A" Licensed Coach, and who was director of the school's courses during the time Beckham was there, had this to say about the footballer: "In addition to his natural ability, David displayed a fantastic work ethic and a great deal of determination, which meant he was continually practicing his individual skills. It was clearly evident to the coaches at Bobby Charlton Soccer Schools that David was completely focused on becoming a professional footballer."[37]

Beckham attended the soccer school at age ten, and says he felt both "lost" and "homesick" at times during his first summer away from his family.[38]

Beckham's second summer at the school seemed to have gone remarkably better. To his delight, there were daily soccer drills and endless hours of practice. By the end, he had advanced to a skills competition. He won the first part—ball-juggling, target shooting, and short passing, which was held in the indoor sports hall of the Cliff, Manchester United's old training ground. For the second stage, days later, Beckham found himself on the pitch at Old Trafford, where the long passing and dribbling part of the competition was staged before forty thousand fans who had seen United play Tottenham. And David Beckham, the United fan from Leytonstone, won![39]

The youngster and his parents then got to meet United legend Charlton, as he made the presentation to the winners in the Europa Suite of the stadium. And the first-place prize for winning the Bobby Charlton Soccer Skills challenge was a two-week trip to Barcelona, Spain. Beckham would not only get to watch FC Barcelona's training sessions, but the eleven-year-old would have his first brush participating in practice with professional football players.

FÚTBOL

The motto of Fútbol Club Barcelona, "more than a club," summarizes the direct connection between the team and the culture of the city in Spain. Founded in 1899, from responses to a newspaper advertisement, the century-old organization has a winning history that includes clashes with rival Real Madrid; struggles to maintain their regional traditions; surviving the Spanish Civil War; and a long string of championships—Copa del Rey, the *Union of European Football Associations* (UEFA) Champions League crowns, and Spanish top tier La Liga titles.[40]

Beckham's journey to the Catalan capital, with its historic landmarks, like the Sagrada Familia and the Castell de Monjuic, took place in the first part of 1987. He was joined by two other boys who'd also won a trip and Ray Whelan from the Bobby Charlton Soccer and Sports Academy. Housing was Barca's youth training compound, a place called La Masia, decorated with pennants and club memorabilia that traced the team's history. The facility, an old Catalan farmhouse built in 1702, was originally used as a workshop for the architects of the nearby Camp Nou stadium. In 1979, the club converted it into a residence for developing young players.[41] Barca focused on molding footballers as young as twelve and thirteen years old, to play for their first team, and would eventually build the reputation it has today, as one of the most productive youth academies in the world.

During a full two weeks, Beckham was surrounded by fútbol. Every day the young boys went out with Barca's youth and reserve teams to train at the latter's 15,000-seat stadium. He described the experience as amazing, including the first time he was taken through the dressing rooms, through the tunnel and onto the Camp Nou field where Barca played.

The experience made an impression on the young David:

De pequeño, Beckham había pisado ya los campos culés, cuando en la escuela de fútbol de Bobby Charlton, ganó una promoción para entrenar con las promesas de La Masia del Barcelona durante dos semanas. Ahí, Becks se enamoró del equipo culé y deseaba fervientemente que el Club le pusiera los colores azulgranas, pero eso no sucedió y en tono de rabia, cuando abandonó la ciudad condal dijo: "Algún día volveré al Barça."

When he was young, Beckham won a training session with FC Barcelona as a prize from the Bobby Charlton Soccer Academy of a two-week trip to the team youth facility. There Beckham fell in love with the team and wanted desperately to wear the Catalan club's blue and red kit. But that did not happen, and when he left Barcelona, a despondent Beckham said: "Someday I'll be back."[42]

A photo with Beckham, Steve Archibald, Mark Hughes, Gary Linekar, and three of the Bobby Charlton School skills prize winners is available on the Internet, and one photo with Beckham and Terry Venables even made it into the photo collection section of his autobiography, *Both Feet on the Ground*.

As impressed as Beckham was with the Catalan football club, the team's then manager, Terry Venables, was equally impressed with the youngster. Venables:

I knew from the first time I saw him that David Beckham would be something special. The way he looked, the way he played and the way he conducted himself on the training pitch around international stars.

Becks, then 10, came over to our training ground as part of his prize for winning a competition run by Bobby's soccer school. He had apparently been his star pupil in the half-term and summer holidays training camp—and when he arrived at our training base it was not difficult to see why.

A quiet lad, we showed him around and posed for the usual photos. Then he watched us train and we invited him to take part in a couple of sessions. Blimey. He raised a few eyebrows that day.

I must have watched thousands of kids in my time but as we said goodbye I made sure I would not forget his name.[43]

THE BOY SCOUTED IN ENGLAND, 1990s

If football managers watched thousands of kids, football scouts must watch millions.

The life of a part time English football scout conjures up images of a track-suited gym teacher, peering from the sidelines of a match or looking over a pitch from the stands, hunched over clip boards and pens and note-filled sheets of paper. They are dispatched to neighborhoods big and small, and to games on grass, dirt, or gravel pitches, all around England. Their job for their club comes down to one simple task—spot and snap up the next big star.

Recruiters log hours and hours watching youth matches and tournaments and cups, scouting, analyzing and looking to recognize potential. Their big get can net a club with the chance to improve and earn barrels of money. Most clubs have a network of recruiters, not only crisscrossing their country, but often traveling farther for a glimpse at a talented young prospect. Assessing a youth's ability includes everything from their playing style, to their areas of physical and mental strength and what concerns they might have about the player. The former Chelsea FC chief scout Gwyn Williams is reported to have used a database filled with the names of as many as 77,000 athletes.[44]

The recruiting process starts early. At Manchester United, that means scouting players as young as nine years old.

Geoff Watson, a one-time chief recruitment officer for Manchester United, relied on several factors when scouting youth talent. His list includes technique, pace, movement, temperament, and finally the X-Factor:

> If you've seen pace, technique and movement, the final piece of the jigsaw is temperament. Will they be able to handle playing in front of 75,000 people at Old Trafford? I'm looking for boys who are in control as well as ones who don't mind getting wet and muddy!
>
> Temperament is a tricky one for a scout. Ideally you don't want a boy who loses it on the pitch, but plenty of temperamental players have made great footballers. If he's got the ability, you have to go with your gut feeling.
>
> So, you might have sat through a thousand games before you find a boy who's got all that, but the hard work is only the beginning. You don't really know what you've got on your hands until you've brought him into the club for a trial and got him playing with boys of a similar standard. At United, we sign our first boys into the academy at nine, although we continue to scout all levels of football for the ones who may have slipped through the net. Scouting is not an exact science. You can never be sure whether a player will be good enough to play for United in a few years' time. But when a player you spotted out on a freezing cold pitch in the middle of nowhere runs out of the Old Trafford tunnel in a United shirt, now that's a great feeling. It makes all those hours of standing in the freezing cold worthwhile. That's what gives the scout a real sense of achievement, something to be proud of.[45]

Roger Skyrme, a scout with Fulham FC:

> It doesn't take a scout to pick out the best player on a pitch. Anyone can spot raw talent, but I'm looking for more than that. A player must have the right attitude. It's ultracompetitive out there, and very few players make it at the top level. To succeed, you've got to have something special in your make-up that will help you rise above the rest.[46]

THANKS, BUT NO THANKS

When Beckham returned from Barcelona, his name and game began to attract the attention of a lot of scouts. With the success of the Rovers, he and his teammates had long been accustomed to seeing recruiters regularly attend their matches. Beckham's skills caught the eye of scouts from West Ham, Wimbledon, Arsenal, and Tottenham.

One by one the offers came. From clubs with deep fan bases in and around London. From clubs with history and tradition, who desire to snag the next great football player from England. And one by one, Beckham turned all of the offers down.

Norwich City was impressed with Beckham both on and off the ball. He spent a week with the Canaries as a youth. Kit Carson, manager, Norwich City Canaries:

> He stood out largely because of his personality. The other lads had come for a bit of fun and something different. They were not really interested in lessons we gave them on professionalism, diet, tactics and the psychology of football. They enjoyed games but not coaching sessions.
>
> David was totally different. We all thought he was a brilliant person and polite and thoughtful as well as highly professional. He was always clean and smart on and off the ball and asked questions and listened. At the end of the week I knew that David was exactly the type of boy we wanted in our very successful youth policy at Norwich City.[47]

Wimbledon approached Beckham too, and also got the answer they did not want to hear. Things looked brighter for Tottenham Hotspur, club favorite of Beckham's Granddad Joe. At least in the beginning. Trips to White Hart Lane with his family meant David already had a familiarity with the team. He had enrolled in the club's school of excellence.

Beckham explained that he enjoyed the years of training with Tottenham, and that he'd had a good relationship with youth development officer John Moncur. An added advantage to joining the team was that White Hart Lane, home of the Spurs, was located in London. He'd be close to home and his family could come see his matches. When Spurs management expressed interest in signing Beckham, the young man accepted the invitation to at least hear the offer.

Moncur's reports and recommendations came as no surprise to new Spurs manager Terry Venables. Two years earlier the former FC Barcelona skipper had witnessed up close the talents of Beckham when he'd made his trip to Spain. Venables vowed then he would not forget Beckham's name. His father,

Fred, ran a pub in Chingford, Beckham's hometown, and Venables had asked him to report any news on the youngster's progress.

Venables says that on the day the Beckhams arrived in his office in 1988, the signing-on forms were waiting on his desk.[48]

Unfortunately, even after offering a deal, Venables and Tottenham received the same reply as the other clubs that had coveted the talented young footballer—"Thanks, but no thanks."

David Beckham had dreams of playing for only one team.

EYES ON THE PRIZE

The recruiter that interested David Beckham the most was the man in the brown Ford Sierra, Malcolm Fidgeon. By day, he was a principal at a school in a town in Essex, England. His love of football filled his time away from school as he was also Manchester United's London scout. Fidgeon tracked the progress of the young prospect in matches he played in with the Ridgeway Rovers and with his District and County teams, keeping tabs on him as he continued to develop. After one match, Fidgeon approached Beckham's mother to express the club's interest. Later the recruiter paid a visit to the Beckhams' home in Chingford. And the good news he'd brought on his visit was an offer on behalf of Manchester United, to train with the legendary football club. Malcolm Fidgeon:

> He [David] was very frail and tiny, but he could do things the other boys couldn't and I thought he wouldn't disgrace himself if he was given the opportunity of a United trial.[49]

The trial with Manchester United consisted of Fidgeon driving David from Leytonstone to the team's training facility in Manchester. Beckham described short stays there, from a few days to a week, mostly during his school holidays and summer breaks. The routine was playing and talking about soccer, morning until night. David loved the routine and everything about Manchester United.

IMPOSSIBLE IS NOTHING

There was cake. This was a celebration after all.

It was May 9, 1988. Manchester United were home at Old Trafford hosting Wimbledon. And it was a week after the thirteenth birthday of the young and promising football prospect David Beckham.

Beckham had arrived with his mother and father to the stadium at the invitation of the club. They had lunch in the same area that the first-team players had their pre-match meal, and David was presented with a red club tie he proudly wore for the rest of the day. But it was after the game, when Beckham and his family headed to the office of United manager Alex Ferguson, that would be a crucial first step in launching David's football career.

The meeting between Alex Ferguson and David Beckham that took place in 1988 was only two years into the manager's term at Manchester United. But the soccer tactician was already making his presence felt, making decisions and setting standards for the next generation of United players.

Alex Ferguson's career as a football player included an impressive eleven years as a forward for a handful of teams in his native Glasgow, Scotland. His first stint at management came at the ripe old age of thirty-two, when he was appointed part-time skipper of East Shirlington. Within a year's time, he'd be invited to take the reins at St. Mirren, a post he held for four years. In that span, he lifted the team from second to first division. From there Ferguson moved to Aberdeen, where, in a seven-year period, he guided them to several titles including three league titles in Scotland and four Scottish FA Cup titles.[50]

As a football manager, his reputation as a winner was growing. He was a motivator with the highest of standards. His players and teams succeeded because they met the disciplinarian challenges he set. In November 1989, when they saw the opportunity, the directors at Manchester United unanimously appointed Alex Ferguson as new manager of the club.[51] Martin Edwards, Manchester United club chairman:

> It was fairly unanimous early on that he was the man we really wanted. Well, really what he had achieved in Scottish football. To take on the might of Celtic and Rangers in Scotland with Aberdeen and to win the amount of Championships and Scottish FA Cups that he did, and of course the success he had in taking Aberdeen to the Cup Winners' Cup final, particularly beating Real Madrid in the final, he had the pedigree. He was young, he was enthusiastic, he had tremendous achievements north of the border and we just felt that he was the right man to take us forward.[52]

On the job, Ferguson set about comprehensively rebuilding the club rule by rule, player by player. In his first season with United, he guided the team to eleventh place, up from twenty-first, second to last, in the league a season before. But despite some key strategic signings in his second year and intentions to shore up the fitness level of the current squad, the club had not made much progress by the time a young recruit named David Beckham was being considered for the academy.

These two lives—one a promising footballer, and the other a promising manager—would shape the destiny of Manchester United for decades to come.

David Beckham often refers to the environment at United as being about family. Even years into his career, Beckham has said he felt Ferguson knew him, had his best interest at hand, and he trusted the manager. Beckham:

> When I first went to Old Trafford as a young boy, you had the feeling straight away of it being a family club with a welcoming atmosphere. It was a big family. That's the reason I wanted to play for Manchester United.[53]

Inside the United manager's office, a young David was accompanied by his parents as well as the London scout, Malcolm Fidgeon. This was the moment he'd been dreaming of for years. To have a chance to be part of a club he'd loved all his life. He'd heard stories about the players of his father's generation, like legends George Best and Bobby Charlton and Denis Law. He knew all about the Busby's Babes greats, the European Cup at Wembley, and the Munich Air Disaster. His own heroes included Gordon Strachan, Mark Hughes, and Bryan Robson. Manchester's history was Beckham's bible and United red coursed through his veins. All of his practices, all of his hard work and dedication—everything came down to this moment, in Alex Ferguson's office.

In the spring of 1988, the Manchester United Football Club offered thirteen-year-old David Beckham a six-year deal to become a member of their organization.

It didn't take the elated teenager long to respond.

"I want to sign."[54]

2

BECOMING A MAN UNITED FOOTBALLER

The view from the second-floor bedroom was a football player's paradise. A lush grass pitch that seemed to stretch for miles, framed by posts that had surely netted the goals of legends, and a sign overlooking the field that read, "Manchester United Football Club—The Cliff Training Ground." It was an awe-inspiring sight for David Beckham, the newest member of the club's famed youth academy.

Home away from home for young David was on Lower Broughton Road, Salford, Greater Manchester. It was the house of United supporters Annie and Tommy Kay, one of many families who regularly opened their homes to host young players in the training academy. There had been weekend tournaments and summer football camps and even trips to other countries all throughout his life so he was no stranger to travel. But traveling was different from moving, and this would be the first time Beckham would live away from his parent's home. He was sixteen years old.

Beckham described landlords Annie and Tommy as a "second mum and dad." They treated him and the other boys as if they were part of their family. Beckham first shared a room with Craig Dean, a highly regarded prospect for Man United. Then he was given a larger bedroom on the second floor. It was just a standard bedroom with room for the basic essentials—a double bed, a chest of drawers, and an armoire. But this bedroom had a history. It was the same room that United player Mark Hughes occupied when he was an academy trainee. Hughes was a hero of Beckham's and he'd had a chance to meet him on the two-week trip he'd won to Spain when Hughes was playing for FC Barcelona. The house was so close to the Manchester training ground that Beckham's view from his bedroom window looked out over the playing fields.[1] It was a daily reminder of the goal he wanted to reach—playing football for Manchester United.

This was David's job now, training to become a professional football player. The young athlete's daily routine began by heading to United's training ground, where there was practice and workout sessions in the morning and afternoon. Once settled he focused all of his energy on football, improving his skills and eventually becoming a pro. Annie Kay:

> When David first came down, I never thought this could be the future England captain.[2] I didn't think he was anything special really. Until a little later on. Maybe when he was about 18 or 19. He was constant then. Then different people wanted to photograph him, Can we come into the house and photograph his bedroom? He did always practice his autograph. All the footballers do that, for when they get famous.[3]

The culture of football that surrounded and nurtured Beckham as a child, was even more impressed upon him as the fresh-faced youngster embarked on the road as a trainee in the Manchester United Football Club's Academy and Reserves.

PARDON THE INTERRUPTION

Life back in London for the teen David Beckham meant doing everything he could to prepare himself for training with Man United. He continued for the next few years as a member of the Ridgeway Rovers team he'd joined as a kid. The youth club had changed its name to the Brimsdown Rovers, but the coaching staff as well as the quality of play remained the same. Beckham's work ethic and discipline for practice hadn't changed either. In 1990, Beckham was named the Rovers' Under-15 player of the year.

In his final years as a Chingford High School student Beckham not only played football, but the athletically gifted teen dabbled in other sports. He was on the school's swimming team and was a member of the cross-country squad. Beckham also played on youth football clubs that represented the Waltham Forest district and Essex County. Beckham credits both of his coaches, Don Wiltshire and Martin Heather, with further developing his football skills.[4] He continued to absorb lessons and structure, building an expansive foundation that would serve him well throughout his career.

With his Essex team coach, Martin Heather, Beckham made his first trip to the United States, to Texas, and the youngster enjoyed his time there so much he claimed he wasn't even homesick. David participated in a soccer tournament called the Dallas Cup, the oldest international youth soccer tournament in the United States. The invitation-only event is held every spring during Easter Week.[5] Beckham spent a week soaking up American culture, complete with McDonald's and pick-up trucks. The thirteen-year-old participated in the tournament's home stay program and lodged with a family whose son also played football, and had a memorable adventure. The family remembered their experience hosting the future megastar, whom they called "Davey." Steve Alcala hosted Beckham when he was in Dallas: "He was just a quiet, polite kid. He enjoyed all the boys in the neighborhood. He was just a kid excited to be in America and experiencing the Dallas Cup."[6]

David's youth squad did not win the tournament's coveted Boot and Ball championship trophy.

While Beckham was pursuing his football dream of playing for Manchester United, he found part-time work one summer at the Walthamstow Stadium. The venue was a dog race track that opened in 1933 in London's East End. Beckham was hired to work in the restaurant and lounge on weeknights, and earned a reported £10-a-night picking up glasses from the tables. It was the youngster's first foray into earning a paycheck.[7] In a handwritten note from 1991 that was sold at auction years later for about $2,000, Beckham revealed to a friend his salary. The letter gave a glimpse at the future pro footballer paying close attention to his finances: "I got my first wage packet the other day and a bonus which came to £120 so that went in my bank and I have got about £250 in there now."[8]

Walthamstow Stadium was where Winston Churchill made an election speech in 1945, and was the venue where Brad Pitt filmed parts of the movie "Snatch." The historic track closed down in 2008.

Work did not distract Beckham from practicing football and reaching his goals. And the better Beckham's skills became, the more attention he drew to himself. He was already pretty well known locally and then in the early 1990s, the talented teen had a chance to make an impression that could shape his future national career.

Beckham's footwork caught the eye of scouts and coaches around the country, and when he was sixteen he was invited for trials to attend the Football Association's School of Excellence. Launched in 1984, the program was essentially created as a center of excellence for training and developing youth players who could then go on to shine for England.[9] Lilleshall Hall in Shropshire, southwest of Manchester, housed the school and young trainees.[10] When Beckham arrived as a not-quite-developed sixteen-year-old, the coaches felt he was too small and he did not make the cut. But for Beckham, the dismissal by the FA's School of Excellence was only a small speed bump along the road to attending the football academy he'd always dreamed of.[11]

MADCHESTER UNITED

Pick one, any one. There's the Trafford, the unofficial team pub. Season ticket holders make the trek to Bishop Blaize, right off Sir Matt Busby Way. Or, there's the Lass O' Gowrie, one of Manchester's many historic pubs. Bursting with United flags and scarves and Red Devil trinkets, doohickeys and knickknacks, packed with passionate United supporters, the watering holes around Manchester city center are the places to be to take in a friendly atmosphere and watch televised Reds matches. In "Madchester" the fan base for United runs deep and wide.

From its humble beginnings, first as Newton Heath LYR Football Club in 1878, to eventually becoming Manchester United in 1902, the club has enjoyed a loyal and devoted following. Through the team's lows—the Munich Air tragedy shortly after World War II, to the highs, the league championship teams of the 1950s and 1960s, the club's fans have stayed true. When the club came up with the idea to recruit families in Manchester to provide housing for youth players who were in the United training academy, there was no shortage of takers. Supporters' clubs abound not just in Manchester, but throughout the United Kingdom. There is a Manchester United foundation that connects the team to the community, Red Cafés where fans can soak up United atmosphere, and a museum at Old Trafford that chronicles the team's rich history. But the museum is not solely a shrine where locals can be found genuflecting before Red legends. Man United happens to be the world's most popular football club.[12]

The love for all things United stretches beyond Great Britain's shores. Besides branches in European countries like Portugal, the Netherlands, and Germany, the Reds reach extends to the other four continents. Millions of fans follow the club and its stars in Asia, with fan clubs found in Tokyo and Vietnam, as well as in South Africa, South America, the United States, and Australia. If there is any question how serious the Red Army takes their support, look no further than Oslo, Norway, where there is a sizeable United following. The Scandinavian branch of the supporters club formed in 1981 and is the largest of the club's worldwide following. In 2013 they reportedly had more than 25,000 members and published a monthly magazine.[13]

In January 2013, Manchester United became the first sports team in the world to be valued at $3 billion. *Forbes* magazine's value of the club was $1.2 billion higher than the next most valuable sports team, Real Madrid.[14] With successes that began shortly after Sir Alex Ferguson arrived, the nineteen-time English champions have steadily built and maintained a presence on the global stage.

ALL IN

As a player participating in the Manchester United F.C. Reserves and Academy, David Beckham could not have known it then, but he was fortunate enough to be involved in something uniquely special to English football. The world-renowned club had a reputation for small-town values. Discipline, dedication, preparation, practice. With all of the players, the club focused on distilling respect for the game, respect for others, and respect for their fitness. The youth system was first established in the 1930s as a way to scout and develop young, local footballers to eventually become part of the professional first team. Alex Ferguson took up the mantle when he became manager in 1986. And Ferguson's policies—hard work, no drinking, no drugs, and a focus on team mentality—were enforced from top to bottom at the famed club.

Beckham describes the atmosphere at Old Trafford as family like. Kath Phillips, a receptionist at the complex, always had a warm greeting for David, and he says as the years went by, she would help him with his fan mail. Joe Brown, who was the United Youth Development Officer, and his wife, Connie, made all of the young players' travel arrangements and would help them with their expenses. But Beckham calls them United's caretakers, as they helped the young players with whatever they or their families needed. Coaches like Eric Harrison, Brian Kidd, and Nobby Stiles treated players as well as families with respect, keeping them involved in their child's emerging career. Equipment manager Norman Davies helped David to a steady supply of the nicest track suits and the best-fitting shoes.[15]

As family values, instilled in Beckham at an early age, have always been important, the atmosphere helped the young player as well as the young man. He was settled comfortably, living in the supporter-hosted home, and although he was from London, he'd fit in fine with the local lads on the squad. He was part of a core of young players who, in their quest to play at the highest level and to win, were forming the foundation of a United team that would rise to an esteemed level of fame.

BAND OF BROTHERS

When Beckham arrived at the Manchester academy, the young man from east London found himself in the company of a talented group of local football players. Gary Neville, Nicky Butt, and Paul Scholes were Manchester natives. The trio had even played together in a local Sunday league. Ryan Giggs, who was a year older than Beckham, would become a first team regular by the time he was eighteen. Like any new kid on the block, David hoped he would fit in. But he says the common bond between all of them was the desire to be the best and the desire to win at Manchester United. It was this bond that evolved into camaraderie and a deep and respectful friendship that not only carried them to football success but still exists between them twenty years later.

Beckham also found these young men were as equally focused on football and succeeding as he was. Years later both Neville and Scholes documented their dedication to the game in their autobiographies. Neville:

> I was willing to ditch everything in my life apart from football and family. So much for my wild teenage years. If there was a game on Saturday, I was in bed by 9:15pm every Thursday and Friday night. I was a robot. I cast off all my mates from school, never saw them again. I decided, ruthlessly, that I was going to make friends with my new team-mates, who shared the same goals as me. As far as I was concerned the lives of athletes and non-athletes were incompatible. Between the ages of 16 and 20, I dropped women completely. They were always going to want to go to a cinema or a bar on a Friday night.[16]

Scholes recalls,

> I was always football daft. When I went to junior school, I would leave home half an hour early in the mornings and spend the time before the bell went for the first lesson kicking the ball around the schoolyard. Occasionally some mates would be involved, but often I was on my own and that didn't bother me in the slightest. I was happy as long as I had that ball.[17]

The group worked hard, trained hard, and only thought of improving so that they could bring success to Manchester United. Along with everyone else, Beckham was continually challenged to follow the Ferguson system and meet a standard. But playing soccer, and playing for United, was all he'd ever wanted. Finally this was his full-time job.

The teens who arrived at the United training academy grew up together on the pitch and eventually became the men who powered Manchester to premier league-prominence. Then the men became legends.

Neville retired in 2011, ending his nineteen-year career having played entirely with Manchester United. The former captain won eight Premier League titles wearing United Red. The Bury, Manchester–born Neville also earned eighty-five caps playing with the England National team. He has transitioned to coaching, joining the England national team in 2012, and began a media career with British Sky Sports and the *Daily Mail*.[18]

Butt was a midfielder and spent twelve years at Old Trafford before moving to Newcastle United in 2004. He ended his career in 2011 also, playing at a club in Hong Kong. He is also a former England national team player who won thirty-nine caps in a seven-year England career. In 2013 Butt became a reserve team coach at Manchester United.[19]

Giggs, who was still playing for United on November 29, 2013, when he turned forty, set many records with Manchester including thirteen Premier League medals and passing Sir Bobby Charlton's 758 appearances. In 1990 he became the first of Fergie's Fledglings to join the senior team. The talented left winger joined the United coaching staff in 2013.[20]

David Beckham's journey to greatness, surrounded on the pitch by a group of equally talented and committed youth at the Cliff Training Ground, had begun.

GOT MILK?

The Northern Ireland Milk Cup is one of the most respected youth tournaments in the world. Contested since 1983, the Milk Cup draws youth teams, in the Under 15, Under 17, and Under 20 age groups, from England as well as other countries. The competition is strong, with future football legends boasting having played in the tournament. The 2002 World Cup featured thirty former Milk Cup tournament players.

In the spring of 1991, David Beckham and the United youth team were just getting a taste of playing together and competing against other teams. Academy coach Eric Harrison had thoroughly prepared the young troops. They had talent, confidence, and a deep desire to succeed. It was this squad that took the pitch for the ninth annual Northern Ireland Milk Cup.[21]

Captained by then sixteen-year-old David Beckham, the Manchester U-18s journey in the Milk Cup tournament included a win over major rivals Liverpool 4–1 in the quarterfinals, and in the semifinal Manchester United defeated Scotland's Motherwell in a penalty shootout, 5–3. In the final, the junior Reds, stacked with future stars that included Beckham, Nicky Butt, Gary Neville, Paul

Scholes, Robbie Savage, and Ben Thornley, faced Heart of Midlothian before a crowd of ten thousand at the Coleraine Showgrounds. They defeated Scottish club Hearts 2–0 in the final with goals from Thornley and Savage.[22]

Capturing the Northern Ireland Milk Cup was Beckham's first taste of triumph as a player in the Manchester United F.C. Reserves and Academy. The young men celebrated their success, posing for team photos on the field with their new trophy, and by drinking containers of milk.

YOU ARE HERE: LOWER BROUGHTON ROAD, SALFORD, ENGLAND

Guiding this group of young phenoms, molding them into men and training them to bring success to United was the responsibility of youth team coach Eric Harrison.

The former winger from Yorkshire, England, had thoughts of coaching even early in his playing career. As a coach, first with Everton, and finally with Man United in 1981, Harrison was determined to make a difference in the lives of the young men he was in charge of teaching. He recalled in his entire playing career—seventeen years and more than five hundred matches—that he'd gotten little feedback in his performance from any of his managers: "There was no one to take you aside, asking you to come back in the afternoon on a one-to-one basis to show you this and that. It just didn't happen."

Under his watch, Harrison made sure that kind of management never existed at United. Behind the big red gates of The Cliff training ground, in Broughton, Salford, United youth players honed and polished their football skills. Harrison pushed the trainees hard in practice sessions, even developing a reputation for his gruffness. Beckham is not the first United player to call him "scary." But Harrison combined his firmness with fairness. Passionate about football, and able to convey that enthusiasm to his players, Harrison made a practice of spending hours with each of his young charges to council them and give them needed feedback. And he gave praise when it was warranted, finding it was the best form of motivation. Guiding the Manchester youth to success led many to seek out Harrison for coaching advice.[23]

In nurturing the talent of David Beckham as well as hundreds of other United players that came through the academy ranks, Harrison followed basic coaching principles that included practice, sacrifice, and building confidence in players.

Harrison's tough-love coaching methods would go on to influence players and teams at United for decades.

Beckham, years later, still has only praise for his former coach. The midfielder acknowledges the coach's methods and style brought fear to the youths during many training sessions. But he also notes there were equal amounts of compassion and understanding meted out, and that Harrison was just as likely to praise as he was to criticize. Beckham credits the master tactician's skills as the reason the group of youths he started out with became as successful a team as they did.[24]

Harrison saw early promise in the young lad from Leytonstone, David Beckham. He could see Beckham's talent—controlled passing and precision shooting. But he also recognized the athlete's drive and dedication. And he knew he was witnessing a special talent. Harrison:

> The only way you find out is when they're integrated into your team, like [David] was in the youth team. Then you see him on a regular basis, in training, Monday through Friday, morning and afternoon. Then you find out whether you think he's going to be a top player. And Sir Alex Ferguson and myself knew.[25]

GLORY DAYS

Eric Harrison had already guided these young men to victory in one tournament. But at the Manchester United football club, work is never done. The youngsters had only a hint of what it meant to be a champion. At United there is a culture of insatiability. Satisfaction at the moment of triumph only leads to searching for the next challenge. Champions want to win more championships. And Manchester's chance at passing another test was just on the horizon.

After World War II, a physically weathered and mentally worn England shifted its efforts toward rebuilding. When football resumed in the country shortly after the war, there was a conscious effort to engage youngsters in the game as well. The England Football Association (FA), the governing body of football in Great Britain since 1863, created the Football Association Youth Challenge Cup for players under the age of eighteen. The competition pairs players from the youth teams of professional clubs against each other. And in its sixty-year history, the tournament has launched the careers of many top British players.

The first FA Youth Cup saw Manchester United defeat the Wolverhampton Wanderers, 9–3 on aggregate. The club would ultimately win the first five of the FA Youth Cup titles, and is still the most successful club in the tournament, having collected ten overall titles.[26]

Legendary United coach Matt Busby once said, "If you want football's finest fruit, then you grow your own."[27] He arrived at United in 1945 after playing professional football for Manchester City and Liverpool and representing Scotland. While building the Red Devils club he placed an emphasis on finding and developing youth players to ensure the first team would have a pool of talent to consistently draw from. It was Busby who trumpeted the creation of a rigorous scouting system, even going so far as coming up with the idea of enrolling Manchester supporters to host the young recruits who needed housing. And all of this was years before the FA Youth Cup had been created, giving United a wealth of teenage talent, a giant advantage over their rivals.[28]

Busby's strategy paid almost immediate dividends as the players of the 1950s youth team captured the first five youth titles, and were the first group of youngsters to earn the attention of Manchester fans. And they had been recruited and developed at the academy. The group was nicknamed the Busby Babes and went on to capture the league championship title in the 1955–1956 and 1956–1957 seasons. But the Munich Air Disaster of 1958, in which eight players from the team died and another two were forced to retire as a result of their injuries, effectively ended the team's chances for what could have been.[29]

The 2012 book, *Sons of United*, details the sixty-year history of the youth teams at Manchester. Authors Steve Hobin and Tony Park, both longtime United fans, painstakingly researched the 576-pages of content, a project that took them nearly twenty years. Summaries of every FA Youth Cup that United played in completes the history of Manchester's involvement in the famed tournament. The writers' work tells for the first time the story and importance of the youth system.[30] Steve Hobin notes, "The fact that we've got this rich history of bringing players through the ranks, of all the club's achievements at youth level . . . there were no records. And our aim was to rectify that situation."[31] Tony Park:

> People just didn't arrive on the first team. They went through a grounding period where they started in the juniors. They'd worked their way through the A and B teams. They'd break into the reserves. Then if they were lucky they'd break into the first team. This is an incredible reference for future generations when they're starting to research—how does the Manchester United system compare to other club systems? Or how did a certain player break through?[32]

In the spring of 1992, Beckham and the young crop of skilled and hardworking athletes on the current Man United reserves team found themselves in a position to contribute a chapter in the club's rich football history.

A winning record during the 1991–1992 season ensured the junior Reds would earn a spot to compete for the FA Youth Cup. While the Manchester United youth team of the 1950s had successfully won the first five championships, the famed football club had not captured a trophy since the 1964 season.

The core four that made up the Class of '92—Beckham, Butt, Giggs, and Neville—had been developing and training together now for nearly two years. The more they bonded off the pitch, the more they developed a synchronicity on it. Playing as if they had telepathy factored favorably for them during the tournament.

On April 14, Beckham's youth team kicked off the first leg, facing Crystal Palace FC, at Selhurst Park in Croydon, London. A goal at the 17th minute by midfielder Nicky Butt put the junior Reds on the scoreboard first. They controlled the tempo of the first half by dominating possession and taking more shots on goal. At the 30th minute, Beckham booted a brilliant, twenty-five-yard volley into the net to give them a 2–0 lead. The Eagles did manage a goal late in the second half, but it was not enough to overcome United. Butt restored the Reds two-goal lead, and Manchester United went on to take the first leg of the tournament, 3–1. Momentum was on their side as they were set to host the second leg in Manchester a month later.[33]

At Old Trafford, the young and promising group of David Beckham, Nicky Butt, Ryan Giggs, Gary Neville, and Paul Scholes gave United fans a first glimpse at greatness. Their stellar performance on the field allowed teammates Ben Thornley, Simon Davies, and Colin McKee to seal the championship, punching in United's three goals. The Class of '92 defeated Crystal Palace on an aggregate, 6–3, and captured Manchester United's first FA Youth Cup title in twenty-eight years.[34]

The headline in the *Manchester Evening News* signaled a bright future for the talented side: "'Long Wait Over as Glory Days Return': The beauty of the second leg of the final against Crystal Palace at Old Trafford was [that] their terrific team work was studded with expressive magical play by creative players."[35]

Steve Coppell, Crystal Palace club manager:

The performance of the United boys is a pointer for a very healthy future. It's clear that the conveyer belt producing young players is rolling again at Old Trafford. There is a quality in the team and they certainly have struck a rich seam with the side which played against us.[36]

Ben Thornley, one of Beckham's youth club teammates, gave the Reds an early lead after scoring the first goal of the final match. Thornley recalled the experience of being part of the FA Youth Cup team in 1992 as one of his greatest accomplishments:

> It slowly started to dawn on us how good we were. From when we first started playing together, we pretty much went unbeaten through those two seasons. Nobody could live with us when we played to our best. Obviously we did lose the odd game, but we knew it took something special to beat us. When we got to the quarter-final stage we fancied we could win it. Spurs were the firm favourites as they'd chucked a lot of money at the lads they'd signed as 16-year-olds but we comfortably brushed them aside in the semi-final and Crystal Palace didn't prove as tough in the final.[37]

Gary Neville has said the team's success, down to a player, is a motivation to always get better, and he gives credit to the coaching staff:

> It becomes very easy to be motivated and determined and maintain your form year in year out when you have a club like this to play for. The manager doesn't accept anything other than repeat performances season after season. The education we received at this club from 16 to 20 is vital. Eric Harrison and Brian Kidd before that instilled in us what it took to be a Man United player. The idea was that you've never made it. With a young player sometimes you hear people saying—he's made it. Our idea was that you've never made it. There's always someone who's done better than you.[38]

Fergie's Fledglings, as this special group of talented young players under manager Alex Ferguson was soon being called, in a nod to the Busby Babes teams of the 1950s, had captured the FA Youth Cup. But the athletes on that team did more than that. They set Manchester United on a course for greatness.

SIX WORKING-CLASS LADS

At first they were a curiosity. The Manchester United wonder kids, who'd just won the FA Youth Cup for the first time since 1964, caught the attention of fans and media throughout England. Then came the scrutiny. There was David Beckham, with a magical right foot. Gary Neville, with great leadership skills. Ryan Giggs, the Welsh wizard. And Nicky Butt, whose good humor reminded the hardworking young men to enjoy every minute of this adventure. The talented Paul Scholes had played in the '91 Milk Cup championship tournament, and Phil Neville, the younger brother of Gary, would play in the '93 FA Youth Cup final. Finally, this special group that brought success to United in the form of premier league championships and UEFA championships, and that earned the adoration of a generation of British and international supporters, became immortalized. The group's achievements would be celebrated for decades in countless articles, books, TV specials, and films. In December 2013, *Class of '92*, a documentary highlighting their accomplishments on the football pitch, was released in theaters in England. The core four players from that team, as well as United legends, reflected on the camaraderie and the bond that existed between that unique and talented group of athletes. Beckham:

> At United, a professional attitude ran through everything we did. There was a sense of togetherness amongst us that I don't think you could ever buy or recreate.[39] My times with these [Class of '92] players at Manchester United were the most special in my career. We came from different backgrounds, grew up like a family playing together through the ranks, all wanting to be successful. In the end, what we achieved was beyond our wildest dreams. I loved making this film and reuniting back with the lads and talking openly about our time together.[40]

Gary Neville:

> For us, we were very fortunate. We came together at the right time as a group, at the right club, with the right coaches, with the right manager. They believed in giving people opportunity, and all you ever ask for in life is a chance. We were given a big chance at the biggest club. It was a dream, it was a special year.[41]

Ryan Giggs:

> You see talent, but it goes deeper than that. We had team spirit, we had quality, we were friends, we were mates, we grew up together. That's why we achieved.[42] When we were approached to do this film, it gave me the chance to think back over all the events in not only my career but all of the lads involved. Hopefully you'll see how personal it is to us all—we're still great mates and who would turn down the chance to make a movie with your best mates?[43]

Nicky Butt:

> It was a special time for all of us growing up and it is only now as you look back that you actually see what an amazing story it is. Everything we did we were together. We trained together, we got changed together, we ate together. The

coaches, Eric [Harrison] made us all know that we're all in it together. It's not individuals here. We wouldn't have gotten anywhere without our teammates.[44]

Paul Scholes:

In our eyes we were just playing a game of football with our mates. We were lucky enough to play well together and at the same time play for the biggest club in the world.[45]

Phil Neville:

If you have someone that's got so much effort and dedication that will always overcome someone that's lazy. And that's what was driven into us by Sir Alex, Eric Harrison, our youth team manager. And it stayed with us throughout our careers.[46] Making the film was a great experience, it got us all together, as we don't often get the chance to these days, to revisit old haunts and reflect over the past.[47]

Alex Ferguson:

It was a great squad of young players, a wonderful period. Those homegrown players carried the spirit of Manchester United inside them. That's what they gave the club.[48]

Bobby Charlton:

A lot of people ask why Man United are so successful. There's a history and with a history there's a responsibility. You have to perform. Alex Ferguson's philosophy was always the work ethic and the long-term, which is why we're always interested in young players. You get them into your blood. The more you get involved in the history of this place—millions have paid to look round an empty stadium—you can connect the Best, Law and Charlton era with Scholes and Giggs.[49]

Eric Harrison:

That so called "golden generation" were easily the best bunch of players I have ever worked with. They didn't just have technical ability, they had the in-built drive and ambition in life to play for Manchester United. They had unbelievable desire, fed off each other's energy and were all totally dedicated. Not one of them ever got into trouble with drink, drugs or anything. To get such magnificent players together at the same time was incredible. Coaching them was fantastically exciting.[50]

The team about to burst onto the England football stage made it back to the 1993 FA Youth Cup title match but were overpowered by Leeds United and lost, 4–1 on aggregate.[51] They did not, however, lose any momentum on their forward progress.

As they stood on the cusp of greatness they took every measure to be prepared for what might come. On the field, that meant continuing to put in the practice and the late-night study sessions. Off the field, that meant media training and guidance for meeting the press. Mock interviews took place in 1993, designed to give the players a taste of the media frenzy that comes with playing for a club the size of United. In the training sessions, BBC broadcasters Jimmy Wagg and Eamonn O'Neal and BBC sports journalist Andy Buckley asked the young members of the Class of '92—David Beckham, Ryan Giggs, Gary Neville, and Paul Scholes—to reflect on their performance in the 1992 FA Youth Cup tournament.[52]

In his mock, post-match interview, Beckham talked about the goal he scored in the first leg of United's match with Crystal Palace, the crowd at Selhurst Park, and how the youth team would be up for the second leg at Old Trafford. He giggled and squirmed as his teammates were looking on and probably teasing, making him more uncomfortable. But he was articulate and demonstrated confidence.[53]

The youth players had probably participated in less than five press conferences between them. The training would help them as they were set to spend a good amount of time in the English football spotlight. It is this kind of attention to detail, this kind of preparation for everything imaginable that great teams, great coaches, and great athletes don't overlook. Success finds those who are prepared when an opportunity presents itself.

David Beckham had spent his life diligently working at making his dream of playing football become a reality. And his work ethic aligned perfectly with that of Manchester United. The young boy who set his sights with laser-like focus on United Red, had become a man on the verge of playing professionally for Manchester's famed football club.

3

FOREVER RED

It was an unusually cool September night, even for predictably chilly East Sussex. The slick and cold weather conditions were more typical of the east coast of the United States during winter than for this seaside resort town on the southern coast of England. The Brighton & Hove fans huddled inside the Goldstone Ground were not about to let the unpleasant weather rob them of cheering on their football club. And those in attendance that September 23, 1992, would become witnesses to the match where David Beckham would make his first team Manchester United debut.[1]

Fresh off an outstanding season with Man United's reserve team, which saw Beckham and Co. capture the FA Youth Cup, the young prospect continued to show progress. He continued to impress with his hard-work ethic and dedication to learn and improve, and began training with the senior team players during the 1992–1993 season. But he was not quite an established regular at Old Trafford. In making that tricky transition from reserve team to first team, Beckham still had a number of steps to take. One of those early steps was being called on to play a match in the fall of 1992.[2]

September 23, 1992, was a travel day for United and the destination this time was to East Sussex, a county a little more than two hundred miles south of Manchester. The Reds would be playing in an early-season league cup match against Brighton & Hove Albion. Along with the first team, this trip included a few of the young reserve players, and in the group was seventeen-year-old David Beckham. By the half of the evening's match Manchester was on top, 1–0. With about twenty minutes left in the game, the young man from East London got the call, the match announcer marking the event: "And young David Beckham coming on, the young, midfield player, as [Andrei] Kanchelskis goes off."[3]

Wearing his red-and-black United kit, the rookie sprinted onto the pitch and into the history books. That night, before a crowd of 16,649, David Beckham recorded the first seventeen minutes of his professional career. Finally, after years of hard work, of practices in the park, of camps and tournaments and cups playing the game he loved, David Beckham played his first professional football match with his beloved Manchester United.

Years later, well into his pro football career, Beckham would reflect on the emotions he'd experienced during his first-team debut.

> That night on the south coast, I was sitting on the bench watching my teammates, who had only months before been my heroes, and I was so nervous. I was desperate to get on, but if I did, would I make a mistake, was I going to make the grade? With 20 minutes to go, the manager turned to me: "Get changed son, you're going on." I was so excited I bounced up off my seat and crack: I hit my head on the dugout.[4]

September 23, 1992, marked the Beckham pro debut, but it did not secure him a permanent spot on United's first-team squad. Instead it put in motion a series of events that led to his eventual promotion and the realization of a dream to finally play for Manchester United.

YOU ARE HERE: OLD TRAFFORD, GREATER MANCHESTER, ENGLAND

The address Sir Matt Busby Way, Manchester, carries all the history of this famous stadium. Opened in 1910 and home to the Manchester United football club, Old Trafford is the second-largest stadium in the United Kingdom after Wembley. World War II bombings left a giant crater on the stadium pitch, forcing it to close for eight years. The stadium has been nicknamed the Theatre of Dreams by its millions of passionate supporters. Reserve teams have trained on the pitch, and first teams played home matches here. United legends Bobby Charlton, George Best, and manager Matt Busby displayed their talents on this stage here in Manchester.[5]

David Beckham, who signed his first professional contract with Manchester United in January 1993, would soon follow in the same footsteps as many of his heroes. After his seventeen-minute first-team debut, Beckham would not get called to play in another senior team match for months. But he continued working hard to achieve his professional football goals. Each match he played was a chance for him to not only gain more experience, but also help him achieve his early career milestones.

First start with United senior team—away game, at Port Vale, September 21, 1994

First home start with United senior team—at Old Trafford, vs. Port Vale, October 5, 1994

First career goal, first career goal at Old Trafford, first appearance in UEFA Champions League match, First start in UEFA Champions League match—December 7, 1994[6]

Manchester was in Group A of the Champions League that season, along with FC Barcelona, Sweden's IFK Gothenburg, and Turkey's Galatasaray. The Reds hovered near the bottom of the pool, and desperately needed a win against the Turkish team to even stay alive on points in the standings. And they also needed help from Gothenburg, which was playing Barcelona that same night.

Previous meetings with Galatasaray had tested the young but fiery squad of United, with each match ending in a draw. This match would eventually go down in history as irrelevant, but what happened in it was anything but. The inexperienced players on the pitch that night played as if they were unaware of the standings or of United's slim-to-none chances of continuing in the tournament. In the end, they did not play as if they were inexperienced.

The nineteen-year-olds—Beckham, making his UEFA Champions League debut, Gary Neville, Simon Davies, and Nicky Butt—performed better than expected. They were impressive. With their dominating 4–0 win, the team's chemistry and the ability to play to each other's strengths that night was a foreshadowing of what would only improve in the coming decade.

Davies punched in the first goal within the first two minutes of the match. Then at about eight minutes before the half, Beckham doubled the Reds' score, with his first goal for Manchester United.[7]

It was the first of a total eighty-five goals Beckham would have for the Red Devils. While it looked like the young rookie was about to permanently reach the first-team ranks, Beckham, still raw around the edges, would need more time to earn his spot on the senior team. He played his sixth match with United in January of 1995. Then in the spring of 1995, Beckham would finally get his shot at more first-team playing. Only it was coming via a loan to another football club.[8]

YOU'RE IN GOOD HANDS

The news from Beckham's team manager was that to reach his ultimate destination his professional career was going to be diverted with a side-trip detour. The young prospect admits the news was at first unsettling, and it left him unsure about his place with Man United. He immediately voiced his concerns with United academy coach Eric Harrison, who recalls, "The club had suggested to David he go on loan to Preston to gain first-team experience and David seemed very down about it. He kept asking if I thought it was United's way of trying to get rid of him."[9]

Preston North End, a club that played in the third tier of the English football league system, had asked if the young Beckham would go on loan with them for one month.

The coach reassured him that the loan was about gaining first-team experience, and nothing more. Beckham's fears were relieved. And when he arrived at Lancashire, he had the good fortune of a chance meeting with Preston North End's most notable striker and former England National team player, Tom Finney, which further helped silence his doubts.

Aside from the undersized striker's tenacity on the football pitch, Finney was widely known for his fierce loyalty to Preston. The revered footballer played his entire career for his local club, appearing 433 times and scoring 187 goals, and remained involved with Preston in retirement, advising younger players and becoming a distinguished ambassador of the game.[10]

David Beckham's debut with Preston North End came on March 4, as the team faced the Doncaster Rovers. He was subbed into the game, but his goal helped the team hold on to a draw. The next match was a week later, and this time Beckham started. And again, fans at Deepdale were treated to the right foot of the free-kick specialist, as the youngster took a corner that this time helped the Lilywhites to a win: "He stood over the spot of the foul—with an unfamiliar number four on his back—before taking his trademark three strides and wrapping his right foot around the ball, curling it into the top left hand corner."[11]

Game 3 and game 4 saw Preston topple Bury and Exeter City. Beckham did not score, but continued to work on getting the kind of first-team experience United had wanted him to have. Then after a 1–1 draw with Lincoln City in game 5 on March 25, the David Beckham PNE experiment was over. His performance during that stretch of games was looked upon as successful.[12] David Moyes, first-year coach, Manchester United:

I was very fortunate to play with David when he came to Preston North End. He was a great lad then. He was very humble, and really just wanted to play. When he came to Preston on loan from United in 1995 I was player/assistant manager there to [PNE manager] Gary Peters. David was frail but he was confident. He had ability and we saw that in his first game. The manager put him on all free-kicks and corners. He was only with us a short while but when he went back he more or less went straight into United's team.[13]

But what may have contributed the most to Beckham's success was that meeting with Preston legend Tom Finney. And according to Harrison reflecting years later, that meeting gave Beckham a welcomed boost of confidence:

Sir Tom Finney, one of the greatest English players of all time, was a Preston legend and still watched all of their matches. After one game, he took David aside and told him what a great prospect he was, how he thought he was a really good player. When David came back to United and told me about that, he was glowing that someone like Tom Finney had done something like that. I do believe it made a difference and the rest is history.[14]

THE YOUNG AND THE RESTLESS

They were young and fearless, a talented group of athletes set to put Manchester United on the world football map, trained in the Mancunian way since they had signed on to the club's farm system at an early age. They were recruited and developed by the club, rather than brought over from other teams or countries. They trained hard and played hard, and the record books showed the success of their efforts. They bled red.

In the 1950s, fans knew them as the Busby Babes. Their talents had been discovered early, and once snapped up by the senior team, they performed brilliantly for United manager Matt Busby. They won premier league titles in the 1955–1956 and 1956–1957 seasons.

Under Scottish manager Alex Ferguson, who took over the club's reins in 1989, the group of ready-to-rumble players was christened Fergie's Fledglings. The first version emerged in the 1980s with the youth team reaching the 1986 FA Youth Cup final. Then in the 1988–1989 season, the Reds won the 1990 FA Cup and the 1991 UEFA Winners' Cup.

But it was the 1990s group of "Fledglings"—a group that included the core talent of Nicky Butt, David Beckham, Ryan Giggs, and Gary Neville, and sometimes

Paul Scholes—that is generally considered the more successful of the two. They captured headlines and hearts throughout England.

When fans, the media, and even the British Parliament filed complaints about Ferguson, who chose to play unknowns rather than the familiar starters for the 1994 League Cup match at Old Trafford, *The Guardian*'s Cynthia Bateman wrote: "What the more astute supporters recognized was that they were privileged to be watching a possibly great United side of the future."[15]

Ferguson, of course, had been observing these particular players for years, as they all had come up under the academy's strict style of training. He had faith in their abilities. These were the same players that were part of the youth team that had won the 1992 FA Youth Cup. Ferguson knew the right amount of playing time on the first team, slotting players into the positions that suited them best, and time to jell as teammates, would only unleash their power. Ferguson:

> I'm convinced six or seven more will reach the very top, that's how highly I regard them. These boys are the best crop I have had in my management career. A lot of people tell me they are the best the club has ever had. To have them all come through like this is very rare. Now it's just a matter of fitting them into the first team when the opportunity arises.[16]

Beckham continued starting that season, collecting more experience and more goals, and fitting in on the field and in the locker room. He describes those first years as if he could scarcely believe what was happening to him. It was in many ways a young man living in a fantasy. And while it seemed impossible, Beckham enjoyed every minute of the journey, including the training sessions and the work he put in to become a member of the Manchester United first team.

It was only a matter of time before the United manager's risk with the inexperienced players would pay off.

BOYS TO MEN

United started the 1995–1996 season with the same core of young, not-quite-there-yet, starting-to-jell players. Beckham had successfully worked his way into the starting lineup, and was finally a regular—the last of the 1992 FA Youth Cup core four to become so. The first match of the season—a 1–3 loss at the hands of Aston Villa—was not a true indication of the talent and fight that would later surface on this squad. United then went on a run of ten consecutive victories, and racked up eighty-two points to capture the team's second Premier League title and the first of David Beckham's career. The twenty-year-old midfielder was as hungry for championship hardware as everyone else on his team. With eyes toward securing a spot in the FA Cup final, United first had to face Chelsea FC in a semifinal match.

United arrived at Villa Park in Birmingham on March 31 at the top position in the Premier League with a four-point lead. In the match, Chelsea scored first and held on to their lead in the second half. But then at the 55th mark, Andy Cole equalized and gave United hope. Four minutes later, Beckham got hold of a misplaced Chelsea pass; then, after drawing the goalkeeper out, slipped the ball past him for a United score. His goal sent the Red Devils to the FA Cup final at Wembley Stadium.[17]

As rivalries go, this one ran as deep and long as the Coke and Pepsi feud. Or for younger generations, Mac and PC. So the FA Cup final on May 11, 1996, was already destined to be heated. Liverpool and Man United, the teams contesting, had a history that brought out the best and worst between players and fans.[18]

Liverpool showed up dressed in their Armani finest—white suits that they paraded around in before the match. United showed up to win a championship. Defense dominated the match as neither club got many scoring opportunities. Finally, at the 85th minute, Eric Cantona took a pass and punched in the goal that gave Manchester the win.[19]

The Reds capped their season, playing on the strength of the young men who'd teamed up to win the '92 FA Youth Cup, by giving that team their first taste of winning a double—the Premier League title and the FA Cup.[20]

HE SHOOTS, HE SCORES

Those who were there, August 17, opening day of the 1996 United season, described the goal as one for the history books.

Credit his great field vision. Or his extensive knowledge of the game. Or maybe it was just luck. Whatever it was, that day, on the pitch at Selhurst Park, David Beckham was at the precise right place at the precise right moment. At the 90th minute of the match, he noticed that the Wimbledon goalkeeper, Neil Sullivan, was not quite protecting the goal line as an alert player might. Beckham saw an opportunity, and like a hound in a fox hunt, took advantage of the opponent's momentary lapse.

From his position on the field, sixty yards from the goal post, Beckham took a few steps, then let loose with his dangerous right foot. The shot sent the ball soaring, and before anyone could do anything, it floated up and sailed over the goalkeeper and under the bar, landing at the back of the net. Cheers erupted in the stadium and everyone was on their feet gasping, including the announcer: "And Beckham saw Sullivan off his line. Oooooh! That is absolutely phenomenal! What an astonishing goal by David Beckham. From the halfway line, Sullivan couldn't get back. . . . David Beckham, surely an England player of the future, scores a goal that will be talked about and replayed for years."[21]

Sullivan:

> It was right at the end of the game actually. As it was on its way, you kinda say, this is gonna be close. And it just dropped under the bar. I thought, I'm nowhere near this. And I looked over and it'd just gone under the bar and into the back of the net. And then I'm looking at the United fans behind the goal and they're laughing. . . . But it was a great goal.[22]

That sixty-yard wonder-goal against Wimbledon is regarded today as one of the best goals of the century. The century! Some say this insignificant goal, in an otherwise insignificant opening match, was the beginning of Beckham becoming a global superstar.

Two short weeks after his impressive Wimbledon goal, Beckham marked his debut with the England national team on September 1, 1996. He started the match alongside United teammates Paul Ince, Gary Neville, and Gary Pallister, and was as active and involved as anyone. It was the match where Beckham became an international soccer player.

SEEING RED

The England national team's newest member, David Beckham, the twenty-one-year-old lad from Leytonstone, fit in with the squad brilliantly. The style of play afforded Beckham even more opportunities to impress. Manager Glenn Hoddle installed him as a starter in all eight of the 1998 World Cup qualifying matches. Beckham's England career started out on solid ground. Finally it was time to head to France, as the defending champions were host of the '98 World Cup.

David Beckham made his World Cup debut coming on as a sub in England's second match of the tournament, then scored his first international, World Cup goal, in the third match.[23] In the end it did not matter how well he played or how many goals he scored, for his name would ultimately be remembered for something much less flattering—*that* red card.

In the match facing Argentina, on June 30, Beckham was involved in a tackle with Diego Simeone, a midfielder from Argentina, that left him face down on the stadium pitch. As Beckham lay there, waiting for a call from the ref, he retaliated with a kick. Simeone, either injured or improvising, immediately went down, the referee pulled out the red card, and Beckham went off. Left with a ten-man squad, England lost and was subsequently eliminated from the tournament.[24] Beckham up to that point had never experienced any negative incidents in his career. That was all about to change.

Beckham had by then met and started dating Victoria "Posh Spice" Adams, a member of the Spice Girls, the hugely successful British pop band. After immediately realizing the magnitude of his mistake, and publicly apologizing, David took off to the United States within hours after the incident to be with Victoria, who was performing at New York's Madison Square Garden. He could not ultimately avoid the backlash, which British fans surely earned an A for, their relentlessness reaching unprecedented levels of viciousness.

The bad press and the bad feelings raged on, and many thought Beckham was going to leave England to escape it, especially after receiving death threats. But he did not. And when Beckham returned for preseason training for United in August of 1998 he did so holding his head high. As high as anyone could with, arguably, the weight of the nation on his shoulders.[25] And what he found shortly after his arrival to Manchester is that the supporters there welcomed him back. Manchester was family, had been since he was fifteen and a half, and he was back home. The fans did not react as the rest of the country had, and his teammates were united—little *u*—unanimously behind him. Beckham scored a goal in his first league match of that season, against Leicester City, and, buoyed by the support of the Red Army faithful, was able to continue playing the game he loved, for the team he loved, and in the country he loved.[26]

THEATRE OF DREAMS

The success Manchester United was having on the field during the 1990s coincided with a favorable upturn in the perception of English football. A short ten years earlier marked a considerably darker era, one defined by hooliganism from fans and generally poor conditions at aging stadia. The top-flight league in the UK lagged behind its counterparts in Spain and Italy in terms of revenue and attendance. In 1992 the Premier League was formed in part to clean up this image and showcase the talent in the country. Since its inception, Manchester United had captured four of the league's title trophies.[27]

The 1998–1999 season for the Manchester United Red Devils started more with a whimper than a bang. Losses and draws were the only highlights of the team's preseason matches as well as the early part of the regular season. But by the start of 1999, United began a stretch of impressive play, which included an 8–1 thrashing of Nottingham Forest. All told, the Reds suffered only three losses in the Premier League that season.

Perennial powerhouse Arsenal Gunners were champions of the league the year before and ran neck and neck with Manchester United for most of the season. Both teams were battling for the title as spring rolled around, and it came down to matches on Saturday, May 16, 1999, to determine who would claim the premiership that season.

Arsenal dispatched Aston Villa, 1–0 at their North London stadium and ended the season with 78 Premier League points. The Gunners needed United to lose or draw to have a chance at the league prize.[28]

A sellout crowd of fifty-five thousand swelled the stands at Old Trafford as United hosted Tottenham Hotspur in the final match of the Premier League season. The announcer summed it up:

> At Old Trafford, the [Arsenal] Gunners' bitter rivals, Spurs, were playing Manchester United. In the 24th minute Les Fernandez lofted one over [Manchester United goalkeeper] Peter Schmeichel to give Tottenham a 1–nil lead. United answered with Paul Scholes' ball to an unmarked David Beckham, who blasted it in to tie the game. And with Spurs needing at least a draw for Arsenal to keep the title, substitute Andy Cole changed all that with this. Final score, 2–1, United, to give them their twelfth league title, and fifth in seven years, by a margin of one point.[29]

Winning the Premier League title had more meaning in 1999 than it had in other seasons. In previous years, when Manchester United had won the title, they were also heading to the FA Cup title match and could hope to record a double championship season.[30] This season, having earned a spot in the UEFA Champions League Final, the Red Devils, by winning all three titles, could make football history, becoming the first English club to win the coveted treble.

With one notch in the win column, could they dare dream of recording two more?

ACT II, SCENE II

Not only was the 1999 FA Cup final the last championship match to be contested in the twentieth century, it marked the second to last time the tournament would be held at Wembley Stadium. The storied shrine to football was scheduled for demolishing and rebuilding over the next few years.

The FA Cup, contested since 1871, is the oldest football competition in the world. In 1923, a newly constructed Wembley hosted its first-ever FA Cup final. Bolton beat West Ham, 2–0, but the match was memorable for the unruly crowds. A mounted police officer controlled an estimated two hundred thousand fans, which gave the match the nickname "White Horse Final."[31]

On May 22, 1999, seventy-nine thousand were on hand to see Man United and Newcastle United face off for the title. Prior to the match, *BBC Sports* had this write-up about David Beckham in its United player profiles:

> The most photographed and talked about footballer in Britain has arguably had his best year for United since breaking into the first team during the 1995/6 double winning season. Responsible for many of the goals scored by Dwight Yorke and Andy Cole with his crosses from right midfield, and has chipped in with the odd goal himself. Has responded magnificently to the criticism he faced after being sent off for England against Argentina during France 98. Along with the Neville brothers, Nicky Butt, Paul Scholes and Ryan Giggs has graduated from the United youth team.[32]

Ten minutes into the match found Manchester on the scoreboard with a goal from Teddy Sheringham, who ninety seconds earlier had just been subbed into the game. Newcastle couldn't mount a comeback, and when Paul Scholes took advantage of a defensive error to give United a second goal at the 53rd minute, the FA Cup title belonged to Manchester.[33]

And then there was one. Alex Ferguson's "Fledglings" had become the first team to complete the "double" in three seasons. There was little time for celebrating though. Manchester United's immediate focus shifted to a date four days later on the calendar, the UEFA Champions League Final, and a shot at history.

THE GRAND FINALE

Wednesday, May 26, 1999, arrived as unceremoniously as any other spring day in May. Except if you were a player with either the Manchester United or Bayern

Munich football clubs, and were about to faceoff for the UEFA Champions League title. The dawn of this championship day stirred emotions in the legions of English and German supporters as well. There was history between these two proud countries, and very little of it was pleasant.

Besides World War II and all of its political ramifications, there were a number of incidents between the two countries that spilled into the football arena. There was the fact that Bayern were from Munich, the German city that was the site of one of the most catastrophic events in United's history. On February 6, 1958, a snowstorm forced a plane to crash on take-off from Munich airport, killing twenty-three of the forty-four aboard, including eleven players and club officials. Elders who remember the news as the disaster unfolded have passed the story down through generations, and school children in Manchester likely learn about it from lesson plans. David Beckham's father, who was a young boy in 1958, grew up with locals talking about the accident and the loss of so many lives. The tragedy of that event is forever etched into the history of Manchester.[34]

Another notable incident was the 1966 World Cup final match. England was the host country and London's Wembley Stadium featured a showdown between the national team and West Germany. The match was level at 2–2 at the end of regulation. In the 98th minute, a rocket by England's Geoff Hurst hit the crossbar and bounced down onto the goal line. "Goooooooal!" The controversial point, and whether the ball crossed the line, has forever caused debate, and the "ghost goal" became part of World Cup history.

England went on to defeat West Germany 4–2. June 30, 1966, marked the greatest day in England's football history, and it was another dagger in Germany's sporting heart.[35]

The significance of this day's match was not lost on Manchester manager Alex Ferguson in the week leading up to the final. "It is Sir Matt Busby's birthday on the day of the European Cup final and we are playing Bayern Munich, the team that reminds us of the tragedy of 1958. There are a lot of coincidences and I hope they all have a meaning when it is over."[36]

The curtain lifted as it always does before every great show with fanfare, setting the stage for the drama that was about to unfold. This highly anticipated performance, the UEFA Champions League title match, was taking place on a grand stage indeed, Camp Nou, Fútbol Club Barcelona's fifty-year-old stadium in Spain.[37]

For twenty-four-year-old David Beckham, starting in his first UEFA final, it would be a back-to-Barcelona experience. It was his exceptional talents as a youth that had won him a prize trip to the Catalan capital, where he had the privilege of training with Barca's reserve team. As an eleven-year-old in 1986, Beckham, wide-eyed with excitement about the pro team's stadium, could only wonder what a professional footballer would feel in an actual game. The UEFA Champions League title match, on the acres of grass of the Camp Nou pitch, was going to give Beckham that answer and more.

Finally it was game time, and the teams competing for Europe's top football title took their places on the pitch. This was the culmination of the forty-fourth season of the UEFA Champion's League, the seventh since the tournament name had been changed from the European Cup. Would Man United capture their first title since 1968? Or would Bayern prevail and reign as football kings of Europe?

The pomp and pageantry played out before a crowd of ninety thousand quickly became a distant memory when, at the six-minute mark, Bayern's Mario Basler curled a free kick into the net to put the German team ahead. United settled down and, playing from behind, remained aggressive. Bayern threats forced United keeper Peter Schmeichel to make some great saves. It could be said that opportunities were squandered by the Reds, but the same would be true for Bayern.[38]

A key component of United's offensive strategy had been a new lineup in midfield. Yellow cards handed out to Roy Keane and Paul Scholes in the UEFA semifinal left both suspended and meant Ferguson had to shuffle his starting XI. He decided to use Beckham alongside Nicky Butt in midfield. It was a role Beckham had little to no experience with. The manager's reconfigured lineup paid off, as Beckham, a player tipped for greatness, more than met the challenge.

Just before this final, Brazilian soccer star Pelé heaped high praise on the English youngster. He selected Beckham as "one of the very great players of this year," and ranked him the third best player in the world behind Ronaldo and Zinedine Zidane.[39] "From my point of view, he is a very important player for the team. He works very hard, he has good vision, good movement and good delivery."[40]

Deep into the first half, Beckham's third free kick threatens to equalize, but it flies just left of Bayern's goal post. Good vision, good movement, good delivery. Man United trailed 1–0 at the half.

Alex Ferguson gave this now-memorable pep talk to his team during the break: "At the end of this game, the European Cup will be only six feet away from you, and you'll not even be able to touch it if we lose. And for many of you, that will be the closest you will ever get. Don't you dare come back in here without giving your all."[41]

In the ebb and flow and push and pull of the second half, United's constant surges were thwarted by an efficient *Die Roten* defense, and they failed on several opportunities to put the ball in the net. They had still failed to score near the end of regulation. Ferguson decided to shake up the offense on his so far ineffective side, and put in subs Teddy Sheringham at the 67th minute and Ole

Gunnar Solskjaer at the 81st. Whether it was a stroke of genius or luck or the football Gods smiling down on United, the subs or the substituting shifted the game's momentum in favor of Manchester.

Bayern, clinging to their 1–0 lead when three minutes of extra time were awarded in the match, were already thinking about celebrating their win. That's when the magic began. Those three minutes would be memorable to millions of Manchester United fans, to players, to coaches, and to David Beckham for decades to come.

THREE MINUTES TO GLORY

In the 91st minute, fortune favored United. They won a corner at the beginning of the extra time, their eleventh of the match. David Beckham sent it in from the left. Peter Schmeichel went for it but Bayern actually got possession. But then Ryan Giggs regained control and took a shot that was redirected by Sheringham into the net. "Goooooooooal!" His shot from eight yards out equalized. Reds fans erupted in the stadium.

Less than two minutes later, Beckham lined up yet another corner. The ball found Sheringham's head, was forwarded to Ole Gunnar Solskjaer and kicked in: 2–1 United. Pandemonium![42]

Munich got the ball at kickoff and had another chance. But what they really needed was more time on the clock. The referee blew the whistle and the game was over. There was shock and awe and shouting from all corners of the stadium. Only on the Reds side it was from joy.[43]

Victoria Beckham: "That was incredible. I have never seen anything like it, anywhere, in my whole life."[44]

UEFA.com: "Solskjaer Answers United's Prayers."[45]
BBC News online: "United Crowned Kings of Europe."[46]
Bild Zeitung: "*Warum?*" (Why?)[47]

It still remains today as one of the greatest moments in Champions League history. The thrill of victory and the agony of defeat were summed up by the reactions and comments of the players and those who were involved:

David Beckham: "It's all a bit hard to take in, it happened all so quickly. We enjoyed the good fortune at the end, and it's an unbelievable feeling to have won in such an atmosphere."[48]

Ole Solskjaer: "It's unbelievable and it's very difficult to describe how I feel just now. But if people still wonder why I stay at United they can see why. The team spirit, it is unbelievable."[49]

Gary Neville: "I remember just collapsing on the floor thinking, 'wow, this is just the best moment you are ever going to have in your life.' It still makes me shiver."[50]

Sir Bobby Charlton, United director and former player: "This has been a marvelous season. It's been marvelous for the fans—the F.A. Cup, the Champions League and in our own Championship, and the players have been just great. I'm really proud of them. English football has been in the wilderness for a long time and now we're back on the world stage."[51]

Bayern Munich president Franz Beckenbauer: "That was the cruelest defeat possible because victory was so close. We already had victory in the bag and there were only a few seconds to go."[52]

Sports columnist James Lawton had this to say:

We have new superlatives now when the conversation turns to extraordinary deeds in sport. We can recall the courage of Ali, the cold-eyed winning instinct of Lester Piggott and Ian Botham's innings at Headingly. But always we will come back to the night United beat Bayern Munich at the Nou Camp. It wasn't a comeback—it swept beyond the limitations of that term. It was a resurrection. They won so dramatically that the history of this wondrous competition has a new and permanent asterisk against the line which records United's 2–1 triumph. It must say: "Won in extraordinary circumstances—possibly divine."[53]

Beckham was down on the field with his teammates, smack in the middle of the shouting and clapping and the chaos. One reporter noticed the midfielder take a minute from his own celebrating, and demonstrate a moment of true sportsmanship. The *Sunday Times* reported:

As [United] got closer to the podium, Beckham noticed [veteran midfielder Lothar] Matthäus and, breaking from the Reds, he walked towards his rival. Seeing him come, Matthäus moved to meet him halfway. They shook hands at first and then embraced.

Their coming together embodied the greatness of the occasion and the manliness of the contest. The young man of English football, the old man of the German game; they had nothing more to give except their respect. One acknowledging that on the greatest sporting nights the margins can be damn fine, the other recognising that no matter how fine, the winner must be congratulated.[54]

KINGS OF ENGLAND

David Beckham had every reason to celebrate. His performance at midfield and specifically in the extra time meant the difference in the game. His corners set up both eventual scores. After such an incredible season, after the whistle had blown and the astonishing reality set in, after basking in the glory David Beckham had his own memorable championship moment.

> Beckham: When the whistle finally blew, I experienced a surge of adrenaline, just enough to propel me toward our fans. Other players were lying on the ground exhausted. Had it really happened? Had a season of miraculous comebacks been sealed with the most astonishing climax of them all? Football would never be the same again for any of us. We had achieved something that we would never forget.[55]

As thrilled as he was to celebrate with his teammates, Beckham was also enormously happy to share this moment with his parents, because he knew how much the win meant to them. For his father who was such a passionate United fan, and for his mother and all of her support of him over the years, this win, this championship, this special moment was for them as much as it was for David.

Back in Manchester, United's treble winning champions were cheered by 200,000 fans as they were feted parading through the city streets riding in open-top buses. Lifting the treble set Manchester United on a course for worldwide recognition and enabled the team to have fans in all corners of the globe. As it turns out, as Manchester United became more popular and a fan favorite, so too did David Beckham. Or was it the other way around?

A STAR IS BORN

Incredible as the past season had been for Beckham in the United kit, off the field had been filled with life-changing moments too. On March 4, 1999, Beckham and his fiancée Spice Girl Victoria "Posh Spice" Adams had their first child, son Brooklyn Joseph. Then, on July 4, in a lavish ceremony in a castle in Dublin, Ireland, David married Victoria.[56] British tabloid *OK!* paid a record 1.5 million dollars for the exclusive rights to cover the event. The magazine sold 1.5 million copies of the wedding issue, more than four times the magazine's normal sales figures at that time.[57] The Beckham marriage was a marketing match made in heaven. The melding of sports and music industry stars piqued British natives with an insatiable curiosity of the celebrity couple's every move.

The paparazzi were more than willing to feed the frenzy as they followed the striking duo step for step.

The famous, married couple were soon dubbed Posh and Becks, and continued to feed Britain's insatiable appetite for their every action. They were everywhere. When Victoria turned up at a local Woolworth's to sign copies of a new record, David accompanied her, and gave out autographs, too. When Victoria attended United matches, the paparazzi snapped away. If the couple went to dinner, even that made the front page of newspapers. By 2002, and the arrival of their second son, Romeo James, the couple had purchased a mansion in the London borough of Hertfordshire, that quickly became known as Beckingham Palace. They counted as one of their close friends Sir Elton John, who became godfather to both Beckham sons.[58] And as Beckham's popularity on the field continued to grow, especially now that he had redeemed himself in the eyes of British fans, and continued to play so impressively, so too did his celebrity status. That in turn increased his sponsorship opportunities, and not just in England. United was already building a huge fan base in parts of Asia. With his good looks and talent on the field, David Beckham was one of the favorite players. As early as 2002, he'd already achieved a marketing coup in being able to crossover and appeal to a global audience.

They were young and beautiful, stylish and sexy. Advertisers salivated at signing David and his rugged good looks. Lucrative deals were struck with German sneaker company Adidas, soft drink maker Pepsi, and hair product Brylcreem that helped Beckham not only earn millions but also be seen by millions.[59]

It was this celebrity aspect, this obsession with fame thing that United manager Alex Ferguson felt was distracting the dedicated player he'd observed since he was a youth. Ferguson seemed convinced that football, at least playing with Manchester, was no longer first on Beckham's list of priorities. It was something that the manager, right or wrong, could not tolerate.[60] And it began to change not just the course of the athlete and manager's relationship, but ultimately the course of David Beckham's football career.

KIND OF BLUE

By the start of the 2002–2003 Man United season, the dream that had come true for David Beckham—to spend his football career playing for his beloved Manchester United—had officially turned into a nightmare. There were a series of incidents that were reported in the press. Beckham was given permission to miss a team training to take care of his ailing son, Brooklyn. But when news reports showed his wife Victoria at an event the same evening, an angered Ferguson proceeded to fine the midfielder.[61] Ferguson later benched Beckham for a few matches in the 2002–2003 season. Journalists who covered United and English football knew a rift between Manchester's star player and famed coach was growing.[62] Depending on what you read, the blame was the celebrity influence of his pop star wife or too many off-the-field commitments. No matter the cause, the rift was growing larger every day.

What happened on February 15, 2003, seemed to force the issue that, one way or the other, something had to be done to come to a resolution.[63]

Beckham watched from the sidelines as Man United was eliminated from the FA Cup at the hands of Arsenal, 2–0. He had left the field at Old Trafford with an injury to his right leg late in the second half of the match. But it was off the field where the more damaging actions took place.[64]

According to published reports and those who witnessed it, Ferguson lashed out at Beckham in the locker room after the game, full-on ranting, seemingly accusing him, and him alone, for the horrendous play on the field. And during his tirade, Ferguson kicked a stray cleat that happened to be lying on the dressing room floor that flew at and hit Beckham on the side of his head.[65] BBC headlines: "Beckham's Cutting Edge; When Managers Attack; Will Becks Give Man Utd the Boot?"[66]

In his 2004 autobiography, Beckham admitted the whole incident seemed unreal. There was no breaking the sanctity of the club code—what happens in the team dressing room, stays in the team dressing room. Neither the manager nor the player was going to violate that trust by running to the media or the public with the complete blow-by-blow. They were both mature enough to handle the situation and move on, despite whatever speculations appeared in the press. Years later, Beckham would reveal that his immediate reaction had called for several teammates to restrain him from Ferguson.[67]

But Beckham also said Ferguson apologized almost immediately afterward. A bandage over his left eye, which covered the two stitches the midfielder needed to close the gash the cleat had made, was now proof to the public of the strained relationship between the player and the manager.[68]

British bet makers placed odds—who would be forced out of Manchester first?—and most had Beckham as the favorite.[69] Whatever Beckham was going through emotionally, and whatever would ultimately happen to him, one thing was certain—the lad from Leytonstone who had only ever wanted to play for United, and who had proved his love and devotion through his stellar performances on the pitch, would remain forever Red.

SAY IT AIN'T SO

As the 2003 summer transfer window opened, the press ran story after story speculating about where United would be shipping Beckham. The two teams that were reported to get in the bidding were both in Spain, rival football clubs Barcelona and Real Madrid. In May however, Real made it publicly known that they were not interested in the English midfielder.[70]

While the trade rumors were swirling, Beckham wore his United jersey proudly, as he finished out the 2002–2003 season with Manchester. When United faced Charlton FC, their final home match of the season, Beckham had every suspicion that this could be his last match at Old Trafford playing for Manchester United. He scored the first goal of the match and in his autobiography vividly remembers his emotions.

> As I wheeled away towards the supporters, the instinctive joy that comes with a goal collided with the thought that I might never be doing this again. . . . I was happy to score but choking back tears at the same time. . . . After I'd changed and had something to drink in the lounge, I took Brooklyn out on the field for a kickabout. Old Trafford was empty, sunshine still creeping over the roof of the stand. If I was going to go to pieces that would have been the moment: the place looked beautiful, still echoing with the voices of the 60,000 fans who'd been jammed in there an hour earlier. It was a bittersweet afternoon.[71]

In the last match of the season, on May 11, United found themselves visiting Everton with the Premier League title on the line. In what would be his final start, and final match as a member of the Manchester United football club, David Beckham drove in one of his famous free kicks for a score. The team went on to win and he captured the sixth premiership medal of his twelve-year United career.

Then in early June, a Man United executive confirmed that the club had indeed spoken with Barcelona's team president about a Beckham trade. The drama between the two Spanish clubs and Manchester went back and forth for weeks. Finally, on June 17, 2003, Manchester United confirmed that they had sold the England captain to Spanish club Real Madrid for a $41 million transfer fee. David Beckham's career with Manchester United was over.[72]

In the end, Beckham may have sensed there was no way to resolve whatever was happening at United, and that the opportunity that was presented to him in Madrid was too good to turn down. While his comments after the trade was announced were all media-savvy correct, the man who as a kid had only ever wanted to play football for Manchester United, made them with a heavy heart.

I would like to publicly thank Sir Alex Ferguson for making me the player I am today. I will always hold precious memories of my time at Manchester United and Old Trafford as well as the players, who I regard as part of my family, and the brilliant fans who have given me so much support over the years and continue to do so. I recognise that this is an amazing opportunity for me at this stage in my career and a unique and exciting experience for my family.[73]

UNFORGETTABLE

Ten years after David Beckham had succeeded in becoming a member of the football club of his childhood dreams, joining the football family and only club he'd ever wanted to play for, he took his final bow for Manchester United.

The love affair with the Manchester United football club started early, and influenced by a father's devotion to the team, it only deepened over the years. Combined with an all-consuming desire to play football, and a work ethic that meant dedication to practice and perfection, David was able to achieve more than he could ever have dreamed. The little boy who hung posters of United players on his wall, now found himself joining the football legends as his photo graced program covers and posters, and he found jerseys with his name on them worn by a new generation of youngsters.

When David Beckham ended his career with Manchester, he left the supporters of the Red Army with plenty of highlights to remember him by. The midfielder made 394 appearances for Manchester, scoring eighty-five goals. United won six Premier League titles with Beckham on board, two FA Cups, and one UEFA Champions League title. And there was the treble in 1999.[74] Beckham wowed with his magic right foot, but he played with his heart and soul, giving everything, willingly, that he had to United. It's how he wanted to be remembered.[75]

In 2005, Gary Neville had this to say about Beckham's departure: "He's still probably upset about the fact that he left United. He loves the club, he grew up loving the club. You can't grow up from the age of four or five, you know, having something as being part of your life and then expect it's not going to hurt you."[76]

The chapter on David Beckham as a player with the Manchester United football club had come to an end. But there was a lot more to come in the story of the football legend's career.

4

POSH LIFE

They were on their feet. Everyone. Screaming, cheering, singing. Girls, boys, teens, tweens, and equally star-crazed grownups. Delirious, ecstatic, ninety-eight thousand fans packed into Wembley Stadium to see them—the Spice Girls, Britain's pop music sensation.

Girl power took on the final frontier with a stage setting that resembled a scene from outer space circa 2198. A massive silver, sci-fi castle has transformed the center of the football pitch. Planets and stars and galaxies whiz by on the giant movie screens on stage. A saucer-style spacecraft makes a landing on the field.[1]

Strutting and shimmying on the stage at the world-renowned venue, Posh, Scary, Sporty, Ginger, and Baby, aka the Spice Girls, are belting out hit single after hit single from their record-breaking debut album, *Spice*. The hot ticket on this hot summer night, September 20, 1998, was for the last show in the last country on the last leg of the group's Spiceworld Tour.[2] Seven months, ninety-seven performances and seventeen countries in Europe and North America. The record-setting tour, with sold-out venues around the globe, wrapped in London, the city that was the site of the group's formation and first recordings. It's the city that launched them into international fame.[3]

WANTED

For any aspiring singer, answering the advertisement was a no-brainer. It was in the *Stage*, the British weekly newspaper that covered the entertainment industry and listed auditions.[4]

WANTED: R.U. 18–23 with the ability to sing/dance? R.U. streetwise, outgoing, ambitious, and dedicated? Heart Management Ltd. are a widely successful music industry management consortium currently forming a choreographed, singing/dancing, all-female pop act for a record recording deal. Open audition. Danceworks, 16 Balderton Street. Friday 4 March. 11 am–5:30 pm. Please bring sheet music or backing cassette.[5]

A reported four hundred women showed up. Four months later, after screenings and auditions, Heart Management had their five-member, all-girl group. One of those women was nineteen-year-old Victoria Adams, before fame and before marriage to footballer David Beckham. Originally given the name Touch, the girls lived together in a house for several months in 1993 learning dance routines and rehearsing songs, reflecting and perfecting an image. The next two years were followed by more hard work. The dedicated and driven quintet recorded demos and performed showcases for industry execs, producers, and songwriters.[6]

Melanie Brown, Melanie Chisolm, Emma Bunton, Geri Halliwell, and Victoria Adams had become the Spice Girls by then, and in crafting their sound and brand they were growing dissatisfied with their management company. The group was eventually introduced to Simon Fuller, the entertainment executive who would go on to create the successful Pop Idol music show and the Idol series. Fuller and his company, 19 Management, took on the group in March 1995, and in September, the Spice Girls signed with Virgin Records. Finally, with a record label behind them, the group proceeded with recording tracks for a debut album.[7]

The Spice Girls released the single "Wannabe" in June of 1996. It was an instant hit. The song rose to number 1 in the United Kingdom and thirty other countries. The Spice Girls exploded onto the public, becoming the fastest-selling British band since the Beatles and rode a wave of global success for several years. They would go on to set a record of nine UK number 1 singles and fifty-five million records sold. Spice Girls-fever defined the 1990s, as the group went on to become the biggest pop cultural icons of the decade.[8]

At Wembley the Spice Girls had also performed "Say You'll Be There," the second single released off the group's debut album. It was the video of this song that caught the attention of a football player with Manchester United named David Beckham. While playing in an away match with the England National team, in his hotel room Beckham recalled his thoughts when he saw the Spice Girls video on TV, "I turned around to Gary [Neville] and said, 'That one there, that's the girl I'm going to marry.'"[9]

Who he wanted as his wife was settled. But Beckham had no idea how he was going to meet *that girl*, Victoria Adams, when the Spice Girls were the biggest pop stars on the planet. Months later, in a charity match with Manchester United facing Chelsea in London, David would have the chance meeting he'd dreamed of. Two members of the Spice Girls were attending the game. Beckham headed for the players' lounge afterward, hoping. When he entered he could not believe his luck to see Victoria Adams and Melanie Chisolm chatting in a corner. His prayers had been answered and his dream was about to come true: "Hello, David. I'm Simon Fuller. I look after the Spice Girls. I'd like you to meet Victoria."[10]

"WANNABE"

It is no secret that watching the movie *Fame* inspired young Victoria Adams to pursue a career in showbiz. The oldest child of Jackie and Anthony Adams, owners of an electrical warehouse business, grew up with siblings Louise and Christian in Goffs Oak, Hertfordshire, England, a working-class neighborhood north of London. Her parents signed her up for classes at a local theater school. Victoria:

> I was an eight-year-old girl with a dream. I was going to be like one of the kids from *Fame*, and as I thought about the bit where the audience get to dance on stage I had literally never been so excited. And you know what? When my mum took me to see Cliff Richard at Wembley a few months later, I said to her, "I'm going to be performing up there one day."[11]

By her own admission, Victoria was verbally and physically bullied at school.[12] She had acne and was unpopular, and that only made high school worse. She never felt like she fit in. But Victoria had a dream, a laser-like focus on fame and unrelenting determination. A quote from her autobiography, repeated often whenever her future aspirations were discussed, was that she wanted to become as widely known as a popular British laundry detergent.[13]

"I wanted to be as famous as Persil automatic."[14]

Years later Victoria studied dance and modeling at the Laine Theatre Arts College. She was single-minded in reaching her goals and committed to achieving them. By the time she'd answered the *Stage* advertisement, Victoria Adams was ready for her close-up. All of her practices, all of her hard work and dedication—everything came down to this moment, at a music group audition.

The self-confessed workaholic put everything she had into making it with the all-girl singing group. And her efforts paid off, with Victoria Adams achieving the kind of success even she likely could not have imagined. Her life story was the ultimate example of how far one could get with hard work, discipline, and keeping your focus on your goals. If Victoria is not officially as well known as Persil, she runs a close second.

Those early steps toward fame also put Victoria on a direct path to be introduced to her husband. And although it would take her twenty years to meet him, when she did, the future celebrity couple discovered they had grown up in towns that were only fifteen minutes away from each other.[15]

INTIMATELY BECKHAM

"I literally didn't know who David was when I first met him. How dim is that? But I soon realised he was the man for me. He is just so sensitive and so not like other footballers."[16]

They tried to keep their romance a secret. Rather than be seen going out to fancy restaurants, the couple's first dates were spent talking while sitting in cars in parking lots. Victoria even shared in her autobiography that the first time David kissed her was on one of their glamorous parking-lot dates.[17] Escaping the glare of the media spotlight, their new relationship was initially as normal as anyone else's.[18] Beckham:

> For the first three months it was amazing because no one found out about us being together, we loved that because we could sneak around. Our first kiss was in the car park of a restaurant. We used to drive to places and just spend as much time together as possible. That was an amazing time in our relationship.[19]

But trying to keep spying eyes away from them was as impossible as keeping a teen from texting. Once the news got out that Posh Spice was dating a Manchester United footballer, Victoria and David became front-page news. There was, they admit, an almost immediate chemistry between the two, and the couple managed to spend as much time together as their busy schedules would allow. David knew Victoria was the one and proposed to her only months after they'd started dating. He gave her a $65,000 three-plus-carat diamond engagement ring.[20] And Victoria gave him an $80,000 three-tiered band of ninety-six diamonds as his engagement ring.[21]

Despite their desire to have privacy, it soon became clear to David that the two were extremely desirable public figures. He grabbed the football headlines and she filled the entertainment pages. In terms of fame and popularity and being recognized, David, at that time, was almost an afterthought to Victoria. The David Beckham as a brand, as an icon was not even discussed at that early stage of his career. His life as a footballer included media intrusion and public interest, but nothing on a grand scale. It was when David entered the celebrity world of global superstar Victoria Adams that he too was thrust into the upper stratosphere of fame.

THE PITTER PATTER OF LITTLE FEET

It is possible that David Beckham's first-born son practiced kicking in the womb, as if he knew what the expectations of his birth would bring. Brooklyn Joseph was born to David and Victoria on March 4, 1999, in London. As the press does with the Royal Family, the paparazzi waited at the hospital exit for the chance to snap the first photos of Baby Boy Beckham. The world, it seemed, was waiting as eagerly for his arrival as was his family.[22]

Having a baby changed many things in the Beckhams' world. Though both were considered young parents, David was thrilled when he learned he was about to become a father. Noted Victoria, "When I told David I was pregnant, he just started weeping. He must have cried for about an hour and I had tears running down my face, too. It was a very emotional moment for both of us."[23]

As emotional as the news had been for the footballer, nothing could have prepared him for the feelings he'd have witnessing the birth of his first child: "I was the first to hold him and it was unbelievable. It was weird, the best feeling in the world and like nothing I ever felt before."[24]

David was all in, for diaper changes and bottle feedings and whatever he was needed for. The young parents did not hire nannies, wanting Brooklyn to be around them and more included in their lives. They also relied on their close-knit family for guidance and when they needed babysitters. And they enjoyed the experience of having a new addition to their family. Said Victoria, "Brooklyn is literally the best baby in the entire universe and David and I just so love him to bits."[25]

Naturally, the Beckham heir was at his mother's side whenever she attended David's football matches, and quickly showed an interest in the game. At a match in 2001, while accompanying his father around the field after Man United had sealed the Premier League title, the two-year-old gave the Old Trafford crowd a thrill when in front of the goal he made an impromptu shot into the net.[26]

Since then his love for the game has only mushroomed. He's played with an apparent attempt at pursuing the beautiful game for a career. Growing up, Beckham junior has had formal training in various different camps and academies.

And he's had the example of his father's commitment to practice and discipline to emulate. By the time he became a teen, Brooklyn would participate in several trials with English Premier League teams' youth academies.[27]

Proud father David spoke of his young son's soccer skills in 2013: "Brooklyn is the most amazing footballer. He's showing great potential and I think he could go all the way. I'd love it if he played for England."[28]

In 2013, unconfirmed reports flourished that Brooklyn Beckham was about to be signed by Manchester United's academy, in the coming year. Any such signings would put the youngster inches closer to continuing his father's footballing legacy.

YOU ARE HERE: LUTTRELLSTOWN CASTLE, CASTLEKNOCK, IRELAND

At first glance, the small stone building looks dilapidated and unwelcoming. But the folly, as it is called, was built to look like it was in ruins as part of its charm. In this tranquil setting, on the Irish countryside, with moss-blanketed steps that led to the entrance, and the soft gurgling of a stream below, it was transformed into something magical. Ivy-covered walls, roses entwined in branches, and thousands of twinkling lights completed the enchanted forest scene.

Luttrellstown Castle, just outside of Dublin, Ireland, was constructed nearly three hundred years ago. Tudor revival and nineteenth-century gothic revival details are prominently featured in the romantic-style building. Former distinguished guests have included Prince Rainier and Princess Grace of Monaco, Fred Astaire, and President Ronald Reagan.[29]

On July 4, 1999, the castle was the site of the wedding of Manchester United footballer David Beckham and Spice Girl Victoria Adams.

Inside the small folly, along with two dozen or so family members and friends, David held Brooklyn in his arms as they awaited the bride. Father and son were both dressed in ivory and white suits. A string quartet began to play the bridal chorus by Wagner, the popular wedding processional known more commonly as "Here Comes the Bride." Then Victoria walked in, and the footballer was overcome with emotion. Beckham:

> Victoria was everything I knew—and knew I wanted—but she suddenly seemed much more than all that, too. I thought I knew how I felt about her but I wasn't prepared at all for how I was feeling right at that instant. Victoria was more beautiful than I'd ever realized or could have imagined.[30]

For her wedding gown, Posh had selected American clothing designer Vera Wang. There had been several fittings and input from the English fashionista, who wanted "to be like a modern Cinderella."[31] The structured, ball gown–skirted dress featured a small-waist bodice. The champagne-colored, satin, strapless gown had a twenty-foot train.[32] It had a price tag of $100,000, earning it a spot on the twelve most expensive celebrity wedding gowns of all time. Kate Middleton's Alexander McQueen–designed gown topped the list at $400,000, while the average American bride spends approximately $1,500 for a dress. Victoria also wore an 18-carat, yellow-gold tiara with brilliant diamonds.[33]

A small number of family and close friends witnessed the ceremony as the teary-eyed bride and groom held hands standing at the altar.

> The Right Reverend Paul Colton, Bishop of Cork, Ireland, asked if, "anyone knows any cause or just impediment why these two should not be joined together" and then placed the couple's hands together before beginning the marriage vows. At 4.49 pm David Robert Joseph Beckham and Victoria Caroline Adams were officially declared husband and wife.[34]

After the ceremony three hundred or so guests, including the Spice Girls and players from Manchester United, joined the couple at their lavish, $800,000 reception. Working with an expert wedding planner, Victoria and David had spent the previous ten months deciding on every detail of their magical day. Victoria called it a dream come true.[35]

Gary Neville, a teammate of David's from Manchester United and the England National team, was his best man. An eighteen-piece orchestra entertained guests. The couple had matching gilded and red-velvet thrones so that they could be king and queen of the castle for the day. During the course of the day, the bride and groom changed into royal purple outfits and made the obligatory round of greeting everyone who attended. As the evening came to an end, everyone poured outside the castle to watch a spectacular fireworks display.[36]

In such a secluded and private location, there were no intrusive paparazzi. But the Beckham wedding was photographed. For the exclusive right to take and publish the photos, Britain's *OK!* magazine had paid a handsome $1.5 million.[37]

Earlier in the evening, Victoria's father, Tony Adams, summed up the couple's new union with a wedding toast:

> Victoria started dance classes at the age of three and was soon rushing home from school to change from her uniform into a leotard to kick her legs about—little did she know that only a few miles away there was a little boy changing from his uniform into shorts to kick a ball around. They continued with enthusiasm and at 16 both

left home to continue their training. Victoria went to dance college in Epsom and we all know where David went.[38] They've each worked really hard to achieve what they have. And now they're really lucky to have found each other after all this time.[39]

TEAM BECKHAM

Romeo James: September 1, 2002; 7 lbs., 4 oz.; London, England
"Romeo's gorgeous. He's got Brooklyn's nose and Victoria's chin."[40]
He may have been the second child born to David and Victoria Beckham, but the media covered the birth as intently as they had the couple's first child, with paparazzi camped out at the hospital entrance for a chance at those coveted first photos.

> I was selfish before—everyone is. Until you have children you don't realize how much it changes your life and how they become your main priority in terms of making sure they are OK, making sure they are happy. Me and Victoria are busy in our jobs and what we do as individuals. But there is nothing that compares to being a father. They are the most special boys in our lives and we would do anything for them.[41]

While the world watches to see if the second Beckham son will also follow in his father's famous football shoes, Romeo showed that he may be leaning toward a career in fashion like his designer mother.

At ten, the second Beckham son notched his first modeling gig when he was chosen to star in the 2013 summer campaign of British luxury fashion house Burberry.[42]

Cruz David: February 20, 2005; 7 lbs.; Madrid, Spain
"He's a healthy little boy. He's got Victoria's lips and nose. He's gorgeous."[43]
The Beckhams had long ago revealed to the world the reason for naming their first child Brooklyn. Romeo, they explained, was simply because the couple considered themselves romantic. With third son Cruz they looked no further than good friend and mega movie star, Tom Cruise, and explained they'd always loved the name.[44]

As he did with his first two sons, Beckham etched his third child's name onto his back. His three boys are also represented as cherubs alongside a guardian angel on David's chest.[45] David:

> It would be easy for our kids to sit back and not work for anything, but they're not like that. They're as competitive as Victoria and me. They want to win.

They want to work at something. They know their values. That's the way we've brought them up so far, and that's the way we'll continue to bring them up.[46]

Harper Seven: July 10, 2011; 7 lbs., 10 oz.; Los Angeles, California

It's a girl, finally! The Beckhams welcomed the newest addition to their family, their fourth child and first daughter, Harper Seven in 2011. Victoria loves the old-English name, Harper, and Seven was the jersey number of David with both Manchester United and the English National team.[47] Victoria tweeted, "Baby Harper is the most beautiful baby girl I have ever seen; I have fallen in love all over again!!!"[48]

Fashion finds Baby Girl Beckham an adorable palette to work with. Could Victoria Beckham's daughter be caught in anything less than a designer's best? Bloggers track Harper's every outfit, and splashed across the Internet are photos of her dressed in everything from Marc Jacobs, Stella McCartney, Burberry, and Hermes. When not being a pint-sized fashionista, Harper is also captured hanging out with her famous football father. The two are snapped attending various events including baseball, basketball, and hockey games, as well as numerous family outings.

At New York Fashion Week in the fall of 2013, where her cuteness got as much attention as the clothing designs, a Harper sighting combined the worlds of both of her celebrity parents. The two-year-old sat in the front row with David as the father and daughter watched Posh's runway show. Finally, on the football front, the world should be pleased to know, that like her three older brothers, the tiny tot has already acquired an interest in the game and has even been photographed playing it.[49] Harper it seems may also have inherited David Beckham's athletic genes. David:

> To have another girl in the family is really incredible. We've got three beautiful, healthy boys already and we're so lucky to have that and now to have a beautiful little girl, it's amazing. Having a daughter is a whole new thing. Having pink in the house and lilac in the house. And you have to be a lot more delicate with girls than with boys and I'm not used to that so it's a whole new experience but it's an amazing experience.[50]

THE BOLD AND THE BEAUTIFUL

The stylish black-and-white photographs created a dramatic effect of smoldering eroticism. The provocative couple in the ad campaign are selling a new line of Armani undergarments. David is shirtless, his toned abs glistening as he lies stretched across a large, coiled rope. Victoria, in simply a bra and panties, lies seductively alongside and on top of him. Together, their beautiful bodies spoke the universal language of sexy.[51]

Initially David signed with Giorgio Armani, which was his first clothing contract, with a three-year deal worth a reported $20 million back in 2007. His campaign ran in January 2008 with billboards that stopped traffic in London, New York, Los Angeles, and Paris. Then Victoria, who by this time was pursuing other areas of work, as the Spice Girls had dissolved the group years earlier, was selected for her own spot. And then the two worked together to create the sizzling and sexy images for the global spots, promoting the autumn/winter 2009/10 collections of the designer's Emporio Armani underwear line. The shots marked the second time the duo had appeared as a double act for Armani.[52]

The Beckham's continued to prove their marketability as a couple. Armani sales for the new underwear line were boosted to nearly $30 million in 2008.[53] The success also helped David form the idea of creating his own line of undergarments, which took a number of years to start, but ultimately manifested in the partnership between the megastar footballer and retailer H&M. This time Beckham's name would highlight the product, as well as be stamped all over it.

Building Brand Beckham, product by product, campaign by campaign, the celebrity couple continue to branch into other businesses. And their calculated ventures keep adding to the pair's fortune as well as making them a household name in countries other than England. And David, as one half of the iconic duo, continues to attract followers with his many off-the-field ventures, widening his appeal with even more audiences.

LEARNING TO FLY

Those who expected the ultra-driven Victoria Beckham to fade into the background after packing up her microphone when her solo singing career flopped, only need to feast their eyes on a different section of the entertainment news. The mom and wife made time for motherhood and for supporting her husband, but the businesswoman shifted into reinvention mode and steered into new ventures. Years earlier there had been the few modeling gigs and ads she'd done for Dolce and Gabbana and Rocawear. So the style icon set out to capitalize on her sense of fashion and poured her energy into design.

At first Posh was asked to design a line of jeans for Rock & Republic. Then with momentum from the positive reviews, Victoria created her own denim line, launched an eyewear line and a new fragrance line called Intimately Beckham, under dvb, the company she owns with husband David.

Marc Jacobs, who chose Victoria as the face of his spring/summer 2008 campaign, has said, "Fashion is about risks, and I think that both of us work very, very hard . . . as people who challenge and who take chances and are willing to push the envelope and who refuse to be categorised by what other people think. That's one of the main attractions of Victoria."[54]

Recognized by her peers, she was awarded two *British Glamour* magazine awards, for Woman of the Year and Entrepreneur of the Year in 2007. Victoria has since branched into a dress collection, coats, handbags, and jewelry, and she does not appear to be slowing down. In November 2011, she was named the "Designer of the Year" at the annual British Fashion Awards.[55]

Despite critics who question her talent as a singer or designer and scrutinize her weight and looks, Victoria seems to defy the odds and still remain as relevant as ever. By employing the same virtues that saw her achieve success as a Spice Girl—hard work, dedication, sacrifice, commitment—Victoria Beckham can now proudly wear a multitude of titles that includes celebrity, businesswoman, style influencer, wife, and mother. The preferred order of importance will ultimately be decided by her. "I never try to follow a trend or fashion; I just do what feels right. Everything I make, from glasses to a handbag to a dress is something I would wear and carry myself," Victoria said at *WWD*'s Apparel and Retail CEO Summit in 2011.[56]

LOVE STORY

When David met Victoria, their fame level rose meteorically to one almost on a par with the British royal family. Where they went, what they wore, what they did—all was photographed and documented for an ever-growing fan base to consume. But along the way, the couple became more than just gossip-magazine fodder. Both forged forward in their careers, reaping success, wealth, and more fame. And while it is no surprise that their actions, together and individually, continue to make headlines, what may surprise some is that their union still exists. In 2013 the Beckhams celebrated their fourteenth anniversary and effusively proclaim to be more in love than ever.

At a time when celebrity marriages more often fail than make it, theirs has defied the odds. Through years of coordinating outfits, rumors of infidelity, public scrutiny and criticism, hectic work schedules, and several relocations, David and Victoria have endured. Unconfirmed reports claim the couple renewed their wedding vows in 2008 at a secret ceremony and location at the suggestion of David. If they did, it remains a secret. In 2009, a British survey named Victoria and David Beckham the "perfect married couple." Their union was held up as "a shining example of marriage" in a Wedding TV survey.[57] He said,

> She comes home and shows me what she's been doing all day and what exciting dresses and bags she's got coming through. And then I say something boring like "I got kicked today." But we listen to each other. We try to go out at least once a week, just the two of us, a quiet dinner somewhere. It's not about wearing a nice dress or a nice suit. It's just going out and chatting and having some time together.[58]

She said,

> Sometimes people throw s--- at us but we get through it. You deal with it, or you don't. You go into a marriage knowing there are going to be ups and downs. We're in the public eye so we have more to deal with than most. We accepted that years ago. It's just about us and the family. We're soul mates.[59]

What still stands after fourteen years, four children, and one fairy tale romance, is a couple deeply in love and committed to being together forever.

5

THE THREE LIONS

Membership in the exclusive club is a coveted achievement. Entry fees are paid with talent and time, dedication and drive, and the relentless pursuit of success. It is a nod to years of commitment, and for consistently striving to be the best. The former football players gathered on the pitch inside Wembley Stadium exemplified all of these virtues and more. One by one, they posed, each clutching their commemorative century cap. It was halftime of a final 2012 European Championships warm-up game between England and Belgium. But the real treat for the crowd in attendance was witnessing the history-making legends that stood on the field, as they were being honored for having played in more than one hundred international matches for England. It was a small but distinguished club, and David Beckham was one of the centurions being celebrated.

The Union of European Football Associations (UEFA) had organized this event, a tribute to the five former players from England who had achieved such a monumental career milestone. A year ago, the organization had launched this initiative to honor European footballers who'd reached the historic century mark. UEFA reserved today for England's Three Lions legends. In addition to Beckham, the football governing body gave awards to Peter Shilton, Sir Bobby Charlton, and the families of England greats Bobby Moore and Billy Wright.[1]

Standing on the grounds of the historic Wembley Stadium, David Beckham could reflect on the years he spent wearing the Three Lions shirt. As he was showered with adoration and applause, he looked proud, humbled, grateful. He could marvel at how dedication to the game he loved had led to achievements and accolades even beyond his dreams. And how those same childhood dreams had brought him to this day, where he joined a group that will forever be classified as football legends.

THE DEBUT OF NO. 7

The highlight reel on David Beckham's illustrious England football career began recording in 1996 in the Eastern European city of Chisinau, in the Republic of Moldova.[2] It is admirable to be recognized as a rising prospect within the English Premier League. Playing for your country takes that recognition to another level. It meant joining your fellow countrymen, and, running side by side on the pitch, all trying to capture a title—the World Cup title—to be crowned football's best. The governing body of English football, the Football Association, or the FA, is the oldest football association in the world, having been founded in 1863, when it devised a set of universally accepted rules for playing the modern game. An early version of the rules allowed players to run with the ball in their hand, but was scrapped after a series of six meetings that firmed up the final rules that serve as the foundation used today, 150 years later. The inaugural match was played using the new FA rules in 1864 between two club teams, and the English National team played its first match in 1872. The Three Lions played their first World Cup in 1950, and won the prestigious tournament in 1966.[3]

The England starting XI commanded loyalty and a complete sense of patriotism among supporters. Some of the legends that have donned the Three Lions jersey include Bobby Charlton, who led England to glory when they won the 1966 World Cup title; Sir Geoff Hurst, who is the only player in history to score three goals in a World Cup final; Gary Lineker, who still ranks as England's second-highest scorer of all time; and Bobby Moore, who is the only captain for the Three Lions to ever win a World Cup title. In the fall of 1996, a twenty-one-year-old David Beckham was called to join those legends and to proudly wear his country's colors.[4]

When England started on the campaign to qualify for the 1998 World Cup it did so with a significantly large number of new faces around the locker room. Running the show was new coach Glenn Hoddle. The former midfielder, who had made fifty-three appearances for England, had replaced Terry Venables, who'd guided England to the semifinals in the Euro Cup championship that took place in the UK the past summer. The wealth of new talent included Manchester United youngsters Gary and Phil Neville, and wearing no. 7, David Beckham. Beckham had so impressed the new manager that he was handed a place in the team's starting lineup when they played their first World Cup preliminary match in Republican Stadium in the fall of 1996. It was the first time he'd sing "God Save the Queen" wearing the Three Lions uniform and playing for the England national team.

One journalist had this comment on Beckham as he made his England squad debut:

> Among the bonuses of Glenn Hoddle's international baptism, one stands supreme. A young English player who can operate on the right side of midfield with a natural authority and excellent distribution. David Beckham is a real find. . . . Hoddle deserves credit for recognising an authentic international.[5]

David played the full ninety minutes of the match against Moldova. And he was actively involved in helping set up two goals—one in the first half, which led to a Nick Barmby score, and one in the second, that saw Alan Shearer find the back of the net. The Three Lions win the match, 3–0, and give new manager Hoddle his first-ever England win. David Beckham took the first steps of his promising international career, and recorded his first England cap.

For the third match of his England career, David would travel to Tbilisi, Georgia, where the course of the twenty-one-year-old's life was destined to change forever. Surely the football and music industry gods must have been chatting about how they could fascinate a generation by giving them the celebrity couple of the next century. On the night before his World Cup qualifying match, Beckham found himself in a hotel room when a video of the Spice Girls, Britain's top pop girl group, appeared on the TV. David spotted one of the singers, Victoria Adams, "the one with the bob," and proclaimed that he had to meet her. He would and they were married only three years after he made that first declaration. The rest, as they say, is history.[6]

In roughly a year and a half as a member of the Three Lions, Beckham had started all eight of the World Cup preliminary matches and had collected a total of fifteen caps as a player with England.[7] Finally the calendar turned to summer, and all thoughts to the World Cup. David headed to France, the host nation, with the England national team, for what would be his first tournament. It would also mark a pivotal moment in the footballer's life and career.[8]

COUP DE THÉÂTRE

France, the summer of 1998, was a whirlwind of World Cup preparations. The European country that gave the world Champagne, was celebrating for the second time as host of the "Coupe du Monde"—the first was in 1938—and was determined to enthusiastically welcome the 2.5 million visitors set to attend the tournament. David Beckham's enthusiasm would come from participating in his first World Cup tournament.[9]

Despite his performance in the run up to the World Cup, the England rookie was surprised to find he was not starting the first match vs. Romania. He'd been told by the coach the reason was because he wasn't "focused." He made his World Cup debut instead coming on as a sub, but Beckham was bewildered by the accusation. He did not let on about any building frustration though, and supported his teammates from the bench as they lost, 2–1.[10]

In the Three Lions' second match vs. Columbia, Beckham was called on to start. The midfielder scored a spectacular game-winning goal, his first in a World Cup, giving a glimpse of what greatness was to come from the rising star in the future. In their next match, England faced Argentina. The score was even at 2–2, when minutes after the second half got under way, Beckham found himself tackled by Argentinian captain Diego Simeone. That's when everything fell apart.[11] The *Independent*:

> The crucial incident occurred a minute or two into the second half of England's second-round World Cup match against Argentina in St Etienne on 30 June, when Beckham, sprawling face down on the pitch following a foul by opposing captain Diego Simeone, flicked up his right foot and deliberately caught his assailant on the leg. This rash retaliation was spotted by the referee who duly brandished a red card, obliging Beckham to leave the field and abandon his teammates to an unequal struggle—a struggle which, despite an epic rearguard action, they ultimately lost.[12]

It was an uncharacteristic reaction. And even Beckham has said that he doesn't know what he was thinking or why he did it. The referee wasted no time pulling out a red card and sending Beckham off. Football purists are convinced Simeone was faking, and that his acting skills are what should have been called out. But whether that was true or not was not the issue. Beckham getting a red card was. And his action had major ramifications for England. The ten-man squad left on the field valiantly held on for the remainder of the match and forced it into extra time. They ultimately lost the battle on penalty kicks, 4–3, and were eliminated from the tournament. All of England, it seemed, blamed David for the loss. The British press fed into the fury, perhaps to a level not seen before, with headlines and stories berating Beckham for his petulance.[13] Gary Neville (England teammate):

It's difficult to describe, really, it happened so quickly. The challenge came and he went down, he flicked his leg out in retaliation, in a "get off me" type thing. It wasn't a nasty thing, it wasn't a violent thing. He was never going to hurt the lad. But the lad's reaction wasn't what you'd expect from a professional football player. And the referee . . . you just knew he was going to send him off. I put my arm around him and said, basically, it's happened. . . . He walks off into the tunnel. It's a lonely feeling, that walk off the pitch. It might be only 30 yards but it feels like 30 miles. I don't think anybody was prepared for what happened after that.[14]

In his official statement issued two days after the match, Beckham apologized to his teammates, management, and all of the England fans, saying he regretted his actions and letting them know how sorry he was. When he spoke to the press later, he shared what he could recall had been on his mind immediately after being sent off. "I stood in the tunnel and watched the last few minutes and the terrible tension of the penalty shoot-out. That was worse than anything else. It was then I fully realized what I had done."[15]

While the media goaded—and at times outright led—the campaign against Beckham, he did have the support of his Manchester United family. He credits that circle of love as a saving source of strength. As Alex Ferguson put it: "It's in the past. Get back to Manchester where people love you and get playing football again."[16] England and United legend Sir Bobby Charlton:

You cannot throw him to the wolves. I saw him after the match and he was terribly affected by it. He realised what he had done. He is a young man who was very much affected by it, I know that, and he will have other World Cups where he can put that right.[17]

Gareth Southgate, former England national team player:

I have every confidence he can win this battle, even though it is going to be hard for him—very, very hard. David seems a quiet lad, yet I have no doubt he possesses the character and personality to come out the other side. He wouldn't have progressed as far as has in the game without a lot of inner strength.[18]

Distraught, David went in search of comfort—at the side of his then fiancée Victoria. Immediately after the team flight returned to London, Beckham headed straight to New York, where the Spice Girls were performing at Madison Square Garden. It helped him briefly escape the fallout. His family in the UK was not as lucky. There were reports of supporters jeering them, photographers harassing them, and the media camping outside of their front door. David has always commented on how upset he was that his family had to deal with the backlash for something they did not do.

Backstage at Madison Square Garden, Beckham was experiencing emotions unlike he'd ever had before. His thoughts were not on football, though, or his recent actions in France, but on a photo Victoria had shared with him of the sonogram of his first child. He was going to be a father. It had not been revealed to the press yet. And it was exactly the kind of news he'd needed to help put things into perspective. When David returned to England, bolstered by the support of his family and friends, he got back to the business of playing football, reporting to preseason training with United, and he soldiered on.[19]

THE MOST HATED MAN IN BRITAIN

The preseason, and with it the season of friendlies, was indeed over by August 9, when Man United were set to compete for the FA Charity Shield in a match at Wembley Stadium. What started with boos every time Beckham touched the ball was the first sign of how angered the English supporters were, and how ugly their behavior was going to become. The first away game for Manchester saw them facing West Ham United in Upton Park, in London, where the taunting received more news and attention than the match.

Police officers met Beckham as the team bus arrived at the stadium. Hundreds of people had been waiting in the parking lot and they weren't there for David's autograph. There was an early indication that the atmosphere might be dangerous when an effigy of Beckham wearing a shirt emblazoned with no. 7 was found hung outside of a local pub. As surreal as that seemed, the taunting that followed once the match got underway was otherworldly frightening. When Beckham approached the touchline, overzealous, patriotic English supporters stood up and rained vicious curses down on him. Grown men spit at him and threw bottles down on the field. What Beckham did not know at the time was that this hateful behavior was going to be repeated at nearly every England and Man United match he would play in for the remainder of that season.

Enraged, the nation decided Beckham was to blame for its World Cup misfortunes. A butcher shop had placed two pig heads in its front window and labeled one David and the other Victoria. Hecklers shouted at him when he drove into gas stations and would give him the finger if they pulled alongside him driving on the road. He revealed in later interviews that he could not believe the hateful things his own countrymen had shouted at him. The worst of the verbal abuse had been comments made about his wife and son. And that didn't even include the death threats he would receive.[20]

On the schedule for Manchester United the following spring was a UEFA Champions League match with Inter Milan, a top flight club from Italy. It would also mark the first meeting between Beckham and Diego Simeone, who played for the Italian club, since the World Cup incident. Before the game, and for the first time, Simeone admitted to faking the injury as he told the press his version of the events that happened on the football pitch the previous summer in St. Etienne, France:

> *Evidentemente, fui muy astuto al dejarme caer . . . , y el árbitro cayó en la trampa al sacar la tarjeta roja. Puede decirse que mi caída convirtió una tarjeta amarilla en una roja.[21]*

Obviously, I was being clever. By letting myself fall, I got the referee to pull out a red card immediately. Let's just say the referee fell into the trap. You could say that my falling transformed a yellow card into a red card. But in fact, the most appropriate punishment was a yellow one. In reality, it wasn't a violent blow, it was just a little kick back with no force behind it, and was probably instinctive.[22]

Though the media cooked up scenarios of retaliation on Beckham's part, there were none. Before a crowd of 54,430, Beckham played the entire match of the first leg of the quarterfinal, which Man United won, and even exchanged shirts with the Argentinian captain at the end. The consummate professional. Always.[23]

Simply Red singer and Manchester United fanatic Mick Hucknall was at the match and commented on his admiration for Beckham's professionalism around his whole ordeal:

He has taken the right attitude with the kind of incredible pressure he was under since the Argentina match at the World Cup. And I thought his gesture to Simeone was brilliant. It was a really good thing to do. It showed great maturity. My respect for David went up ten-fold—for the gesture and for the commitment he showed throughout the match. [Things] could all have so easily gone terribly wrong for David this season, but he has focused any anger or frustration that he has had on football.[24]

Trouble continued though, and at one point within months after the red card penalty Beckham recalls in an autobiography how unsafe he felt when he found himself home alone and spooked by a stranger peering into his house. The alarm system was fully functioning, but that did not stop Beckham from being frightened when he was awakened by a loud sound coming from outside. He found what turned out to be someone at the back fence of his home. A brief staring contest took place between Beckham and the man before the footballer called the police. The intruder was nowhere to be found by the time they arrived.[25]

Another particularly hateful outing Beckham recalled was at the first match of the European Championships in Belgium in 2000. England lost, but this time when the abuse was lashed on Beckham, he retaliated, giving the hooligans in the stands his finger. It was the first time he'd "lost it." He was later reassured by the England manager, Kevin Keegan, that he had done no wrong in his actions while continuing to weather this seemingly unending storm. David said that helped him, more than anything, stay strong throughout the ordeal. He would not crack or crumble from the weight of the pressure. David Beckham remained a proud Englishman, and relished the opportunity to continue playing for his country.[26]

LEADER OF THE PACK

Through all of the public taunting and hatred that contributed to David Beckham's personal hell, the professional athlete had the will to keep playing football. The national team had replaced the management from their 1998 World Cup disappointment, and the new coach kept Beckham in his starting lineup. Work was underway to lay a successful foundation for a run at the 2000 Euro Cup Championships in Belgium. David also started all four of the group matches in the tournament, recording his first appearance in the Euro Cup. Unfortunately the Three Lions were unable to gain any advantage over their European opponents and were unable to make it past the first round. England dealt with the disappointing finish by once again bringing in a new coaching staff.

By the end of 2000, David found himself playing for the fifth coach since he'd joined the national team. And when Peter Taylor, who had enjoyed a successful career as a winger before turning to coaching, took the helm on November 15, 2000, before a friendly international with Italy in Turin, he handed the captain's armband to David Beckham, asking the lad from Leytonstone to lead the players on the field. "If someone had said in 1998 after my sending off in the World Cup that I would be leading my country out within three years, I would have laughed in their face."[27]

The more telling moment came in early 2001, when, with yet another new England coach on board, Beckham was asked to keep the title. It was the beginning of another astounding year for him.

2001: THE YEAR OF THE COMEBACK

The Kings of England, otherwise known as the Manchester United football club, were still riding a wave of notoriety as top dogs within the English Premier League. David Beckham's team earned the nickname in 1999 after winning Europe's honor of capturing the treble, three prestigious titles—the English Premier League title, the FA Cup Championship, and the UEFA Championship title.

The English midfielder was clearly beloved by the supporters of the club, as Old Trafford was one of the few places he could escape the vicious name-calling that followed him after the red card incident. United followed the treble season with another Premier League title, and in April of 2001 captured their third title in three seasons. David made thirty-one league appearances and scored nine goals.

Later that same year, Beckham was part of the England team that faced Greece in a World Cup preliminary match. Despite the prospect of the outcome of the match—automatic qualification for the World Cup—England did not appear up for the challenge. The team had battled Greece all afternoon, before a loud crowd at Old Trafford, but trailed, 2–1. Throughout the match captain David Beckham summoned his leadership skills and encouraged his teammates to keep fighting. Then he used his athletic ability to show them how to never give up. Minutes into stoppage time, England was awarded a free kick. Beckham waived off teammate Teddy Sheringham. With the confidence that comes from practicing thousands of free kicks as a youth, and pro matches with United and with the Three Lions, that found him prepared when the moment arose, Beckham used his magic right foot to send a rocket swerving wide of the Greece goalkeeper. The tie gave England the points they needed to land a berth in the 2002 World Cup.[28]

> There is something incredible when you strike a football in just the way you want to. It feels so satisfying, the tiny thud of the ball against your boot, and then the fizz of the ball as it speeds away. When you get it right, you hardly feel the impact. It is like kicking a feather.
>
> But the goal was the icing on the cake. It was as if all the lingering doubts about me as a player and as a person vanished in an instant. All of the pain, all of the bitterness, all of the hatred, all of the recriminations. I knew that one of the most difficult chapters in my life had come to an end.
>
> I was forgiven at last.[29]

Once hated, berated, and blamed for all that was wrong with the English national football team, David Beckham was suddenly celebrated.[30]

Two months after his Greece goal, the fervent and faithful England supporters showed David even more love. More than 75,000 fans took part in a phone vote and named Beckham the BBC Sports Personality of the Year. The prestigious honor, awarded by the public service broadcasting company that since 1922 has been recognized as the country's most respected news organization, had previously gone to such sports legends as Daley Thompson and Steve Redgrave.

In three years, Beckham had overcome adversity and on this occasion was overjoyed. On stage at the award ceremony, he held the trophy—a mounted silver-plated four-turret lens camera—and thanked his family and teammates: "It's a great privilege to receive this award. This award was voted for by fans and people in the country who watch the England and Man United teams play. That is who I thank for this award. It is amazing."[31]

THE ARGENTINE REDEMPTION

The hand of fate intervened in David Beckham's life once again in the summer of 2002. By this time, the star midfielder was playing for Real Madrid. In Japan, with his England teammates, David would face old foe Argentina in the second match of the World Cup. This time, captain Beckham scored on a penalty just before halftime that gave the Three Lions a 1–0 lead. They held on and David was hailed as a hero. England was knocked out of the tournament in the quarterfinals by eventual winner Brazil. But Beckham had scored a personal triumph. And the England fans, whose passions ran deep whether it was love or hate, reversed opinion on the London native and cheered on his performance. This moment, more than any other in Beckham's storied career, has been credited as the turning point for the football legend, where his star power started edging toward another galaxy.[32]

WORLD CUP 2006—GERMANY

In the summer of 2006, Beckham and the Three Lions arrived in Germany to compete in what would be his third consecutive World Cup tournament and second as captain. At 31, the midfielder showed little sign of slowing down, and he started all of the England matches. After two wins and a draw in Group play, England advanced to the second round to face Ecuador in Stuttgart. On June 25, 2006, Beckham would be involved in another World Cup play that would again gain him worldwide recognition. Unlike in 1998 in France, this time the attention was welcome. In the 59th minute, Beckham scored on one of his patented free kicks, and put his team ahead, 1–0. The goal, the seventeenth of his career with the national team, gave him the distinction of becoming the first England player to score at three separate World Cup tournaments.

The win placed England into a quarterfinal matchup with Portugal. It was a tough battle for the Three Lions, made worse by a Beckham right-ankle injury shortly after halftime that left the midfielder sidelined for the remainder of the match. But despite the cheering England fans, who made the arena in Germany feel like a home match, there would be no happy ending for the Three Lions at Arena AufSchalke, Gelsenkirchen.[33]

In pain and visibly distraught, Beckham could only watch as the drama of team UK's final 2006 World Cup match unfolded. First teammate Wayne Rooney received a red card. Then with ten men on the field, England succumbed 3–1 on penalty kicks. Reliving the nightmare of 1998, their World Cup title dreams would once again have to be put on hold for another four years.[34]

Any agony David felt that night was about to be replaced with an even acuter sense of sadness.

The next day, dressed in his England-issued, navy blue blazer, Beckham's somewhat hunched body language gave the hint that a sobering message was about to be delivered. At the morning press conference he nervously fumbled with the sheets of paper he was reading from. But more memorable than anything on the morning of Sunday, July 2, 2006, was the emotion in his voice. Less than twenty-four hours ago, an injury had forced the thirty-one-year old Beckham out of what, in the end, had been England's final match of the 2006 World Cup. Today's emotion was for a different reason. The midfielder, who'd played for England since 1996 and had been captain for fifty-nine total matches, and during three World Cups, was handing in his armband. With tears in his eyes, he read his notes and gave everyone his reasons why.[35]

On 15 November 2000 Peter Taylor gave me the greatest honour of my career in making me captain of England and fulfilling my childhood dream. Now almost six years later, having been captain for 58 of my 95 caps, I feel the time is right to pass on the armband as we enter in a new era under Steve McClaren.

It has been an honour and a privilege to have captained our country and I want to stress that I wish to continue to play for England and look forward to helping both the new captain and Steve McClaren in any way I can. I came to this decision some time ago but I had hoped to announce it on the back of a successful World Cup—sadly that wasn't to be.

This decision has been the most difficult of my career to date. But after discussing it with my family and those closest to me I feel the time is right.

Our performance during this World Cup has not been enough to progress and both myself and all the players regret that and are hurt by that more than people realise. I wish to thank all the players for their support during my time as captain, as well as Peter Taylor, Sven and all the coaches. I would also like to thank the press and of course the England supporters who have been both great to me and my teammates and I want them to know for me it has been an absolute honour.

Finally I have lived the dream. I am extremely proud to have worn the armband and been captain of England and for that I will always be grateful.

Thank you.[36]

Beckham left the press room to applause from the attending international media. Peter Taylor, who first asked David to be captain of the team before a friendly international with Italy in Turin in November 2000, later remarked, "I feel he has been a terrific captain and he's played very well for us. He must have thought about it long and hard. There have been a couple of dips in form but overall he's been outstanding and should be proud of the last six years."[37]

OFF AGAIN, ON AGAIN

The coaching carousel was still revolving in England, and shortly after the national team's 2006 World Cup elimination a new coach was on board. Steve McClaren reached out to let David know the Three Lions were headed in a new direction, and it was one that did not include Beckham. For the first time since he'd joined the squad in 1996, Beckham was officially dropped from the England National team. Beckham:

> I had to come to terms with what had been said and the situation. But after maybe a day or two after speaking to my friends and to my family, I said, okay, this is the situation, now how do I get myself out of it? It felt as if it was [no chance to ever return to the team], with the conversation and the things that were said, that was it.[38]

Beckham professed his passion for representing his country remained "as strong as ever."

Life after being dropped from the England squad was at first not significantly different for David. The talented midfielder continued playing with Real Madrid, completing his third season, one that saw the team finish in second place in the top Spanish league. But it was the following year where a series of highlights combined to make 2007 another eventful year in the career of David Beckham. It started with a rumor that the English midfielder was leaving his Spanish club, Real Madrid. The rumor turned out to be true and by the summer, Beckham and his family moved to the United States, where he became the highest-paid and biggest-name player to join the country's young but promising soccer league. But before he landed in Los Angeles, Beckham received news that he was recalled to play for England.

McClaren made the announcement on May 26, 2007, and Beckham played his first match the next month, a start against Brazil in England's initial match at the new Wembley Stadium. Later that same month Real beat Mallorca 3–1 at the Santiago Bernabéu Stadium to capture the La Liga Spanish championship, and Beckham, still with the team, had now won the league title in two different countries.

Then on November 21, 2007, Beckham made his ninety-ninth career appearance for England in a Euro Cup preliminary match vs. Croatia at Wembley Stadium. The Three Lions lost, 3–2, and did not qualify for the championships being held the next year. They also sacked McClaren. Beckham reiterated that he had no plans to retire and that he wished to continue playing for England and hoped to be in the new coach's plans for the team.[39]

LADIES AND GENTLEMEN, IN THE GOLD BOOTS, DAVID BECKHAM

By 2008, England had hired yet another new manager, the third in seven years. The new skipper was Beckham's former coach from Real Madrid, Fabio Capello. Beckham was called on to participate in the club's first team, and it put the soccer superstar in a position to once again make history. The young dreamer from Leytonstone, the dedicated athlete who'd won championships with Manchester United, and titles while playing for teams in two different countries, the former captain, was reaching a career milestone of receiving 100 caps for the England national team. An impressive selection of English former players and coaches, as well as Great Britain's prime minister, weighed in on his achievement.[40] Peter Shilton, England's most-capped player remarked, "There are only four of us in the England 100 club and it will be a pleasure to welcome David into it."[41] Sven Goran Eriksson, former England manager said, "I hope he makes it to 100 at least because I know what it means to him to play for England.

He loves his country and he's a very proud man. He has one of the best right feet in the world—if not the best. He is still a great player."[42] Rio Ferdinand, former Manchester United teammate agreed: "[Beckham] has never stopped working hard, he has been a great servant and he fully deserves to win his 100th cap. He is with some illustrious names, some icons of the sport and he is a worthy member of that list."[43] And even Prime Minister David Cameron weighed in, hailing Beckham as "a fantastic role model" and adding that "getting 100 caps for England is an amazing achievement for which he should be very proud."[44]

Beckham recorded his 100th cap with the UK national team when he entered the game for England as they faced France in a friendly at the Stade de France in Paris. With 100 national team appearances, Beckham became the fifth to join an elite group of distinguished English football players. On this occasion he had been wearing gold boots, specifically created by Adidas. The sneaker company's Predators shoes were custom inscribed with the date of the match and had the number 100 stitched on their tongues.

> Becks will keep every memento of his special night in Paris' Stade de France. If it is not nailed down it will be swept up into his kit-bag.
> [Beckham] said: "I plan on keeping my shirt, the slips, the socks and everything possible I can grab in the changing room. I've been lucky to swap shirts with some great players, but I'll be keeping it this time. I've always had that passion for playing for my country and belief. I've been proud to wear the shirt for many years."[45]

Beckham's family—his wife and three sons, his parents, and two sisters—all watched proudly from a VIP box at the stadium as David recorded his century milestone. After the match, Beckham reportedly continued celebrating, at the lux restaurant Baccarat in Paris, where he was feted with a cake in the shape of a soccer ball.

"This is a moment which will remain in my memory forever. I'm very proud," Beckham told *Le Parisien* newspaper after the match.[46]

Two months later, on May 11, 2008, in a match where England faced the United States at the new Wembley Stadium, Beckham had the honor of receiving an honorary gold cap representing his 100th national team appearance from Sir Bobby Charlton himself. At age eleven, a young David Beckham shined, playing at the Bobby Charlton Soccer and Sports Academy in Manchester. Now he joined the English legend in the exclusive 100 caps club.[47]

The Century Club, as of May 2008, comprised of British national players who had made 100 team appearances:

Peter Shilton, GK (1970–1990), 125
Bobby Moore, DF (1962–1973), 108
Bobby Charlton, FW (1958–1970), 106
Billy Wright, DF (1946–1959), 105
David Beckham, MF (1996–), 100[48]

A WORLD OF PAIN

The calendar rolled on, and as 2008 became 2009, Beckham collected fifteen more caps with the Three Lions. The headlines at the start of 2009 could have been that there was no coaching change at England. David was used as a sub in a match that saw England face Belarus at Wembley Stadium in a World Cup preliminary match in the fall. He rejoined his Galaxy teammates to finish out the remainder of the season. And as he had done the previous year, as part of his strategy to retain his match fitness while playing at a higher professional level than was afforded him in the MLS, he once again went on loan to Associazione Calcio (AC) Milan.

At the beginning of 2010, Beckham reported for duty in Italy, to start a second loan with AC Milan. It was all part of his playing and fitness strategy to increase his odds of being selected as part of Capello's team that would travel to South Africa for the World Cup. He arrived in time to join the Black and Whites at their midseason, and in his first match back played seventy-five minutes in a 5–2 defeat of Genoa. A significant match for Beckham in the early part of that year included playing against Manchester United for the first time since he left the club in 2003. Then on March 14, David was called on to start a Series A match at San Siro Stadium against Chievo Verona. But it was the end of the match that would get the most news coverage.[49]

The England midfielder pulled up sharply with no other players around him and signaled to the bench he had a problem with his left ankle. Beckham hopped to the sideline for medical attention and was later seen lying on the ground in agony. He was lifted onto a stretcher and taken to the dressing room.

Beckham later told ABC News: "It was like being hit by a hockey puck. I thought someone had kicked me and then I looked around and no one was there. I saw my foot was just hanging. I knew straight away what had happened."[50]

It was confirmed shortly after that the thirty-four-year-old had torn his left Achilles tendon. The injury—a rupture of the strong tendon joining the muscles in the calf of the leg to the bone of the heel—is serious, the kind that can end an athlete's career. The immediate concern was that Beckham would miss the World Cup in South Africa and a shot at becoming the only English player to compete in a fourth World Cup. Beckham left his hotel the following day on crutches and headed to Finland for surgery. The prognosis was positive though: Beckham's recovery was likely to see him running again after four short months, jumping and kicking after six, and a full comeback was predicted after he completed his rehabilitation. Fans around the globe rejoiced. There would be more chances to see the superstar bend a football again.[51]

The day after his surgery, Beckham posted this message on his Facebook page:

> I'd like to take this opportunity to thank everyone for their messages of support, they mean a lot to me. The operation was a success and I'd like to thank Dr. Orava and all the medical staff who looked after me during my time in Finland. I'm feeling positive and now concentrating on getting back to full fitness over the coming months.[52]

YOU ARE HERE: ROYAL BAFOKENG STADIUM, RUSTENBURG, SOUTH AFRICA

While recovering from his Achilles injury and dealing with the disappointment, David Beckham received unexpected good news. England manager Fabio Capello, recognizing the value of the veteran midfielder, extended an invitation to the thirty-five-year-old to still be a part of the squad that would travel to South Africa for the World Cup, though he would be unable to play. His role with the England squad involved him being a role model for the younger players, acting as a mediator between them and management and as a member of the coaching staff. Capello said, "I want David in South Africa because he's an ambassador for football, sport and England. It is important for him to set an example. Some players like this are really important to me both as part of the group and when they play."[53]

Soon after the tournament began it became clear this was not merely a mission assigned to Beckham as a way of drumming up publicity. It was reported that Beckham was asked to be a pundit for TV stations covering the tournament but that he had turned those offers down. He also steered clear of the press during his time in South Africa, preferring to focus on the team and the task at hand. Reporters who covered the Three Lions in training would note Beckham's commitment to England was real, as the veteran was one of the first out on the practice field, and warmed up every day with the rest of the players. James Pearce, blogger, BBC Sports:

What I would say, is this: Put any cynicism and jealousy aside for a few minutes and you will probably see that Beckham is a man who is proud to be English and a man determined to do what he can to help his country. There is no evidence at all to the contrary. He is a rare breed. A sportsman who is happy to put his country first.[54]

When England arrived at Royal Bafokeng Stadium in Rustenburg, South Africa, on June 12, 2010, to face the United States in its first match of the 2010 World Cup, David Beckham was there. He assumed his duties as team liaison, sitting alongside the squad and coaching staff on the bench, in a three-piece suit with the Three Lions crest over his breast pocket. The tournament ended for the Three Lions after only three matches. But the veteran Beckham had once again successfully taken on a task and role that further established his legend in football circles.[55]

"YOU LIKE ME, YOU REALLY LIKE ME."

What had shaped up to be a see-saw kind of year for David Beckham, swinging back and forth between good and bad, was going to close out with a swing in the positive direction. In mid-December, the former England captain received the BBC Sports Personality Lifetime Achievement award. The award was given annually by BBC Sport to a sportsperson "who has made a major impact on the world of sport during their lifetime."

Beckham was recognized for being England's most capped outfield player, winning six Premier League titles and the Champions League title with Manchester United, as well as his roles in the London 2012 Olympic bid and in attempting to bring the 2018 World Cup to England.

At the star-studded ceremony at the LG Arena in Birmingham, Becks was applauded by 12,000 admirers, many of whom were well-known athletes in the UK. His wife, Victoria, teared up as she clapped while sitting in the front row with all three Beckham boys; David's mother, Sandra; father, Ted; and sister Joanne Beckham.

Before the honoree took to the stage to accept his Lifetime Achievement award the audience had been treated to a video montage showing HRH Prince William paying tribute to the footballer:

His contribution to football in 18 years has been exceptional. During his career he has had highs and lows but has always remained determined. Most importantly, he is an example to young and aspiring footballers of how to play the game with skill, integrity and determination.[56]

On stage, Sir Bobby Charlton handed Beckham the prestigious award. The standing ovation and applauding and cheering went on for more than two minutes. Beckham was visibly emotional taking it all in. Behind the podium on a giant video screen, images of him at various stages of his career played, including a photo of an eleven-year-old Beckham, with the Manchester United legend. David wiped a tear from his eye while Bobby Charlton was making the presentation. He then gave the following acceptance speech, a dedication to the British troops in Afghanistan, whom he had visited earlier in the year.

I am obviously really humbled because to receive an award for something that I love doing and always have loved doing—I'm very humbled.

To receive it from Sir Bobby Charlton, who was there when I first started with Manchester United, [I am] truly honored.

Football's a team game. Without the teams and players' support I've had over the years, players like Ryan [Giggs] and the other greats, I wouldn't be here without the support and skill of them.

Playing for England is one of the highlights and biggest things of my career. And I've always been able to play for some of the best coaches throughout my career.

I have to thank so many people—my parents, who sacrificed so much over the years to support me, who always have done and always will do, my family and friends. And of course my wife and my children. Not only has she [Victoria] given me three amazing boys but the support she has given me, inspiration every day. Thank you.[57]

UNDER ST. GEORGE'S CROSS

The match scheduled for October 14, 2009, at Wembley Stadium between England and Belarus would probably not stand out as memorable if it were not for one thing. It is the match where David Beckham ended his international career. England won, 3–0, and Beckham, who came on as a sub at the 58th minute and finished out the World Cup preliminary match, headed off the pitch playing for the last time wearing a Three Lions uniform.

After earning his historic 100th cap in 2008, David spent the next two years playing for the Fabio Capello–led England squad as often as he could. Now wearing no. 17, the former captain even managed a few starts in that span. He would go on to earn 115 caps, the second-highest of all time, and the most for a midfielder. He never officially announced his retirement from the team, and even appeared at another England match, in March 2010, but was an unused sub. Then came his horrific Achilles injury, and missing the World Cup in South Africa. After England's eventual ousting in the tournament, a new manager was brought in who did not have the thirty-five-year-old Beckham in the team's rebuilding plans. Beckham may not have closed the chapter on his international career on the most pleasant note, but it did not overshadow the excitement he brought to England fans and the contribution he made to the history of his country's national football team.

Some triumphs from David Beckham's eighteen years playing with the England National team:

- Captained England for a total of fifty-nine matches, including three World Cups and two European Championships
- First Englishman to win league titles in four different countries (England, Spain, United States, France)
- First England player to score at three World Cup tournaments
- First British footballer to play 100 Champions League games
- His 115 total caps is the all-time record for outfield players
- Has twice been runner-up for FIFA World Football Player of the Year, 2000 and 2001
- Named England Player of the Year in 2003
- Named to the FIFA 100 list in 2004
- Has the joint, second-most goal assists in European Championship finals history
- Inducted into the English Football Hall of Fame in 2008[58]

As in any career, there were highs and lows. What was remarkable was how David Beckham handled pressure, hung on to his passion for playing football and his pride for his country, and demonstrated on the field how his talent did match up alongside the England greats. And in the process of playing with his heart, and delighting with his magical right foot, he regained the respect and admiration of not only his countrymen but increasingly fans from all over the globe.

The Facebook post from the David Beckham page was updated on May 16, 2013, with this message to his fans:

> To this day, one of my proudest achievements is captaining my country. I knew every time I wore the Three Lions shirt, I was not only following in a long line of great players, I was also representing every fan that cared passionately about their country. I'm honoured to represent England both on and off the pitch.[59]

As his good friend HRH Prince William put it, "[David Beckham's] contribution to football in 18 years has been exceptional."[60]

6

FAME, FORTUNE, AND FASHION

It was the sound, the "thwump-thwump" of the two bullets hitting the cushion of the pool table as they fell from the opened envelope, that Beckham can still hear when he remembers it. He was in his home, in Manchester, and reading the mail. There was no misunderstanding the message. But just in case, the perpetrator had etched Beckham's name on the side of the metal cartridge and sent a note that there was one for David and Victoria. It's a memory that still gives Beckham chills.[1]

"I never go out without being recognized. It's better in places like L.A., but in Britain and Europe it's impossible to be anonymous. It's frightening."[2]

Not your typical letter. But then David Beckham, the world's most recognized footballer, is not your typical athlete. With gobs of money, movie-star looks, a model's physique, and a wife who is a gorgeous celebrity, the megastar lives an enviable life. But it has its downside: "I have a camera up my backside almost 24 hours a day. If I do anything, I have to be prepared for it to be in the newspapers. It can be a hell of a pressure to live with sometimes. I know I will be judged for everything I do."[3]

The kidnapping plot had been foiled and the would-be assailants were arrested and charged. David had just come off the pitch from a match at Old Trafford and was surprised to be escorted into Alex Ferguson's office before he could shower and change. He was even more surprised to find three officers from Scotland Yard along with his wife when he got there. The good news of the arrests was some solace over the awful news of the attempted crime.

A group of art thieves had hatched a plan to kidnap Victoria, taking her with or without the couple's two sons, three-year-old Brooklyn and infant Romeo, and hold them in a safe house for a ransom of £5 million.[4] News coverage revealed that some of the members had been as close as the gates of the Beckhams' home. And there were details of what they planned to do to Victoria if David was unwilling to comply with the ransom demands. Reporters at a British publication had gotten close enough to the group to learn of the kidnapping and alert the authorities.[5]

While Victoria joked the kidnappers would have to take her hairdresser as well, both she and David, sufficiently and understandably frightened, took the threat as serious. Police were dispatched to their home in Hertfordshire and a new, upgraded security system installed. From that moment on, they have had to increase the level of security in their families' lives, as they had entered into an era they had never expected nor were fully prepared for.

SOCCER AND SPICE

Football purists will debate for centuries whether Beckham's free kick and crossing skills were enough to earn a spot on the lists of football's greatest ever. What is most certainly true is David Beckham was born to play football. Playing with Manchester United, one of the biggest clubs in England, and known all over the world, fame was sure to follow him as his career took off. But when he married Victoria Adams, at the time one of the biggest pop stars in Great Britain, the public interest was accelerated, and the duo were catapulted overnight into a never-dimming spotlight.

As a celebrity couple they were instantly, doubly marketable. Exclusive rights to cover their wedding saw *OK!* magazine fork over a record £1million.[6]

And this was during the period when a large part of England National team supporters were still hating on David for the red card he received in England's loss in the 1998 World Cup. He was able to redeem himself with his play on the field both with Manchester United and the national team, and the better he played, the more endorsement opportunities presented themselves. Beckham had deals with Sainsbury's, a UK-based supermarket, and British retailer Marks & Spencer.[7] The seeds for the Beckham Brand had been successfully planted.

The photo book, *Beckham: My World*, released in 2000, gave fans a behind-the-scenes look into the intimate side of the life of the celebrity newlyweds and their young son, Brooklyn. Dean Freeman spent one year with the Beckham's taking more than 1,000 shots, mostly of the footballer. With portrait-like images Freeman intended to portray Beckham as a modern-day icon. Shirtless, lounging in bed with Victoria, in a bathtub covered with bubbles, and lots of him with his smoldering, steely-eyed gaze. The photos sent female Beckham fans into a frenzy and gave marketing execs all kinds of ideas about how to use the heart-throb to sell for them. Dean Freeman:

> I discussed doing a classic book on him that was picture-led and represented him as the sporting icon of the times. In my mind I had the old Elvis and James Dean type pictures. Since George Best, I don't think there has really been a sporting icon of that type. David is brave enough to set fashions, rather than follow them.[8]

In a documentary in 2002 fans got a peek inside "Beckingham Palace," a seventeen-acre mansion that David and Victoria had purchased in Hertford-shire, England, shortly after getting married.[9] The $4 million property has seven bedrooms, a recording studio, a snooker table, and a golf course.[10] It also has its own Wikipedia page entry. While it looked very much like the Beckhams lived a lavish lifestyle, they maintained that they were grounded, and a regular couple who just happened to be famous.[11]

When it came time to leave Manchester United and Great Britain, and venture into the unknown world of Madrid, Spain, marketers, media, fans, and Beckham himself were likely curious to see if the fame machine would keep churning for the English hunk.

THE CROWD GOES WILD

In Spain, a different country, a different team, and a different language represented a chance to "bend it," the Beckham brand that is, in a new market. And with the reception he'd received within the first two days in the Mediterranean country—paparazzi trailing his car, five hundred accredited journalists at his signing-day press conference and more than one hundred fans at the media-day training session—it was clear the world-class athlete remained a fan favorite and a media mainstay.

It was no secret how well Real did in merchandise sales with the signing of Beckham. The famed football club reaped huge profits when sales of the no. 32 jersey soared in Asia. But they were also successful in pushing the shirts in Spain, with *madrileños* from school kids to senior citizens wearing Beckham's name on their backs. Victoria and David quickly joined the celebrity regulars who popped up in the Spanish entertainment magazines, *¡Hola!* and *Diez Minutos*. David commented about the intrusive press, as "stalkerazzi" in cars camped outside the gates of the family's home in a Madrid suburb: "These are the guys that follow us, day in and day out. Follow your kids, follow your family, follow your wife. For me it's taking it one step too far."[12]

And the Beckhams still had the British media hanging on to their every word. Victoria at that point had been travelling back and forth to England as she continued to pursue her solo music career. David had a mini-entourage of reporters who had been dispatched from English newspapers as correspondents to cover the star midfielder's adventures in Spanish-league football. After just one season, four books—a total of 1,385 pages—had been written about Beckham's first year in a Blancos uniform.[13]

When Beckham moved to the United States, he made the obligatory appearances on TV talk shows, including the *Late Show with David Letterman*. The late-night talk-show host had been whooping it up with celebs, musicians, athletes, politicians, and anyone the public is likely to be interested in hearing from for more than three decades. Beckham made his Letterman debut in July of 2010. He walked onto the set of the New York City studio using a crutch to support himself after his Achilles injury. He also walked into a minefield of jokes about leaving L.A. to play for AC Milan. There was more banter about the surgery and then Letterman shared a lovely photo of Beckham's calf, cut open and bloodied as it looked during his surgery.[14] Beckham made appearances to several other talk shows. On *Ellen*, he played a hidden-camera prank on an unsuspecting masseuse.[15] On *60 Minutes* Beckham showed Anderson Cooper how to kick a soccer ball.[16] And on *Sesame Street*, the footballer taught children a lesson on persistence with the help of Muppet Elmo.[17]

Meanwhile, in Asia, where David had never lived or played, Beckhamania flourished. There were ever-expanding United supporter clubs in Japan, Thailand, and Vietnam. And for anyone who hadn't heard of the English midfielder, in 2002 a little film called *Bend It Like Beckham* made its debut, and introduced him to non-football audiences.[18] As rabid fans of the beautiful game like billions of others around the world, a number of fans in Asia put their support of footballers and teams in other countries because their country's teams have not yet reached the talent level of their European counterparts. Clubs that realized this were quick to capitalize on the easy money revenue streams. Teams organized tours, bringing English Premier League and other European league teams to Beijing and Tokyo and Bangkok so fans could see them play in person.

Manchester United's popularity combined with David Beckham's appeal equaled massive sales in Asia. Both team and player had cultivated a solid fan base. The English icon became so adored in Asia, there is a gold-covered bronze statue of him in a Thai Buddhist temple, a ten-foot statue built of chocolate in Tokyo, and a Japanese chain of beauty salons adorned with his picture.[19]

David Beckham has been photographed so much an exhibit of the images could fill the length of the Great Wall of China. But the football legend and cultural icon has been immortalized in other forms of art as well. In 2002 the lad from East London reached a pinnacle of pop culture when he was selected to become a wax figure in London's famed Madame Tussaud's museum. Beckham was in his England national team uniform, and the scene re-created his spectacular kick against Greece that had sent the Three Lions into the 2002 World Cup. After attending a single sitting, where they were photographed and measured, the figures of both Beckham and England coach Sven Goran Eriksson were sculpted by Stephen Mansfield in two and a half months, a job completed in a hurry to meet the WC deadline.[20] Mansfield commented, "Both Sven and David were great to work with—they were fascinated by the process."[21]

Beckham has since been molded for several scenes, including in his Los Angeles Galaxy uniform, and has appeared in Madame Tussaud's in several countries. He's also been sculpted with his wife, Victoria, most notably when they were depicted as Joseph and Mary in a re-creation of the nativity scene.[22]

In 2004, while he was sleeping, an English artist was commissioned to create a piece of work for the National Portrait Gallery in London. Sam Taylor-Wood wanted to create an image of David Beckham in a way that had not yet been seen. She came up with a deliciously wicked idea that would let millions of fans each imagine they had slept with the handsome footballer.[23] Sam Taylor-Wood:

> At first, I thought I didn't want to do it. He's been photographed in so many ways. We've seen him in so many magazines, on so many covers. What can you do that's new? I had to do something I was proud of. And not just something for the thrill of doing something with Beckham.[24]

One afternoon in Madrid, after a training session with Real, she checked into a hotel room with the footballer for siesta. Then, on crisp, white Spanish linen—the better to show off his tan—Beckham dropped off into a deep sleep. The camera was intimately angled to give the illusion that the viewer is lying with him in bed. Taylor-Wood filmed and the world got to see Beckham as they had never seen him before. The footballer rests with one hand tucked under his head, his nose twitches ever so slightly, he licks his lips, his chest rises and falls as he breathes . . . [25] And all who watch are hypnotically drawn into a fantasy of powerful feelings where they can let their imaginations of themselves and David Beckham run wild.[26]

The sixty-seven-minute video, named *David*, like the great work of Michelangelo, went on display at the National Portrait Gallery in April 2004. Visitors watched the continuous loop, peering at David Beckham, and thrilled to get that close to him.[27]

FOR A SQUIGGLE ON A PIECE OF PAPER

"It's not him, is it?"

"I think it is, you know."

"No, no, it can't be."

"Should I go and get his autograph on a napkin?"[28]

It *was* him, basketball legend Michael Jordan, and David Beckham admitted that he was nervous about approaching him."I was like a little kid, I couldn't think of what to say to the bloke."[29]

In his career and travels, David has met and been photographed with numerous celebrities, politicians, and sports legends, and in 2011, David and Victoria were among the select dignitaries invited to the Royal Wedding of Prince William and the future Duchess of Cambridge, Kate Middleton.

When it comes time to give his own autograph, Beckham is generous. Even when his meal is being interrupted. Even if overanxious fans are poking and pawing. And especially with young fans, because he remembers how great he felt getting them from his own United heroes. Beckham is gracious and accommodating, and although he is admittedly shy, comes across as warm and likeable. Those charismatic qualities are also present when the megastar speaks, either at a press conference or an event. Early media training prepared him for a future of public speaking. Even before a mass of camera crews and photographers, Beckham remains a model of elegance and calm. It is evident from his body language—smiling, open, straight posture—that he accepts the responsibilities that come with fame.

YOU ARE HERE: BANGKOK, THAILAND; COPENHAGEN, DENMARK; SIERRA LEONE, AFRICA

With celebrity and fame, comes a sense of responsibility to contribute to the lives of those less fortunate. Athletes take up the cause as heartily as any famous person. Manchester United, in keeping with their long tradition of giving back to the community and working with charities, began the "United for UNICEF" partnership in 1999 to raise awareness and funds for the international children's charity. David Beckham began supporting the organization's work immediately while in England, participating in fund-raising activities that helped bring football to children around the world. Then in 2001, on a pre-season tour with the team to Bangkok, Thailand, the midfielder made his first overseas trip to work when he met with young victims of exploitation and trafficking.[30]

On January 10, 2005, the former England captain was appointed UNICEF Goodwill Ambassador with a special focus on UNICEF's Sports for Development program. Beckham also helped launch a global appeal for the children affected by the 2004 earthquake and tsunami that left thousands suffering in South Asia. The English superstar has made many trips to countries around the world and continues today as ambassador, providing fund-raising and awareness efforts on behalf of causes regarding youth education and health.[31] He points out, "I think it is important to raise awareness to many issues around the world, many worries around the world. In my position, thankfully, I can create that kind of interest and awareness to things that are happening around the world."[32]

MANTASTIC

Watching a shy, somewhat awkward teen in 1993 filmed in a media training session wearing a light-blue polo shirt gave the world no clue of a fashion icon in the making. Five years later, Beckham landed in the crosshairs of fashion followers and critics when he was photographed wearing a sarong. The fashion world has been documenting his style ever since.

The Jean Paul Gaultier-designed sarong that David wore in 1998 while out to dinner with his then fiancée Victoria made worldwide headlines. The boutique that sold the skirt reportedly sold out of it shortly after.[33] Beckham revealed he liked the sarong so much he bought several in different colors.[34] He later admitted his personal style reflected his long-held desire to be well groomed and presentable. The media picked up on this, and slapped the label metrosexual on him.[35] But Beckham owned his feminine side and boasted of his grooming habits. There were occasions when David collaborated with his wife when it came to making a fashion statement. Once at a New Year's Eve party for the designer label Versace, the Beckham's were dressed in matching leather Gucci outfits. In 2004 David wore a velvet jacket accessorized by four chains of rosary beads around his neck to an event in England. A Christian bookshop reported selling more than one hundred rosaries within a six-week period. Normally around Easter they would sell a total of twelve, and that was for the entire year.[36] Beckham:

I've always liked fashion. I might not have always worn great stuff, but I always knew what I liked. I've definitely worn stuff that maybe someone else wouldn't wear, but I wear what I think looks good.[37]

It has helped that Beckham is adventurous and comfortable taking a risk when it comes to style. It also helps that his good looks and physique make him the kind of man who can pull off a look and be equally attractive whether he's in a tuxedo or T-shirt. Being photogenic has helped Beckham land advertising deals and appeal to football followers as well as others. Any Beckham images away from football give the Beckham Brand a longer shelf life for when the athlete retires from the game.

COVER BOY

As David was photographed in everything he wore as he experimented with fashion, his image as a style icon was further enhanced by the various magazine covers he appeared on. The English superstar has been the cover photo choice for more than a hundred magazines around the world and across all types of genres.[38] Men's? *Details*, *GQ*, *Italian Homme*, *Men's Health* and *Esquire* just to name a few. Sports? Of course. There was *FourFourTwo*, *MARCA*, *ESPN*, *Sports Illustrated*. Women's? Yes, David Beckham has appeared on the cover of several women's magazines. In June of 2002, David became the first man to appear on the cover of *Marie Claire*, in a break from the publication's fourteen-year tradition. Editor Marie O'Riordan explained, "When it came to putting a man on *Marie Claire*'s cover for the first time, there was only one candidate—David Beckham. He represents something for every woman—father, husband, footballer, icon. In a word, he's the ultimate hero."[39]

Then in June 2012, British *Elle* elected Beckham to be on the cover of its Olympics issue. It too marked the first time a man had appeared on the cover of the mag by himself. Lorraine Candy, editor-in-chief:

> He is an icon and *Elle* is known for featuring icons on its cover. This is a first for us on the newsstand and I believe he is loved by men and women alike. Anyway, who doesn't want to see a picture of one of the world's most handsome men on the front cover of a magazine? It will be a collector's issue.[40]

For an *Esquire* magazine shoot, Beckham was groomed and styled, primped and posed, and finally took his place before the cameras. In one session he was dressed in an all-white suit. Even a white tie completes the picture—all business, albeit in Miami 1970s. Later, he's dressed in black. This look was more casual—gone is the tie, and this time his shirt is unbuttoned.

Editor Peter Howarth wanted to do two shoots, with two looks for the cover of the magazine's June 2000 issue. Howarth:

> We talked about who we could do. And it came down to, who is the most famous sports man in the country? And across any sport, it's David, really. If you say, name a British sportsman that everyone's interested in, and equally interested in their life off the pitch as on the pitch. It's unusual to find a sportsman who has such an iconic status beyond the stadium. He is quite special.[41]

AGENT PROVOCATEUR

In becoming an international style trendsetter, all Beckham had to do was use his head, literally. The heartthrob once shaved his golden locks and his fans followed suit, filling up barbershop chairs all throughout England.[42] Snapshots of the many styles that came later include cornrows, ponytails, a Mohawk, and bleached blonde. Beckham proved he was unafraid to take a risk, even if sometimes his choice did not catch on.

He provides eye candy to billions around the world. But some David Beckham covers have stirred controversy as they've touched on issues that have little or nothing to do with his good looks.

For the cover of their May 26, 1999, issue, *Time Out* magazine photographed Beckham in white trousers and a white, see-through shirt in a pose evocative of Christ and the crucifixion, with the caption "Easter Exclusive: The Resurrection of David Beckham," making the religious reference explicit.[43] This was a year after the footballer had received the penalty in the World Cup, and had rebounded from the awful public outcry, winning the treble with Manchester United. In conveying that there were signs that his career was not dead, the media had portrayed Beckham as having suffered enough at the hands of the relentless British fans. Through his handling of the incident and by soldiering on, he had in a way, arisen anew.

Then in 2002, the captain of a men's national soccer team appeared on the cover of *Attitude*, a British magazine that catered to the gay community. And just like that, the heterosexual footballer, married to one of Britain's most fashionable women, who'd repeatedly flaunted his femininity, came out, revealing his antihomophobia, and was embraced by yet another demographic. In 2007 in an interview with BBC, Beckham declared he was thrilled to have gay fans.

"I'm very honoured to have the tag of gay icon."[44] Author and journalist Chas Newkey-Burden:

> What David Beckham did [by appearing on the cover of *Attitude*] was break the long silence about homosexuality in football. Before Beckham came along, it was basically a taboo but he changed all that. He openly courted his gay fan base, saying he loved being a gay icon and was happy for his wife to broadcast that around. He was the first to give interviews to gay magazines—before that, no footballer would have done that. He also changed the way footballers were looked at. Beckham said to the world: "I'm straight, I'm the England captain and I think it's cool people are gay." One day it will be common place for footballers to come out and David Beckham will have played a part in that.[45]

Nick Carvell, *GQ* fashion editor, put it this way:

> Beckham was the antithesis to the God-awful, lad culture of the late 90s. Being a footballer who was clearly motivated by fashion trends and absolutely loved clothes, he turned the idea of what it meant to be a stylish sportsman at the time on its head. Sure he made some mistakes along the way (cornrows), but that's what made him a trendsetter—he always led and never followed.[46]

Another style statement Beckham makes, intentionally or not, is with his body.

It has become an addiction. Not the harmful, need-to-have, will-surely-die-without kind of addiction. But the obsessive, craving-to-have-another, even-though-it-hurts-like-hell, just-because kind. And for David Beckham it only took one visit to a tattoo parlor and the footballer was hooked.

Beckham admits he'd been thinking of getting inked but had yet to decide on just the right design. Then in 1999, after first child Brooklyn was born, Beckham chose to have his son's name be his first tattoo. The tat was done in chunky, block lettering across David's lower back. He went back for a second within months. This one—a large, male, guardian angel, drawn with its wings open, across David's back and shoulder blades. Pain? What pain?

> After I had the angel done, I got up from the bed and there were teeth marks in the pillow. I was sweating and shaking from two and a half hours of pain and I swore I would never have any more tattoos done because it absolutely killed me. But a week later, I got the urge to have another one.[47]

While other athletes are often called out in the media for their tattoos, Beckham is considered cool to be covered in the body art. In 2012, San Francisco

49ers quarterback Colin Kaepernick, for example, was criticized for his tattoos, though many contain Bible verses.[48] Beckham's tattoos are prominent, even on magazine covers and in print ads. It does not seem to hurt his appeal and wholesome image, nor has it stopped him from being wooed by advertisers. Beckham: "I have 32 and I don't regret any of them. They all have a meaning. I think that's what's important about tattoos, if they have a meaning you'll never regret them."[49]

MILLION DOLLAR BABY

On May 12, 2002, David Beckham signed a contract with Manchester United that netted the footballer a significant raise. In addition to the salary terms of the new deal, a reported £70,000 a week, there was a proviso.[50] In what was a precedent-setting deal, the English footballer had negotiated a guarantee on earnings for the club's use of his image. The bonus pay, running alongside his salary, would guarantee him earnings for rights such as the club's use of his photograph and marketing of his famous no. 7 shirt. Beckham's deal did not give Manchester exclusive right, but allowed the organization to use his image in joint commercial deals. In much the same way that actors are compensated for marketing tied to their work, Beckham was able to capitalize on and have control of how his image and name were used commercially.[51] As the Beckham Brand gathered steam, this is the kind of smart-business deal that if successful, would find others following the model.[52]

Within a year of scoring such an unprecedented deal, David was on his way to Spain to play for Real Madrid. Then he parted ways with his management company. In signing with the Simon Fuller-backed 19 Entertainment agency that had successfully managed the Spice Girls and Victoria Beckham, David formed a partnership that would focus more on his brand and image, planting the seed for marketing opportunities in areas outside of football, outside of England, and further cementing his status as a true, global football icon.[53]

One of Beckham's longest-running and most lucrative endorsement deals has been with German sport shoe maker Adidas. He struck a deal with Adidas in 1997,[54] early in his career with Man United, and has only worn the manufacturer's boots. Throughout his career, limited editions of those shoes have been made, such as to commemorate his 100 caps, and upon retiring.

In 2004, Beckham signed a multiyear contract with Adidas. The shoe maker then rewarded Beckham with his own football-inspired logo.[55] The black-and-white logo's design was inspired by Beckham's trademark free kicks, and is easily recognized by his fans all over the world. It mirrors the midfielder on the pitch as he steps into a kick—his left arm is outstretched for balance and his right leg is drawn back ready to kick. The Beckham, free-kick logo later appeared on Adidas products.[56]

By the time Beckham had arrived in the United States, his marketing power had stretched light years beyond the sports industry and football fans.

BRINGIN' SEXY BACK

The National Football League pulls in a whopping 111 million viewers for its annual Super Bowl—the American football championship game. It is why the astronomical price tag of $3.5 million dollars can be charged to purchase a thirty-second commercial that will air during the big game.[57] But with that many eyes on your product, companies can see the return on investment is worth it. During Super Bowl XLVI, in a stylish black-and-white, thirty-second spot filmed in Hollywood, the athlete celebrated for his global football talents was placed in full view of the American football audience.

David Beckham's multimillion-dollar face is what gets zoomed in on first— the latest, lacquered hairstyle, the you-know-you-want-to-be-me-stare, the chiseled jaw barely hidden by two-day-old stubble. With the 1965 hit "Don't Let Me Be Misunderstood" by the Animals set as the soundtrack, Beckham appears Adonis-like on a pedestal, posing for a painting while the audience is treated to panoramic views of his exquisite physique. Slowly a camera glides from left to right, caresses his bare chest, lingers to let everyone enjoy his toned abs, drapes around his tattooed back and settles on the champion's ass in a pair of body-hugging, white trunks. David doesn't talk. What could he say that the images don't already? Eventually the sexy athlete is rotated forward again, the audience sees the face, and across his upper body block letters appear with the words—David Beckham Bodywear for H&M.[58]

The Super Bowl advertisement kicked off the North American launch of the sports superstar's own collection of underwear and a multiyear partnership with Swedish retailer Hennes & Mauritz. One of the world's most successful fast-fashion retailers, H&M opened its doors in 1947, in Vasteras, Sweden, originally called Hennes. The company, which began expanding into the United States in the early 2000s, is lauded for its innovative marketing campaigns and celebrity and designer partnerships. In 2013 H&M had more than three thousand stores in fifty-three countries around the world.[59] Conversations with Beckham began in 2011 when the company got wind that the athlete and his management company were already working on a product in an attempt to continue to explore opportunities to move from hugely successful athlete to equally successful entrepreneur.[60] While David and his wife Victoria previously had been featured as spokesmodels for Giorgio Armani underwear, this particular deal worked a little differently. This time Beckham's name would be on the product, and he would be considered a partner in the two-year deal.[61]

David Beckham's H&M Super Bowl ad was the overall top commercial, with 109,000 comments in social media within forty-five minutes of airing. There were eighty-five thousand tweets alone.[62]

By September, as H&M was set to debut the fall items of the David Beckham Bodywear collection, the retail giant reported the group's sales had increased by 11 percent.[63] David Beckham, footballer turned model turned full-fledged entrepreneur might signal the direction the international soccer star was heading as he entered the phase of his post-athletic career.

Beckham as pitchman has evolved over the length of his career. In addition to his entertaining commercials for Adidas—for new shoes or events, like the World Cup and Olympics—there were early international spots with Pepsi, then with electronics giant Samsung, and finally David became the face for upscale Swiss watch manufacturer Breitling. And the English heartthrob filmed commercials for Target, Burger King, and Sharpie for American markets.

MASSIVE

It is not hard to believe that professional football players who become global superstars earn megabucks, and David Beckham is high on the list of top earners. The numbers are staggering. His contracts for the teams he's played for alone would guarantee him an untold bounty. With Real Madrid, $41 million seemed astounding.[64] Then came the unfathomable $250 million figure that was reported for his L.A. Galaxy deal.[65] Finally Beckham's whopping paycheck for playing five months with France's PSG—$5 million—was a gift. The multimillionaire donated the entire salary to a children's charity.[66]

As is evident by his earnings and personal fortune repeatedly printed in the news, Beckham can afford to make these types of generous donations. In 2013 his sponsorship and image-rights company, Footwork Productions, collected a cool $23 million from his many commercial endorsements with sponsors, including Adidas, Coty, H&M, Sainsbury's, Samsung, and Breitling.[67] Combine it with the salary he earned for actually playing football and Beckham landed eighth on the *Forbes* Highest-Paid Athletes List.[68] The Goal Rich List 2013 had

Beckham number one on the list of the fifty richest players in the world, with a personal fortune of £175m.[69] And on the *Sunday Times* Sport Rich List, global brands amassing £165 million helped Beckham remain the highest earner in British sport.[70]

The Beckham portfolio has the former footballer positioned to continue in his earnings potential as his appeal away from the playing field keeps growing. After all, without football taking up the majority of his time, Beckham has all the time in the world to focus on partnerships, becoming a more strategic business-man and ultimately building an empire.

David and Victoria also continue to contribute, aware that their celebrity offers them a platform to make a difference. In 2013 David was honored with the Global Gift Philanthropist award, recognizing his personal and professional commitment to charitable causes, most notably his extensive work with UNI-CEF, the Malaria No More UK Leadership Council, and the Elton John AIDS Foundation.[71] The Beckhams' acts of charity included a donation of designer clothes that were sold to raise money through the British Red Cross for victims of Typhoon Haiyan in the Philippines.[72]

The skills David Beckham learned early on, from his father as a youth, from his Manchester United coaches, from his business partners, have proven use-ful to him throughout his career both on and off the football pitch. Hard work, dedication, and smart decision making have helped David Beckham record memorable moments that will forever guarantee his place in football, fashion, and cultural history.

> I never wanted to be a star. I never wanted to be famous. I just wanted to be a footballer. I wanted to be a professional footballer and I wanted to play for Manchester United and play for England. Obviously, though, I have been very privileged—and I am very proud of everything that has come with that.[73]

7

SPANISH KICKS

The David Beckham entourage zigzagged its way through the Madrid traffic, headed downtown with a distinct sense of urgency. Sirens wailed, blue-lights flashed. Six policemen on motorcycles escorted a black Audi carrying the English footballer. The group finally reached its destination—Hospital La Zarzuela.[1] Beckham emerged smiling, his blonde hair in a *Samurai* ponytail, dressed in a crisp, white collar-less shirt, half unbuttoned, a white blazer and jeans fashionably torn at the knees. There was no medical emergency. Just reality for the athlete with celebrity status, as he knew it, in a new country, with a new fan base and a new media market to conquer. It was Beckham's first day in the Spanish capital.

The recently acquired player for the Real Madrid Club de Fútbol made his way past the snapping paparazzi, a horde of journalists—from Spain, England, and Japan—and a mob of fans waiting anxiously at the entrance. Once inside, Beckham stopped to pose for photos with hospital staff and sign a few auto-graphs. Then he headed to where he was scheduled to have a team physical completed. Every millisecond of the day was captured on camera, courtesy of a paying sponsor, and filmed to feed the desire of an ever-growing audience's constant fascination with every action the international footballer made.[2]

That Beckham's arrival to the clinic, and what could be filmed of his physi-cal and his interactions with staff and patients had become a "'show'," sold to a sponsor solely for the pleasure of being associated with the Beckham phenome-non, was nothing new for the football player. He'd been introduced to fame in a big way being the husband of pop superstar and now ex-Spice Girl Victoria. But with his talent on the field, his rugged good looks, and his savvy endorsement deals off the field, Beckham himself had by now reached full-on soccer celebrity status. The athlete with the magic right foot, and an international following, was only hours away from landing at a private military airport after a flight from London. He hadn't yet put on a Real uniform, hadn't yet stepped inside the famed Bernabéu Stadium. Yet his mere presence on Spanish soil gave the sports media and the gossip papers their top news story for the day. It should be noted that Beckham passed his physical and was deemed in perfect health by the Real club physician, though this was buried way beneath the headlines.[3]

LET'S MAKE A DEAL

The rumors about which team Beckham was transferring to and if he was leaving Manchester United at all had started so long ago it was impossible to pinpoint exactly when or who first put the word out. The trouble that had started brewing between Beckham and his longtime manager Alex Ferguson had ultimately boiled over. When it became certain that the two could no longer both remain at the club, United opened talks with other teams to gauge their interest in the talented midfielder. The bidding opened in early March of 2003, in Spain, with FC Barcelona expressing great interest. Real Madrid, a team with several high-profile, high-salaried players—Portugal's Luís Figo, France's Zinedine Zidane and Brazil's Ronaldo—was not interested. But in two months the highly publicized transfer story would turn into a battle between the country's top two teams before David Beckham officially signed with his new ball club.

THE TIMELINE OF THE BECKHAM TRADE

There are reports that along with jerseys on sale at the Real Madrid store, David Beckham's face has been superimposed over team photos.

March 30—Real president, Florentino Pérez: "We are very happy with our current team and will never, ever sign Beckham."

FC Barcelona's presidential candidate Joan Laporta claims he has agreed to a £23m fee with Manchester United for Beckham. No deal is confirmed.

June 6—Joan Laporta: "We have shown a business plan to Manchester United which they think is very solid."

Laporta is officially elected as FC Barcelona's new president on June 15.

Manchester United announces that they are ready to accept an offer from Barcelona if a few conditions are met.

June 15—Jon Holmes, the head of SFX, Beckham's management group: "Manchester United will not decide where David goes. David will decide what he does."

Two days later, the deal was done—with Real Madrid!

The club issued the following statement on June 17, 2003: "David Beckham has agreed to personal terms with Real Madrid and expects to sign his new contract with the club on completion."[4]

Madrid, led by Pérez's business acumen and vision, swooped in and made an offer of a reported $41 million transfer fee that Beckham could not refuse. That they had stolen him from their archrivals was all the sweeter. Beckham was about to experience life for the first time as a footballer for a team not named Manchester United.[5]

BECKS IN THE CITY

Real Madrid announces the signing of a new team member with a small press conference, typically held in a small room inside the Bernabéu stadium, which introduces the player to the media and the public. For David Beckham, this turned into an event. On July 3, more than five hundred accredited journalists, including thirty-nine TV stations, attended the announcement held at the Raimundo Saporta Pavilion, the five thousand–seat stadium of Real Madrid's basketball team. The theatrical presentation included an unveiling followed by a photo op with the midfielder in his white Real kit. Beckham was presented his no. 23 jersey—number seven was not available and Beckham opted for the number of his favorite athlete, Michael Jordan—then he thanked the Madrid execs as well as his wife. Then it was off to the locker room, briefly, where he dressed for the first time in his new uniform. The midfielder stepped onto the training pitch to applause and cheers of a few hundred fans who were thrilled to see him. Beckham smiled, shook hands, and then kicked the ball around on the field.[6]

All that remained was for Beckham to do what he loved—play football.

YOU ARE HERE: OLYMPIC STADIUM, TOKYO, JAPAN

Undeterred by the pouring rain and the fact that the match was only a friendly and meant nothing, 65,000 fans packed the Olympic Stadium in Tokyo, Japan, to cheer the Real Madrid football club and everyone's favorite footballer, David Beckham. Undeterred by a yellow card in the early minutes of the match, los

Blancos' newest acquisition scored from one of his trademark free kicks in the 38th minute, his first for Real, and in a largely lopsided event, helped the team to an easy, 3–0 victory.

Only three days earlier in Beijing, China, the English footballer had started his first-ever match with Real, when the nine-time European champions defeated the Chinese Dragon Team. It was the last day of their tour of China in what was a planned eighteen-day trip to Asia where Real would play four exhibition games.[7]

The preseason friendlies were aimed at capitalizing on Real's newest mega-star, David Beckham. It was an unquestionable success. Adoring fans camped out at the team's hotels when they could, took every opportunity to get autographs and photos of the English hunk, and the matches themselves were filled with thousands cheering every time Beckham touched the ball. Real benefitted enormously from the exposure to the lucrative Asian market, and earned a reported €10 million for playing the exhibition matches.[8]

Training for the upcoming season was tough, made only more strenuous by the miles logged on the Asian trip and the marketing demands put on the players. But there was no complaint from Beckham, who commented that the road trip was just what he needed to ease into his new surroundings. He recalled the warm reception he had gotten from his new teammates and considered the entire exhibition trip a successful bonding experience.[9]

BENDING IT AT THE BERNABÉU

David Beckham's venture to the Mediterranean was not the first time an English-man had played football on Spanish soil. In addition to a handful of players who transferred in the modern era, it was English expatriates who can be credited with bringing the beautiful game to the country in the late nineteenth century. Seville was the sight of the first official football game played in Spain in 1890; the Spain football governing body formed in 1913 and received FIFA affiliation in 1904.[10]

In his book *La Roja: How Soccer Conquered Spain and How Spanish Soccer Conquered the World*, Jimmy Burns states that Spaniards quickly developed their own style of the game, making their first World Cup appearance in 1934.[11] But the national team lost in the 1982 Mundial, then made a priority of investing in youth development, and slowly started to turn things back toward a favorable direction. At the 1992 Barcelona Olympics, the national team took gold, a fore-shadowing of the team's rising dominance that would leave them the envy of the football world. La Roja would go on to win their first-ever World Cup title in 2010, preceded and followed by European Championships in 2008 and 2012.[12]

Historians note the 1992 Olympics as a catalyst for the emergence of Spain on the international sports stage. Athletes were succeeding in tennis, cycling, basketball, and motor sports.[13] And in soccer, Real Madrid Club de Fútbol were Spanish kings. The club was founded in 1902, but became a major force in the country and Europe in the 1950s under its president Santiago Bernabéu. With Argentine legend Alfredo di Stéfano Madrid dominated the European Champion's Cup, a precursor to the UEFA Champions League, winning the trophy five consecutive seasons. The team benefited from the country's renewed focus on sports, quickly becoming one of the most popular teams in Spain. Florentino Pérez was appointed president in 2000, and promptly set out to return Real to eminence, signing superstars Zinedine Zidane, Ronaldo, Luís Figo, Roberto Carlos, and Raúl.[14] The club had won a record twenty-nine domestic league titles and nine European trophies, as well as operating a successful merchandising enterprise, selling replica shirts and nurturing a strong following in both North and South America. Real Madrid has been consistently ranked by Brand-Finance Football 50 list as one of the world's most valuable football brands.[15]

Would an English football player, who'd only played with one club his entire career, be a fit in the Real club of superstars' culture? Team management was betting it would be a seamless transition. Jose Angel Sanchez, head of marketing, Real:

> Buying Beckham is like buying into a business. He brings with him a whole range of customers, not just because of his value as a soccer player but as a celebrity, he is an icon of modern society. Real Madrid is not going to abandon its Spanish roots, but right now it's a club with many followers around the world, and this is a source of pride.[16]

All of the club's history was impressed on Beckham as he was prepared to make his Real debut on August 27, 2003. Los Galácticos, the Spanish nickname for the superstars because they were out-of-this-world talented, were hosting the second leg of the Spanish Super Cup at the Bernabéu. Madrid pounced on RCD Mallorca early, and by the half had taken a 2–0 lead. At the 73rd minute, an advancing Beckham took a cross from Ronaldo, then headed the ball in past the goal keeper, scoring his first Real goal. A roar erupted from the crowd and Beckham's teammates rushed to applaud the excited adoptive madrileño.[17] Author John Carlin captured the moment in his book, *White Angels: Beckham, Real Madrid and the New Football*:

> It was as if he had metabolized all that pressure and transformed it into high-energy fuel. Ten minutes into the game he had the Bernabéu fans—the most

exquisitely fussy fans in the world—in his pocket. Real Madrid got a free kick on the edge of the Mallorca penalty area, but wide out to the left, nearer the corner flag than the "D." Few other players would have considered a shot on goal from there. Beckham did, sending the ball skimming over the point where the bar meets the post, with the goalkeeper quite beaten. . . . The whole stadium cried, "Uuuuuuuuuuy!"

For the rest of the game he didn't put a foot wrong. He dictated the tempo in midfield behind Zidane. . . . He made three or four of his trademark pin-point passes, fifty yards long from the right touchline to the left . . . but added to his game a new propensity to tackle back. That desire won over the fans.[18]

Having scored in his first home match with Real, Beckham followed in the footsteps of his fellow galacticos teammates Luis Figo and Ronaldo, who also had punched in goals in their highly anticipated debuts.

During the next few months, Beckham gave the fans in Madrid plenty to cheer about, scoring five goals in his first sixteen matches, as the midfielder settled into his new Spanish surroundings.[19]

ENGLISH ROYALTY

Since 1917 the United Kingdom has been awarding the military and everyday civilians with a high honor for their contributions to and impact on the country. There are more than 100,000 living members who have received one of the six categories of the yearly awarded British orders of chivalry. Musician Paul McCartney, actor Michael Caine, and author J. K. Rowling all have one, as do former athletes Daley Thompson, Roger Bannister, and Bobby Charlton.[20] On November 27, 2003, twenty-eight-year-old David Beckham was bestowed with the British honor OBE, Order of the British Empire, for his services to football.

David and his wife, Victoria, and his maternal grandparents, whom he invited to attend the ceremony, arrived at London's Buckingham Palace in chauffeur-driven Bentleys. The pair sported formal morning dress—he in a black top hat and tails, she in a tailored, knee-length outfit. After receiving his emblem and after meeting the Queen, Beckham met up with the rest of his family, including his mother and father and two sons, as well as members of Victoria's family, for a lunch to continue the day's celebration.[21] "I am honored and privileged to receive this recognition. It's not just for me but for Manchester United, England, all of my teammates and my family," Beckham said on the occasion.[22]

Since 2003, given the work he's done as an ambassador with the London Olympics, with UNICEF, and with his own soccer academy, plus his stellar performance on the football field, it did not take long for the superstar to be nominated to become a knight. As the years went by, anyone who followed Beckham's career knew it was no longer a question of *if* it would happen but *when*. In 2013, it was announced the David Beckham was in the New Year's List for knighthood.[23] If and when it is approved, in addition to calling him a London native, England captain, international star, father, husband, fashion icon, sex symbol, football legend, he'll have a new title: Sir David.

Those first few months in Spain had gone well. Beckham was pleased with how his teammates and the fans had treated him, and was settling into the Spanish lifestyle nicely. He carried those good feelings off the field as well, deciding that Christmas to treat Victoria and Brooklyn and Romeo to a trip to Lapland in the Arctic Circle. And despite the cold—the average temperature in December is minus something °C—the doting father had a memorable time. The boys met Father Christmas and his reindeer and the family enjoyed sleigh rides. Back in England by Christmas Eve, Beckham was especially pleased to be able to carry out the small rituals that put the Christmas in Christmas for kids. He was sure to drink from a glass of milk, and take a bite out of the mince pie he'd leave out for Santa.[24]

THE CONTENT OF HIS CHARACTER

At age thirty, the England captain continued to train and play as hard and as effectively as ever. Off the field Beckham extended his brand further into philanthropy when he announced the launch of the David Beckham Academy.

The soccer school had been a dream of David's for a number of years. He'd attended his share of schools and training camps as a youth, and he drew his inspiration for his academy from those lessons. In particular he wanted to provide the same kind of high-level training opportunities that were provided to him at the Bobby Charlton facility he attended years ago.

> It's about achieving something for the kids to come down and have fun and have the ability to learn about sport, to learn about football, learn about healthy eating, learn about different parts of the body, about injuries. And it's about learning about life and responsibilities. It's not just a soccer academy. I'm very proud to have my name above the door.[25]

The David Beckham Academy opened in 2005 in London, in a facility located nearby the O2 Arena.[26] It was backed by sponsors Adidas and Volkswagen. Along with the two full-sized artificially turfed playing fields, there was an education center and a sports medicine center for kids aged eight to fifteen.

The center also housed memorabilia from Beckham's football career including signed and framed jerseys. A second academy opened in Los Angeles that same year. There was a big celebration, with cake—and cameras—at the London location marking its second anniversary.[27] But in the end, attendance never reached the high levels originally anticipated, particularly as the global economy worsened. Beckham's Midas touch was not enough to keep the academy afloat. Both facilities were shut down in 2009, leaving Beckham and the brand to shelve international expansion thoughts, while they regrouped to determine the best way the footballer could fulfill his desire to give back to youth.[28]

LEAVING LA LIGA

Everything was going right for Beckham in Madrid. Until it wasn't. There were a number of distractions that the English midfielder had to deal with in addition to concentrating on football. There was the weight of the first season with Real, the stress of spending enormous stretches of time away from his family, the rumors of infidelity, the demands of the European Championships, coaching changes at Madrid, and nagging injuries—each on their own a great deal for anyone to handle. By his own admission Beckham said for the first time in his career, his overall state of mind was having an effect on his football performance.[29]

His arrival in the summer of 2003 brought with it a high level of excitement. Joining a side with football megastars Raúl, Roberto Carlos, Luís Figo, Zinedine Zidane, and Ronaldo, Real was expecting to maintain their winning form. But after four seasons, without a Spanish League or Champions League title, it appeared the formula was not working.

The reports in the Spanish press hinted that Beckham was considering leaving Real Madrid. Negotiations for renewing his contract, set to expire by the end of the 2006–2007 season in June, had been talked about throughout the year. Only no one knew how they were going.[30]

Then a story ran with the club's sporting director, Predrag Mijatović, confirming Beckham was out. But Real's communications director Gaspar Rosety restated there had been a misunderstanding, and that Mijatović had only stated that Beckham's contract had not yet been renewed. Then new manager Fabio Capello benched the English midfielder for a Copa del Rey match.[31]

Behind the scenes the Beckham business team was as busy as Santa's workshop at Christmas. Shortly after arriving in Madrid, David opted to sign with 19 Entertainment, run by Simon Fuller, and the management company that had successfully steered Victoria's career.[32] Setting the course of the Beckham

Brand, Fuller's work had kept the international star relevant and focused on marketing that would enable Beckham to further establish his legacy. Fuller was reportedly a key figure in the Real contract negotiations and was driving Beckham's next deal as well.

Did the Mijatović statement cause Beckham to reconsider his commitment to Real? Did his management team feel the prolonged contract negotiations were not going to net them what they wanted? Or did Team Beckham already have their sights set on conquering another continent in football?

The announcement was made on January 11, 2007, that David Beckham had signed a multimillion-dollar, multiyear deal to play in the United States in Major League Soccer, the country's fourteen-year-old professional league.[33] The news that he would be leaving Real Madrid was not well received by the team's management. Real Madrid coach Fabio Capello told the press on January 13, 2007, that Beckham's career with the club was over:

Beckham aunque seguirá entrenándose con el equipo, no jugará más. Es un gran profesional, pero él ya tiene un contrato muy importante con otro Club . . . no podemos contar con él. Yo creo que uno no puede tener las mismas ganas cuando ya estás en otra casa.

Beckham will train with the team but he won't play. He has always been a great professional, but if a player has such an important contract with another club you cannot count on him. You can't have the same enthusiasm when your mind is on other things.[34]

Ramón Calderón, Madrid Real president remarked, "David Beckham will be a B-list actor living in Hollywood."[35]

The atmosphere those first few weeks after the announcement was difficult for the English footballer. Beckham recalled that at Real practice sessions, once the press had gone, he was told to go train alone. "It was tough to take, not just as a footballer, but as a man. I felt belittled."[36]

But rather than lash out at his critics or make comments to the media, Beckham maintained his professionalism. "*Get up and get on with it,*" his father's words echoed in his head. He had every intention of honoring his commitment to the Spanish club. He pushed past the doubt and past the unlikely, focused instead on the possible and the how, concentrated only on his play, and found himself back in the Real starting XI.

Within weeks, Capello reversed his original statement, not coincidentally after the team had lost two La Liga matches in a row, and put the midfielder back in his lineup. After missing six matches, Beckham rejoined the team in San Sebastian, for a game against Real Sociedad on February 10. He scored a goal from a twenty-seven-yard free kick to tie the score at 1–1.[37]

TERRESTRIAL

The Beckham's moved to Spain and adapted to the new culture as best they could. David was accepted by both his teammates and the fans of los Blancos. The English midfielder even took on learning Spanish to truly immerse himself in his adoptive culture. In a documentary on the footballer and his life in Madrid, which aired in 2005, Beckham is having a meal at one of his favorite restaurants, Asador Donostiarra, where he places his food order in Spanish. Later in the same film, at the Bernabéu, fans who were lucky to be on a stadium tour that day swoon and call out the international sex-symbol's name when they see Beckham on the pitch.[38] The move to Spain would be an interesting entry in the footballer's diary, and one that will leave Spaniards recalling for decades that David Beckham once played for our Real Madrid. Sid Lowe, staff writer for the *Guardian*:

> On one level he was the embodiment of a project that failed, the galáctico signed as much for his image as for his ability. Beckham grew tired of insisting that he had not come to sell shirts. The thing was that, as far as the club was concerned, that was part of the reason why he had come. From his perspective he had come to play football. He felt the reduction of him to a question of image was unfair. He was right too: he came to play and, mostly, he played well. Team-mates insisted that he was serious, committed, a hard worker. Figo calls him "a phenomenon . . . the image he has is totally different to what he is really like as a player and a person."
>
> Beckham quickly won over the Real fans, scoring on his competitive debut against Mallorca in the Super Cup. But what really impressed them was his effort. One columnist summed it up when he admitted: "We expected a pretty boy but this guy scraps and fights." There was none of the ego they had expected.
>
> Small, simple details helped: he was polite and dignified, respectful. When he stood in the middle of the pitch and applauded the fans after each game, his team-mates had invariably long since disappeared down the tunnel. There is still admiration in the way supporters talk about him, even if they know he was not as talented as Zidane or Ronaldo and if they analyse his time there they will see a good footballer but probably not a star, three decent enough years bookended by two superb spells. Some players were held responsible for Real's decline, Beckham was never one of them.[39]

Guillem Balague, journalist and author who covered Beckham in Spain:

There was the impression that we were getting a pop star. But he won everyone over with his hard work. Guti [José María Gutiérrez Hernández] has been whistled at the Bernabeu, so has Zidane, so have all the talented people. But the ones who try really hard are the ones that the Santiago Bernabéu clap for, and that's what they did with David Beckham from the beginning. Some of the biggest friends he's still got at Real Madrid are the officios (staffers), the cleaning lady. He treated everybody equally. For him to deal with the fame and everything that goes with it and still have time for everybody just shows the class of the guy.[40]

When Beckham was honored with the BBC Sports Personality Lifetime Achievement award in 2010, Zinedine Zidane praised and congratulated his former teammate in a BBC interview:

I was able to spend three or four years with him in the changing room in Madrid and I saw him develop. I noticed he was first and foremost a great person before being a great footballer. It's true that he is a role model on the pitch, but I think this was shown in the fact that he arrived one hour for training before everyone else and he left practically one hour after everyone else. His behavior was exemplary both on and off the pitch.[41]

Just as Beckham's arrival in Spain had made headlines, so too would the global superstar's departure. The English midfielder had appeared on forty-seven covers of *Marca*, a Spanish sports weekly publication, in his four years with Real.[42] As an experiment his risky move to a European club may not have been viewed as a roaring success, but it was by no means considered a monumental failure either. On the field he always gave everything—it was his signature style, ingrained from his youth. And off the field he proved his brand was as strong as ever, continuing to broaden as a fan favorite with new audiences, and growing his status as a global icon.

BECAUSE EVERYONE LOVES BUBBLES

Beckham's final start and final match with Real Madrid ended on a bittersweet note. June 17, at the Santiago Bernabéu Stadium eighty thousand–plus fans witnessed an exciting season-ender. Though they were down 1–0 to RCD Mallorca when Beckham headed off the field, slightly limping, Los Blancos came back to win 3–1 and capture the La Liga title, their first since acquiring the

English midfielder.[43] Beckham was loved in Spain and would be missed. It was written in *Forbes* magazine later that year that Beckham had been largely responsible for the club's huge increase in merchandise sales, a total reported to top US$600 million during Beckham's four years with the club.[44] Just as he'd done in 2003, when he left Manchester United, winning the English Premier League championship title, Beckham had gone out on top, riding a wave of optimism as he approached the next stage of his career. Even if he was about to start that stage on less than solid legs.

All the elements of a celebration were present. There was the victory and the trophy presentation, tears and hugs, a final bow at the Bernabéu and a walk around the pitch with his three sons. Then Beckham joined his teammates for a ride atop the Real Madrid "campeones" victory bus as it paraded through the streets of downtown Madrid. The fans were cheering, deliriously happy, celebrating their heroes as they went by. It was the final chance for David to acknowledge and thank them for accepting him those past four years and to savor the memories of his Spanish journey. *"Gracias por todo."*

> For me it couldn't have ended any better than it has tonight. To win La Liga has been the best ending, and the only ending that I could have ever had. I've been written off for playing for my country, written off for playing for my club, and to come through that, and to come over that, that's going to be one of the biggest highlights of my career. For me the fans have been absolutely incredible to me, for a year. That's one thing that I'll never, ever forget about this country and the people.
>
> It's been an amazing four years, something that I've been proud to be part of. It's the end of this chapter. Now I am moving on to another one in my life.[45]

Beckham, with the Manchester United Youth Academy, before the 1991 Northern Ireland Milk Cup tournament. *Photo courtesy of the Northern Ireland Milk Cup.*

Victoriously lifting the Milk Cup trophy. *Photo courtesy of the Northern Ireland Milk Cup.*

Beckham, lifting the 1999 FA Cup trophy, spent twelve years with Manchester United, the team of his boyhood dreams. *Photo by Colorsport.*

The former captain of the England National team, Beckham made 394 appearances for the Three Lions. *Photo by Colorsport / Andrew Cowie.*

Beckham visited U.S. and British troops in Afghanistan at Camp Leatherneck in 2010. *Photo by Corporal Khoa Pelczar, USMC.*

The international soccer star posed with US Marines while on a morale-boosting trip to Afghanistan. *Photo by Corporal Khoa Pelczar, USMC.*

The documentary *Class of '92* highlighted a young Manchester United team and its journey to becoming a global sporting success. *Photo courtesy of Image & Artwork © 2013 Universal Studios.*

Beckham brought in fans by the bucket loads as a member of Major League Soccer's Los Angeles Galaxy. *Photo courtesy of FameFlynet Pictures.*

8

IN THE U.S. OF L.A.

The rookie posing in the Los Angeles Galaxy jersey had already won two championship titles with top-level football clubs, demonstrated commanding leadership as captain of his country's national team, and scored more than one hundred goals in a career that spanned fifteen years. But those moments were fading snapshots of the past, the David Beckham before photos—with Manchester United, scoring a spectacular goal from the halfway line against Wimbledon, in tears giving up the armband he'd proudly worn for England following a loss in the 2006 World Cup, hoisting the La Liga trophy after a triumphant season with Real Madrid. Today's photo shoot was reserved for framing the present and the future of Beckham, and what was on the horizon as he prepared for his new role as a member of Major League Soccer in the United States.

Old and everyday routines were suddenly going to seem unfamiliar. The smell of the grass on Game Day, the sound of footsteps pounding the field during practice, and the feel of kicking the sweet spot on the ball would all be somehow slightly different for the football legend as he recorded history-making firsts in this country, in this league, in this uniform.

A team photo shoot was scheduled for the Los Angeles Galaxy players and coaching staff, and one by one they took turns getting their headshots taken. It's the first year, too, for the Galaxy photographer, Robert Mora, though he's worked for Getty Images and covered high-profile events like the Emmys, the Golden Globes, and the Academy Awards, as well as the NBA's Los Angeles Lakers and NHL's Los Angeles Kings.[1]

Mora raises his camera to his right eye, over and over, gently directing, focused on getting the perfect shot. "I'm gonna count to three, okay? Give me one big smile. Ready? 1, 2, 3. Perfect. Smile, a little to your left, and chin up, big smile. Ready? 1, 2, 3. Last one, big smile, ready. Here we go, 1, 2, 3. Great."[2]

The athletes were all dressed in the updated Galaxy uniforms, which featured two stars above the team crest representing their league championships, and showcased the new team colors—collegiate navy, gold, and white.[3] These photos were for the Galaxy media guide, the MLS monthly magazine, and screensavers that fans could download. When it is Beckham's turn, no. 23 takes his place in front of the light stands. Cameras have been a constant in the star footballer's life ever since he was sixteen years old. Sports media covering matches, uninvited paparazzi, and commercial photo shoots have guaranteed there is more than enough furnished evidence for future generations to experience David Beckham. Where will these images fit in the scrapbook of the legend's life? And is the world's most photographed football player aware of the significance of this moment?

Here we go. Chin up. Okay, last one. Big smile. Ready? 1, 2, 3. Perfect.

David Beckham, famous English footballer, global sports icon, cultural phenomenon, was ready for his American close-up.

SOCCERATI

Anyone who knew anything about soccer knew of David Beckham. His announcement on January 11, 2007, surprised many, and flat-out stunned others in the sports, business, and entertainment industries. It became instant fodder for sports trivia: On what day did David Beckham make his most famous statement?

Had there been a more important announcement since courier Paul Revere's fabled cry of 1775 declaring, "The British are coming, the British are coming"? This twenty-first-century invasion was equally monumental.

David Beckham told the world on January 11, 2007, that instead of re-signing with Spain's Real Madrid Club de Fútbol, he would be taking his famous right foot to kick goals in another country. The English midfielder had agreed to a guaranteed, five-year deal to play for the Los Angeles Galaxy of Major League Soccer in the United States. The terms of the contract—$32.5 million, profit sharing on a percentage of Galaxy jersey sales, and an undisclosed share of ticket revenue, plus a provision that would give him the option to buy an MSL franchise at a fixed price when his playing days came to an end[4]—were eye popping, not to mention unprecedented. But even larger than the projected salary was the task Beckham would be taking on upon his arrival—transforming the perception of soccer across an entire country.

At thirty-one, Beckham, with his years of experience, could give the Galaxy needed sub minutes, or would be used sparingly as a starter if he had life in his aging legs. And no one knew for sure which it would be. But the sports media hyped Beckham's impending arrival, and what playing in the United States would do to raise the worldwide visibility, popularity, attendance, and prestige of the young American soccer league.

Even people who didn't know anything about soccer would soon know of David Beckham. News headlines and magazine covers spread the word:

BBC America: "Yes, It's True: David Beckham's Coming to America!"[5]
Washington Post: "David Beckham Set to Invade America"[6]
Sports Illustrated: "Coming to America"[7]
ESPN Deportes: "Preparen la fiesta"[8]
NPR: "David Beckham, the New Star in L.A.'s Galaxy"[9]
Details: "Will America Buy David Beckham?"[10]

Major League Soccer owners and executives added to the hyperbole.

Alexi Lalas, Galaxy president and general manager: "There will be an interest in Beckham over here that exceeds anything else. Tiger Woods has that international appeal, but with due respect to Woods and Michael Jordan, David Beckham is at an entirely different level."[11]

Don Garber, commissioner, Major League Soccer: "David Beckham is a global sports icon who will transcend the sport of soccer in America."[12]

Tim Leiweke, president and CEO of the Anschutz Entertainment Group (AEG), the company that managed the Galaxy and two other MLS clubs: "David Beckham will have a greater impact on soccer in America than any athlete has ever had on a sport globally. David is truly the only individual that can build the bridge between soccer in America and the rest of the world."[13]

Beckham made this statement announcing his new deal with Major League Soccer:

I am proud to have played for two of the biggest clubs in football and I look forward to the new challenge of growing the world's most popular game in a county that is as passionate about its sport as my own. This week, Real Madrid asked me to make a decision regarding my future and the offer to extend my contract a further two seasons. After discussing several options with my family and advisers to either stay here at Madrid or join other major British and European clubs, I have decided to join the Los Angeles Galaxy and play in the MLS from August this year.[14]

What the soccer superstar did not say was that his signing, his move to the U.S. of L.A., had not been a decision he'd made on a whim. The elaborate plan to bring the world's most recognized football player to America began years ago, when a grown man simply allowed his inner child to imagine the impossible.

RED, RED WINE

It was 2002, and AEG's president Leiweke had just met with Terry Byrne, a trusted friend of Beckham's, to discuss starting a soccer school in the United States. A year later Leiweke had a conversation with Simon Fuller, the founder and CEO of 19 Entertainment, and Beckham's business manager, where Leiweke casually asked if Fuller could imagine David ever playing in America. In 2004, Beckham and his wife, Victoria, invited Leiweke and other AEG executives, as well as Fuller and Byrne, to their mansion outside of London. There, over dinner and a bottle of red wine—a favorite of David's—the AEG boss was more than just pitching the budding American soccer league, he dangled the idea of making soccer a top sport in America.[15] Leiweke: "It would be amazing for the sport in this country if he played for the Galaxy. It would be amazing for the legacy of David Beckham."[16]

Leiweke was convinced that night he'd piqued the football icon's interest, or at least appealed to his pioneer spirit, enough to continue having conversations with him and Fuller whenever possible in the coming years. Then in the fall of 2006, Major League Soccer passed the Designated Player Rule, which allowed the teams to sign top players without regard for salary cap restrictions. It set the table for acquiring higher-level players who also commanded higher salaries. Leiweke was well aware that Beckham's contract with Real Madrid was set to expire at the end of the 2007 Spanish league season. On January 1, the date the Galaxy could officially enter talks with the English legend, they moved quickly. Exactly ten days later, at 6:10 AM, Leiweke received a call from Spain with the news he'd waited years to hear: "We've got a deal. We had the meeting. David's made his decision. We've informed Real Madrid that he's leaving."[17]

STATE OF MAJOR LEAGUE SOCCER—2007

It was a major coup, signing the high-profile English midfielder, and the Galaxy was looking at financial profits even before Beckham ever appeared in a match for the team. Thanks in part to the media frenzy and attention his signing created, the club was able to broker a new uniform sponsorship deal, worth $25 million, with nutrition company Herbalife.[18]

The Galaxy sold one thousand new season tickets the day after announcing Beckham's deal.[19] By early July, before Beckham was set to make his debut on the field, the Galaxy reported 250,000 no. 23 jerseys had been sold.[20]

Even the L.A. Galaxy owners AEG saw an immediate spike in their business. The global sporting and music entertainment company was already selling its Beckham association in China, where the company had been applying strategies for building arenas in Shanghai and Beijing. AEG's CEO Tim Leiweke said: "Suddenly, we're known as the company that owns the team that David Beckham is going to play for, so our world changed."[21]

But while most of the MLS headlines included David Beckham's name, it was a mistake to assume the twelve-year-old soccer organization was some obscure, semipro sideshow. Though young and scraping to find and hold on to American sports fans, what Beckham was signing up for was a league with credibility and a solid foundation. There were thirteen teams, with the league's average attendance at the end of 2006 at 15,504.[22] Two cable channels, Fox Soccer Channel and GolTV, covered soccer exclusively, and TV ratings overall were on the rise—viewership on ESPN2 rose 18.2 percent, with an average of more than two hundred ninety-nine thousand tuning in. Fox matches pulled in an average thirty-three thousand viewers.[23] The TeleFutura channel, a Spanish broadcast television network in the United States, continued to provide the growing fan base of Hispanic viewers with a Major League Soccer game of the week.[24] There already were several small stadiums sized specifically for soccer crowds that helped eliminate having enormous arenas with thousands of empty seats, and more were scheduled to be built. In short, MLS had a promising if not prospering future before Beckham was crowned its savior.

While U.S. fans waited anxiously, marketers continued spinning to keep Beckham's name in the spotlight.

AMERICAN HUSTLE

The English soccer star wrapped up a successful campaign with his former team Real Madrid by winning Spain's premier league title. Capturing the La Liga trophy with Los Blancos gave Beckham the honor of having won a championship title with teams in two different countries.[25] Back in the States, while the media was still buzzing about the celebrity couple's impending arrival, questions were raised as to whether the Beckhams would become new Hollywood royalty. Converting Brand Beckham into a household name in the United States could turn out to be a major marketing challenge. *Marketing Weekly* reported findings from a study suggesting that Beckham was recognized by 99 percent of Britons and 93 percent of Asians but only by 40 percent of Americans.[26]

But making the transition from the back pages of the Spanish sports weekly *Marca* to gracing the front cover of fashion publications was as easy for Beckham as one of his trademark corner kicks.

"*POSH + BECKS, determined to become the new American idols,*" the magazine headline seemed to shout from the page. Above the words, a bare-chested David and a bikini-clad Victoria posed seductively on the hood of a car. This was the cover of the August 2007 *W* magazine.[27] The issue hit newsstands on July 9, perfectly timed to be available two weeks before Beckham's first scheduled Galaxy game.

All sultry stares, sensuality and attitude, the Beckham Brand was officially launched in the United States.

W, a thirty-five-year old, oversized fashion glossy, in the stable of magazines owned by media giant Condé Nast, had a reader base of half a million in the United States.[28] The provocative images of the English footballer and his wife that made up the twelve-page photo spread were taken at a rock quarry outside of Madrid, and were geared to whet the celebrity gossip-crazed appetite of an American audience. The photographer Steven Klein was chosen specifically by the Beckhams for this assignment.

Klein's photographs, says Anna Wintour, editor of American *Vogue*, are "clever, conceptual and ultimately lyrical." At the same time, Klein has an uncanny knack of capturing—and even preempting—the cultural mood in his pictures, according to Murray Healy, managing editor of *Arena Homme +*, which had published earlier Klein photographs of Beckham. "He has the power to remake people's reputations," said Healy. "Those photographs of Beckham made him a fashion face and gave him a cultural significance outside of football for the first time."[29]

If the Beckhams had any hopes of living as normal, anonymous Angelinos— taking the kids to school, hanging out at the beach, making trips to In-N-Out Burger—they were likely shattered after the *W* issue.

VERBATIM

David, Victoria, and their three sons, Brooklyn, Romeo, and Cruz, arrived in the United States to start their American adventure when they landed at LAX on July 12, 2007. A crowd of nearly three hundred greeted them at the terminal. This made both the print and broadcast news, and photos were snapped of them as security shuffled them to an awaiting black car.[30]

The few hundred fans gathered at the airport was miniscule compared to what was in store for Beckham the next day. The L.A. Galaxy–David Beckham media day attracted five thousand fans and seven hundred media from twelve countries.[31]

The spectacle capped six months of hype and hope about the storied football player's arrival and the start of the American chapter of his career. Since Beckham's announcement of his jump from the premier leagues of Europe to play for the fledging soccer league of the United States, everyone from pundits to prognosticators had weighed in on the famous footballer. Sky Sports football commentator Ian Darkes:

It was cruel and maybe it wasn't fair, but I think the English media saw it as him going to a sort of semi-retirement home and that it was a decision based on furthering the message of Brand Beckham and breaking into the United States market.[32]

Ivan Gazidis, MLS deputy commissioner:

He is a figure that has the ability to give soccer more cultural relevance in this country, and that's really what's driving this from our standpoint.[33]

Kristine Lilly, former member of the U.S. Women's National Team:

I think it's great. Any time you get a stud like him to come over to the States to help the sport, it's great. He's a top-class guy. He's coming over to bring attention, but he's also coming over to play soccer. That's what he takes seriously. And all the hoopla around it helps the sport.[34]

Executive director of the USC Sports Business Institute David Carter:

To the extent that he creates so much curiosity from soccer moms and casual fans and can help generate some interest in MLS, it will work. However the quality of play had better be up to their expectations and the level of customer service had better be high. He's going to drive them to the turnstile, but then it's going to be up to MLS and its franchises to keep them coming back.[35]

President of the U.S. Soccer Federation Sunil Gulati:

I think Beckham brings a tremendous amount of skill and leadership on the field, and certainly a huge measure of notoriety off the field. Those things are clearly beneficial and should exist throughout David's time with the Galaxy. The goal moving forward will be to ensure that the momentum created by his coming to play in MLS endures and continues to positively impact all aspects of the sport, whether that means other good players following in his footsteps, increased media attention, or improvement on the field.[36]

German football legend Franz Beckenbauer, who also played for the New York Cosmos back in the 1970s, said that when he played, announcers had to explain the rules over the public address system. "Now, more than 20 million Americans play the game. I think the whole country's waiting—because now, soccer in the United States is different. . . . The soccer family is quite big in the United States."[37]

Scott Branvold, a professor in sports management at Robert Morris University in Pittsburgh, said the Beckham brand goes well beyond the game of soccer. "The fact that I would recognize who he is, and he hasn't really played in the United States, probably is commentary to the fact that his name is probably somewhat bigger than soccer itself."[38]

John Carlin, author of *White Angels*, which covered the Beckham phenomenon in Spain, said, "What he did was boost the brand and the visibility of the club. Manchester United failed to get the point, which is why they let him go. They based their decision on their evaluation of him as a football player. But that wasn't the point at all."[39]

Jeff Bliss, an independent sports-marketing consultant says a deal for global television rights, as well as the prospects of attracting other big-name players to the United States is much more likely now. "If you look at Beckham as just a soccer player, then they're paying way too much. That's absolutely correct. But he's much more than a soccer player. He is a Tiger Woods, Michael Jordan, Jack Nicklaus type of athlete who doesn't just transcend his own sport. He transcends sport itself. He's going to attract a whole new demographic of casual sports fans and of women and girls in particular. Even people who don't care much about soccer."[40]

SHOWTIME IN L.A.

The big media day before the big game day arrived with an official presenting of the international soccer star. The David Beckham Media Day, held at the Galaxy's Home Depot Center in Carson City, California, just south of downtown L.A., kicked off at 10 AM on a sun-splashed, ninety-degree day. Drum beats and blaring trumpets from the University of Southern California's band filled the stadium with full, fiesta-mode music. From the stands, thousands of

Beckham—and Galaxy—fans, carrying signs and wearing team jerseys, cheered, chanted, and enjoyed the pep-rally atmosphere.

In a corner of the stadium, out on the pitch, a stage was erected. And it was there that David Beckham sat, cameras trained on him from the visiting media, waiting to be announced. Galaxy president and general manager Alexi Lalas MC'd the ceremony:

> And now, the moment we've all been waiting for. We are here to witness a historic event. Not just for the Galaxy, but for Major League Soccer and for the sport of soccer in the United States. Ladies and gentlemen, it is my distinct pleasure and honor to introduce to Los Angeles, and the world, the latest member of the LA Galaxy, Mr. David Beckham.[41]

Blue and white confetti pumped from cannons on both sides of the makeshift stage floated around Beckham and the MLS execs. Becks lifted his Galaxy jersey and the crowd roared. He adjusted the microphones at the podium and then thanked the fans for coming out to his presentation:

> I've always looked for challenges in my career and something exciting. This is one of the biggest challenges I've taken in my career. To move to a different country, the other side of the world. I'm looking forward to it. I think potentially in the States, soccer can be as big as it is everywhere else around the world. And I'm very proud to be a part of that. I'm looking forward to starting to train next week, I'm looking forward to the first game. So thank you for supporting me for all these years. Thank you to everyone who helped me to make my dream come true.[42]

Two weeks later, David Beckham would make his long-awaited debut, playing soccer for MLS on American soil.

WHEN SATURDAY COMES

On the afternoon of July 21, Beckham pulled up to the players' entrance at the Home Depot Center in his black Cadillac Escalade at 3:53 PM.[43] But the filming and the photo taking had started hours before. Photographers continued to snap shots of the football legend before he dressed, at the media pregame event, and recorded his every move once he walked from the tunnel out onto the stadium ground.

The game was technically only a "friendly," vs. the English Premier League team Chelsea, which meant it would not count in the Galaxy's league record. But for the twenty-seven thousand fans packed into the stadium, "friendly" was not part of their vocabulary. The game had sold out back in March, within days after the date of the match was announced. On the Galaxy sideline, David Beckham sat in his blue warm-up jacket waiting to get into the game. Though there were other players on the bench, the roughly fifty photographers elbowing for position had surrounded no. 23, and had their lenses aimed only at him. The bull's-eye was on Beckham's back. In the 65th minute, with Chelsea leading 1–0, the home crowd stood on its feet in unified appreciation as Beckham rose to ready for warm-ups. His ankle was a bit wobbly, but he jogged up and down the sideline to get loose. Then, he removed his jacket, and in the 78th minute entered the game and sports history books everywhere.[44]

The stadium erupted. Beckham slapped hands with Alan Gordon as he was subbed into the game, then ran out to take center stage, and the center of the pitch at the Home Depot Center.

For the next twelve minutes Beckham booted the ball, passed it to teammates, was tackled and sent to the ground by Chelsea midfielder Steve Sidwell, and had a single corner kick shot.

The game ended in defeat for the Galaxy and Beckham walked off the field having made his first appearance playing for the American soccer league.[45] He was emotional when he spoke with the media following the match.

> It felt nice to kick a soccer ball. I haven't trained all week but it was nice to get out on the field with the lads. I was proud and delighted with the way people have reacted to me personally. It was nice to see a full stadium; it was amazing.
>
> The reaction when I just took my top off or kicked a ball was incredible. Almost embarrassing at times. It was a very emotional occasion and to get that reaction was incredible.
>
> The ankle has swollen up slightly but I expected that.
>
> I don't think I have had such an extraordinary year. This last week has been one of the most remarkable in my life. The attention on the team, my family and me has been remarkable.[46]

Beckham had been cheered on by Victoria, their three children, and a host of A-list celebrities that included Tom Cruise, Katie Holmes, Eva Longoria, Mary-Kate Olsen, Governor Arnold Schwarzenegger, Jennifer Love Hewitt, Alicia Silverstone, and Drew Carey, among others. His twelve-minute cameo was another among the first significant steps toward converting the United States into a soccer-mad country.[47]

COVER TO COVER, COAST TO COAST

Ankle and knee injuries, sustained during the first half of the year while he was playing with England and Real Madrid, would hamper the all-star midfielder for the remainder of the second half of the MLS season. Beckham made his first MLS regular season appearance on August 9, coming on for defender Quavas Kirk in the second-half, in a match at D.C. United. Beckham played twenty-one minutes, and although he did not score, his mere sighting gave the 46,686 fans packed into Washington's RFK Stadium reason to cheer. The excited crowd applauded every touch the thirty-two-year-old English midfielder made on the ball. It marked the biggest debut for a non-American star in a U.S. soccer league since June 18, 1975, when Brazil's Edison Arantes do Nascimento, Pelé, made his first appearance in the North American Soccer League with the New York Cosmos.[48]

But the ESPN-televised game had only a 0.4 ratings share. Put into perspective, just the weekend before, the 2007 Scrabble All-Star Championship received a 0.5 on ESPN.[49] Beckham made his first Galaxy start six days later, on August 15 in the SuperLiga semifinal against the same D.C. United club. In the match he recorded his first goal for the team, scored off a free kick in the 27th minute, and the Galaxy advanced to the final after a 2–0 win. Later Beckham wrote on his personal blog page a message to his fans that read: "It was incredible to finally start the game against D.C. United, but to actually score a goal in my first proper home match was more than I could have hoped for, and an intensely amazing moment for me."[50]

Then 66,237—what turned out to be the largest crowd in franchise history— came to see Beckham play his first full ninety-minute game, a 5–4 loss, at the hands of the New York Red Bulls in Giants Stadium.[51]He even collected two assists and appeared to be adjusting to the rhythm of the Galaxy. But in the SuperLiga final, on August 29, Beckham injured his right knee, later confirmed as a sprained medial collateral ligament,[52] and was forced out of the match.[53] By the time the season wrapped, Beckham had made only five league appearances and two starts in his highly touted rookie campaign with MLS.[54]

Taking stock in Beckham's history-making year would not be complete without including a review of how his brand had fared. Notable media placement from the year included a full-page, black-and-white ad that ran in the *New York Times* on January 11. The photo of Beckham, wearing his England uniform, in full, post-goal pose, is beneath this brief message: Summer 2007, Beckham Comes to America.[55]

Then in June, Adidas, the German multinational footwear manufacturer and the company that Beckham had endorsed since playing for Manchester United, launched their new global campaign on the U.S. market. "Fútbol vs. Football," featured Beckham and New Orleans Saints running back Reggie Bush of the National Football League. The two athletes are on a field in practice, matching athletic skills, or not, by playing each other's sport—Beckham dresses in American football gear and gets tackled, while Bush gets a lesson on how to kick a soccer ball. The campaign's goal with Beckham, per Stephen Peirpont, VP of brand marketing for Adidas America, was to draw more people, more American families into the sport of soccer.[56]

In the weeks leading up to the football icon's U.S. debut, ESPN rolled out a major TV ad campaign. A thirty-second spot featured several Real Madrid fans, all shedding a tear at Beckham's departure, while in the United States, fans are cheering his arrival, and it is filmed over the Beatles' song, "Hello, Goodbye." It closes with the line: "Say hello, America. Beckham arrives July 21."[57]

Finally, an hour-long ESPN-produced documentary, *David Beckham: New Beginnings*, aired the day of Beckham's first Galaxy appearance, which was then followed by the sports network's live coverage of the match.

While advertising was aimed at boosting Beckham's appeal across the United States, every mention of the football legend brought newfound attention to Major League Soccer around the world. In one year, the signing of David Beckham and the massive media coverage that followed immediately expanded the reach of MLS. News of the English athlete's move to the American soccer league appeared in media markets that likely never previously mentioned MSL, thanks to media wire suppliers BBC, CNN International, AP, and ESPN that assured the item was picked up and carried into even smaller markets. And specialty media like the Al Jazeera TV network broadcast the news into the Arab-speaking nations of the Middle East. The media mentions went beyond the sports pages, appearing in the business, style, entertainment, and pop culture sections of publications and websites.

In 2007, young football fans in remote corners of the world learned of MLS because that's where David Beckham played. While this was indeed great news for the Beckham Brand, it was also adding to the legacy of Major League Soccer.

BEVERLY HILLS, 90210

The fancy invitation had gold script lettering on a red envelope and read: "*Tom Cruise and Katie Holmes and Will Smith and Jada Pinkett Smith request your presence . . .*" It was to a welcome party for David and Victoria Beckham, thrown by their new celebrity friends at the Museum of Contemporary Art's Geffen Contemporary gallery in Los Angeles.[58] It was the party of the summer, held the weekend after Beckham's Galaxy debut, and attended by celebrities from the sports, music, and film industries—Ron Howard, Quincy Jones, Eva Longoria, and Ashton Kutcher, to name a few.[59] It's the kind of jet-set lifestyle David and Victoria, who were already accustomed to being treated like royalty in England, would easily slip into once they arrived in America.

The celebrity couple also found and settled into a $22 million, six-bedroom home in swanky Beverly Hills. The nature of their new zip code meant living in the same neighborhood as Jay Leno, John Travolta, Priscilla Presley, and Tom Cruise and Katie Holmes.[60] Within days, Victoria posted news on her blog that her time was filled with decorating and with getting the couple's three sons—Brooklyn, eight; Romeo, four; and two-year-old Cruz—ready for the new school year. "Just adding some of the finishing touches to it actually," she said, "and then it really will feel like home. On top of that the weather here has been amazing too so we are all a happy bunch."[61]

As both David and Victoria were frequently quoted as being very concerned about their children having a normal lifestyle, they would reportedly rely less on nanny's and more on family as caretakers and with helping as they adjusted to their new environs. And depending on their schedules, both parents would plan to take turns driving the kids to and from school.

Victoria also kept her name in the spotlight, further establishing her burgeoning design career, and with the release of *The Spice Girls Greatest Hits* album in November 2007, closing out the year participating in the Spice Girls Reunion Tour.[62]

2008—LET'S TRY THIS AGAIN

The English football icon, who'd made headline news in the United States only a year ago, began 2008 performing duties for his native UK. The previous two years had been anything but stable for Beckham in terms of securing a place on the English national team. After England's 2006 World Cup elimination, Beckham famously handed over his armband and left the captaincy of the team after thirteen years. At the time he was less than six appearances shy of reaching the 100 caps milestone. When he was dropped from the team altogether several months later, it appeared the goal of reaching the milestone would have to be pushed back, if reachable at all. But then new England coach Steve McClaren recalled Beckham and the midfielder participated in several matches as England readied itself for the 2008 Euro Cup.[63]

In a Euro Cup qualifying match on November 21, 2007, Beckham earned his ninety-ninth cap while playing against Croatia. In the 65th minute, striker Peter Crouch collected Beckham's right-wing cross on his chest and volleyed it into the corner of the net to level the game at 2–2. But England fell to Croatia in a 2–3 loss, and the national team failed to qualify for the Euro 2008 Finals.[64]

Just shy of achieving the historic feat of making 100 appearances for the England team, likely to have been made in the run-up to the Euro Championships, Beckham was not discouraged. This was not the end for Beckham, as he indicated immediately afterward that he had no intention of retiring from the national team. When asked by the British press did he want to play a part as England took a new direction, Beckham had this response: "Without a doubt, I'm not retiring. I've said that from the moment I was taken out of the team, and from the moment I came back into the team. I'm not stepping down."[65]

MLS SEASON OF FIRSTS—2008

Despite his national team duties, a healthy David Beckham was ready to embark on his second season with his new American squad. After what could be summed up as a largely disappointing first year—Beckham played in a total of five games as a rookie with the Galaxy, did not record a single league goal, and had only two assists—he was on track to deliver the kind of year both MLS execs and Galaxy fans had originally hoped for.

L.A.'s no. 23 showed signs of his old Real Madrid form playing in MLS arenas around the country. He scored his first MLS career goal just nine minutes into the Galaxy's opening match against the San Jose Earthquakes at the Home Depot Center. At Real Salt Lake in May, Beckham pulled off a double, driving the ball into the net twice in a 2–2 draw. He recorded his only multi-assist game of the season on April 19 against Houston, when he passed twice to teammate Landon Donovan. Beckham was named the MLS player of the week on two occasions during the season.

The Galaxy finished 2008 with their first winning record in two years, but did not qualify for the league playoffs. Beckham's totals for the season, his first complete with L.A., included twenty-five games, a team-best ten assists, and two goals.[66]

Ticket sales soared and sellout crowds awaited the traveling Beckham circus at nearly every stadium stop across the country.

YOU ARE HERE: TORONTO, ONTARIO, CANADA

It did not take long for the English all-star to be named an all-star in the United States. It was perhaps the most favorable indication that Beckham was having a measure of success in his second MLS season. An eighteen-man roster would represent the MLS All-Stars in a match against the English Premier League team West Ham United. David Beckham, who received an overwhelming number of votes from fans, players, media coaches, and general managers, was in the starting lineup.[67]

The mid-season summer exhibition match was being televised in nearly one hundred countries and approximately three hundred media credentials had been issued.[68] The thirteenth annual talent showcase took place on July 24, at the BMO Field in Toronto, Ontario, home of the MLS's most recent franchise, the Toronto FC. Dressed in navy blue, with Pepsi logo–emblazoned jerseys, the MLS All-Stars took the field before a sell-out crowd of 20,844, signaling that an MLS with David Beckham had greatly boosted awareness of the American soccer league.

West Ham scored first, but the MLS All-Stars tied it quickly after. Then a midfield pass from Beckham, and a back heel kick by the Chicago Fire's Cuauhtémoc Blanco, helped set up a goal that put the U.S. squad ahead 2–1 at halftime. The English Premier League team scored again to draw level in the 67th minute, but Dwayne DeRosario's penalty kick put the all-stars on top for good, and they went on to win 3–2.[69]

And had Beckham's performance measured up to the enormous amount of votes he'd received?

In his first MLS All-Star appearance Beckham played the full ninety minutes, notched an assist and came close to scoring in the 40th minute, but West Ham defender Calum Davenport headed it away from its path. The English midfielder took all seven corner kicks for the All-Stars.[70]

I'd read about the last five years not losing so I was kind of nervous and hoping that we would win. As soon as we started I knew we were capable of winning it because of the quality we've got in the team.[71]

After All-Star duties, Beckham played in four games for the Galaxy, then was permitted to leave Los Angeles so that he could fulfill obligations he had as ambassador with the London Organizing Committee of the Olympic Games.

In his role with the British Olympic Committee, Beckham travelled to Beijing and the site of the Closing Ceremonies of the 2008 Summer Games. The pageantry involved the host nation China and a handover ceremony to London, which was scheduled to host the 2012 games. Led Zeppelin's guitarist Jimmy Page, pop star Leona Lewis, and David Beckham entered the Olympic Stadium riding on top of one of England's iconic red, double-decker buses. Then Becks kicked a football into the stands as London began its official countdown to the 2012 Summer Games.[72]

AND IN OTHER NEWS . . .

While Beckham's personal earnings were strong, the world's economy in 2008 was not doing nearly as well. In January, stock markets around the world plunged amid growing fears of a U.S. recession fueled in part by the 2007 sub-prime mortgage crisis. In the next month the U.S. stock market dropped more than 3 percent after a report showed signs of an economic recession in the service sector.[73] By September, 158-year-old global financial services firm Lehman Brothers, a Wall Street behemoth, had filed for Chapter 11 bankruptcy.[74] Then on September 29, the Dow Jones lost 777 points, the biggest one-day point decline in its history.[75] The drop was a foreshadowing to the economic recession that was hitting with a vengeance. Would a sluggish economy affect Brand Beckham's goal to push soccer onto the American forefront?

In a year that also saw historic changes in government marked by Barack Obama being elected the first African American president of the United States and Cuba's president Fidel Castro stepping down, David Beckham managed to make some headlines of his own.

FORZA MILAN

The English midfielder, first and foremost, has always trumpeted his love of playing the game of football. The higher the level of competition, the better. Beckham had made it clear throughout 2008 that he had wanted to maintain his form so that he could be selected for the 2010 England National team and participate in the World Cup in South Africa. He intended to do that by actually playing with a top European club team. Italy's AC Milan football club had been in the mix before Beckham eventually signed with the Galaxy. This time around he was able to make a deal that would see him play for the top Italian-league team on loan for two months, starting in January 2009 and returning to L.A. in time for the start of the MLS regular season. Milan made the announcement on

October 30.[76] Despite this and other speculation, Beckham reaffirmed that the move was not a signal that he had intentions of leaving L.A. He fully intended to return to the Galaxy in time for the start of the regular 2009 season in March.

> One of the reasons I want to train and play in Milan for a few months is that the MLS season doesn't run as long as the European season and my body is pro-grammed to actually not have that amount of time off.
> AC Milan is one of the biggest clubs in the world. I've been lucky enough to play with one of the biggest clubs in England, one of the biggest clubs in Spain and now I'm being given the chance to play with one of the biggest clubs in Italy. I can go there, keep fit and play with some of the best players in the world. But it doesn't mean I'm leaving the States. I'm still very committed to being a Galaxy player. I came to the Galaxy to win trophies for the club and I still want to do that. I'm also very committed to my role as the MLS ambassador.[77]

Associazione Calcio Milan is one of the most successful football clubs in the world, having won a total of twenty-nine major trophies, including four World titles and more than five European Championship titles. Not only would Beck-ham play alongside superstars Kaká, Ronaldinho, and Andrea Pirlo, he'd put himself closer to being viewed by England coach Fabio Capello.[78] There was no guarantee he'd make the national team, but his chances seemed to improve when he opted to spend part of the season playing in Italy.

Soccer aficionados in the United States and Europe began to wonder about Beckham's future with MLS. Near the end of the year, when asked to assess his experience with the league over the past two seasons he replied:

> I've enjoyed the experience of obviously being in the MLS and being the ambas-sador of the MLS. . . . The frustrating part has obviously been the Galaxy's per-formances and the Galaxy's success, because we haven't had any."[79]

Then he was off to Italy. Beckham was unveiled at Milan's training facility by the club's chief executive Adriano Galliani on December 20, 2008. [80] The next day, Beckham was introduced to the Italian club's fans at the home teams' stadium San Siro by walking out on the pitch before a match and proclaiming "*Forza Milan.*"[81]

Though there was cheering and applause from some, Beckham's mini-loan to one of Europe's top-level football clubs was about to ignite a firestorm on two continents that threatened to damage the soccer star's athletic career as well as his highly polished brand.

9

L.A. TAKE 2

The chanting from the fans inside the Home Depot Center was typically loud and spirited. And as usual, it was unmistakably directed at David Beckham, the megastar midfielder of the Los Angeles Galaxy who arrived from Europe to thrill American Major League Soccer audiences with his precision ball passing skills and specialty free kicks. What was different about this shouting though was that it was actually jeering rather than cheering.

It was July 20, Beckham's first home match of the 2009 season after returning from his loan to play for Italian football club AC Milan. Just two years ago Galaxy fans were excited about the newest team acquisition. The luster was starting to wear off the glittering athlete. And it did not help that he'd publicly admitted that he wanted to remain in Italy and void his MLS agreement.[1] Contract negotiations broke down, and Beckham was back in a Galaxy uniform honoring his multimillion-dollar deal. But fans who had originally supported him had not gotten much in return from the well-paid but absentee superstar. While many in the stands still applauded the English midfielder, it was the minority at the match who were the most visible and vocal. They lashed out at Beckham with a barrage of catcalls and boos.[2]

Among those in the sellout crowd of twenty-seven thousand, several held up signs that let Beckham know they were displeased with his performance to date and with his loyalty to the team. Messages like "Go home fraud," "Hey Becks, Here Before You, Here After You, Here Despite You" and "Commitment ≠ Part-Time Player," conveyed their frustration and disappointment.[3]

In two years, thanks to injuries and his loan to play in Europe for part of the MLS season, Beckham had only played in thirty Galaxy matches,[4] and had failed to make the kind of splash with the team or the league that his headline-making deal originally predicted.

Then as the teams headed off the field at halftime, Beckham approached the sideline and appeared to extend his hand to shake that of a heckler in a gesture of "no hard feelings." Some reports have either the same fan or another equally disenchanted heading down the stands to approach Beckham, yelling obscenities. Others have Beckham as the instigator of the confrontation. In the end, Beckham was about to hop over the railing before being held back by several teammates. One unruly fan was escorted out by security.[5]

Beckham makes headlines. Beckham's performance steals the show. Everyone's talking about what Beckham did last night at the game. But this was not the media attention MLS execs envisioned when they signed the English superstar. The savior of all things soccer in the United States, the shining MLS ambassador, the unbendable brand was suddenly less than brilliant. The ever twisting Beckham career saga, a page turner for any sports fans, had taken a turn in an unexpected direction.

BLURRED LINES

The first whispers of a U.S. defection surfaced in the Italian media by mid-January, almost immediately after Beckham appeared in his first match for football club Associazione Calcio Milan.

He made his Serie A debut on January 11, when coach Carlo Ancelotti surprised everyone by including the midfielder in his starting lineup. Beckham wore no. 32. The England captain arranged for his mother, Sandra, to be on hand at the Stadio Olimpico to watch as he played eighty-nine minutes of a 2–2 draw.[6]

Italian newspaper *Corriere della Sera* focused on Beckham's physical condition. "The key question prior to the match was how much time would Beckham have on his legs and the answer was ninety-one minutes, including the two minutes of added time in the first half. He is no [Gennaro] Gattuso, but he is not a figurine either."[7] Beckham's second game was his debut at the famed San Siro Stadium, the soccer temple on Via Piccolomini 5 in the San Siro district of Milan, with a history that dates back nearly a century.[8] Beckham excited 65,692 fans as he took the pitch as one of the starting XI for AC Milan as they faced Fiorentina on January 17. AC Milan's 1–0 victory cemented their third-place position in Serie A.[9]

By his third game, where he scored his first Milan goal,[10] Beckham played with his new team with an ease that suggested not only that he'd been with them for a while, but that he might want to continue. His impression of the level of play in the MSL seemed to be wavering. Indeed his own word for his experience the past two seasons in the league had been "frustrating." That's when he hinted his interest in staying with Milan if it was in any way possible.

"Beckham Torn Between Lure of AC Milan or Completing American Dream at Galaxy," *Daily Mail*[11]
"Beckham: Milan 'Special,' MLS 'Frustrating,'" *Soccer America Daily*[12]
"David Beckham Leans to A.C. Milan," *New York Daily News*[13]

The news hit the Los Angeles Galaxy offices and was about as welcome in the health-conscious city as a bacon cheeseburger.

The report in an interview in the Italian newspaper, *Corriere della Sera*, on January 28 conveyed much of David's dilemma:

The Americans are doing everything they can to improve the level and reputation of their game. It's a young league, and I think it needs another 10 years to become successful. I have to admit that, having played in Europe, sometimes it was frustrating playing in certain games. Playing here is the dream of every footballer. But deciding isn't easy. It's a question that takes time. I'm under contract and I have a lot of respect for the Los Angeles Galaxy. But the chance to play for Milan is something special. I knew I would enjoy it, but I didn't expect to enjoy it this much. But in terms of character, I'm a very respectful person.[14]

The next few weeks were a scramble of conversations and negotiations between Galaxy and Milan execs and lawyers and the management company of David Beckham, to try and salvage what sports writer Grant Wahl had called with his book title, the Beckham experiment. The phrase had caught on since the book was published earlier in the year, and it roughly summed up the experience of the English star in Major League Soccer and his impact on the game in the United States. Beckham's admission that he'd wanted to remain in Milan, effectively ending his commitment to the Galaxy, was the nightmare scenario the MLS management had hoped would never happen. Finally on March 8, the exact day the Milan loan was scheduled to end, an agreement was reached. The "Beckham experiment," although far from following the predicted script, was salvaged. The question still remained whether it would have a happy ending.

And David Beckham appeared to come out on top. The L.A. Galaxy conceded to allow Beckham to remain with Milan through the remainder of their 2008–2009 season and would plan for the superstar to return the United States to finish the MLS season by July. But Beckham took a hit in this deal also. First, he would have to give up a portion of his Galaxy salary. In addition, the opt-out clause that had been in his original contract, allowing him to terminate the final two years, was no longer a free option. If Beckham ever considered terminating it again, it would be a substantially costly buyout.[15] And getting what he'd wanted meant committing his thirty-three-year-old body to a grueling schedule with three professional football teams, not to mention traveling between at least three countries.

On the plus side for the Galaxy—they got to keep their star player, and there still was hope that the Beckham experiment would be all that they had originally hoped and that there would be a Galaxy happy ending.

By the time July arrived, the atmosphere in Los Angeles was heavy with discontent. Beckham had played in eighteen matches for Milan, and made five appearances for England in 2009. He played seventy minutes in a win at Giants Stadium against the New York Red Bulls in his first match back with the Galaxy.[16] Then came his home debut, that fateful match at the Home Depot Center on July 20. In part of Beckham's L.A.-Milan deal, the Galaxy had negotiated an exhibition game with the Italian club. Considering his blatant admission that he wanted to sign with Milan, no one could have been surprised by the Galaxy fans' reaction to the English all-star during that match.

TROUBLE IN L.A.

The poor record and the lack of championship titles in Los Angeles spoke for themselves. But what the public did not know was that away from the field, the Galaxy organization was dealing with an array of internal problems. Just a year ago, Alexis Lalas, the team's general manager, and Ruud Gullit, the coach, had been let go. They hired Bruce Arena, a former player and coach whose pedigree included winning the first-ever MLS Cup as coach of the D.C. United back in 1996, to fill both positions and turn things around. Los Angeles had not made the playoffs since 2005, and finished the 2008 season 8–13–9. Arena focused on beefing up the team's porous defense—the Galaxy had finished thirteenth out of fourteen teams and let in a league-high sixty-two goals—as well as drafting players that could help on offense.[17] For a player accustomed to winning, and winning at a high level, it was not surprising to find Beckham might have a change of heart about playing in the MLS.

Earlier in the year, when Grant Wahl's book, *The Beckham Experiment*, was released, came the damaging news that Landon Donavan had questioned David Beckham's commitment to the Galaxy.[18] Any tension that might have been building between the teammates likely included how Galaxy management had handled the role of captain. When Beckham arrived, Donovan was asked to give up the armband, and the coveted role was handed to Beckham.[19] If there was any animosity, Donovan acquiesced for the good of the team. But Beckham's actions and absence in the past two years was enough to make any teammate wonder where his priorities were.

Back in January of 2009, Lalas had predicted the Beckham backlash:

> Galaxy fans are very knowledgeable and they recognize there has been good and bad in David coming to the team, but they just want a good team and the current situation is not ideal, to say the least. [But] anybody who says that the signing of David Beckham has been a failure is delusional and is not seeing the bigger picture.[20]

With new management in place there was hope of stability and consistency in Los Angeles. In Arena's first season L.A. made it to their first postseason though they eventually lost to Real Salt Lake, 5–4, on penalty kicks in the 2009 MLS Cup final. Arena was named MLS Coach of the Year, in a sign at least that management had regained control of the club.[21] Now all that was left was to give the fans what they wanted—an MLS championship title.

THE SECOND ITALIAN TOUR

By early January 2010, Beckham was back in northern Italy, sporting his no. 32 red-and-black shirt, and ready to start his second loan stint with AC Milan. This, too, had been arranged after the negotiations that took part the past year regarding Beckham's time with the Italian club.[22] He had always made it clear that he needed to play at a high level to stay match fit to play with the England National team and that he would be able to accomplish that in Italy. And his strategy was paying off. Beckham had been called on by England coach Fabio Capello, who had managed him in Madrid, and suited up for England in nearly a dozen matches the past year. The midfielder was scheduled to play the second half of the Milan season and then had hoped to be called to represent the England National team at the World Cup in South Africa.

In his first game with *i Rossoneri*, on January 6, Milan faced Genoa in an Italian league Serie A matchup. It turned out to be an impressive season premier for Beckham, as he continued to prove to Capello that he was worth a spot on England's squad for the 2010 World Cup. In front of Capello, Beckham played a strong seventy-five minutes, slotting back into the Milan team he represented eighteen times last year as if he had never been away. The Red and Black outpaced Genoa 5–2 at the San Siro stadium. In the 75th minute, a smiling Beckham came off to a warm reception from the Milan fans.[23]

But the match that likely stood out on the Milan schedule for Beckham that year was on February 16, when the Italian club hosted Manchester United for the first leg of a UEFA Champions League clash. It was the first time Beckham would suit up to play against his beloved Reds, the team he'd grown up dreaming to join, since leaving the club for Real Madrid in 2003. Keeping his emotions in check, David's free-kick within minutes of the start found its way to Ronaldinho, who put Milan up 1–0. Beckham came off at the 76th minute but Milan would lose the match, 3–2.[24]

Then came the second leg, and David Beckham found himself heading to Old Trafford to once again play football in the place he will likely always consider home. Only this time he would not be sporting a Manchester United uniform.

The former England captain was mobbed the minute he touched down at and stepped inside the Manchester airport. United supporters cheered on their beloved David Beckham, asking for autographs and hoping to snap his picture. At Old Trafford, on March 10, the former Manchester United star received a hero's welcome. Red supporters, thrilled to see one of their own out on the United pitch again, gave Beckham a standing ovation.

When the London native was asked how it felt to be back "home" in Manchester, he stated it had been a "really emotional night."

I never underestimate the Manchester United fans. The way they supported me through my whole career is incredible and tonight surprised me even more. It was an unbelievable reception. I didn't think I'd get here again. After a few years, you think it's not going to happen seven years on, first time back. As much as it was disappointing [to lose], it was really an incredible night.[25]

When the match was over, applauding the fans, and taking in their heartfelt appreciation, Beckham, in his Milan no. 32 shirt, left the pitch, taking the familiar walk into the tunnel at Old Trafford.

And a handful of supporters left comments on a BBC blog paying tribute to Beckham:

"Brilliant night of footie. Great performance by Utd and it was especially good to see the old hero Beckham return."

"Before Beckham was famous, he was a die-hard United fan who as a kid would prefer to stay in and watch match of the day rather than go out. The way Beckham plays football and the way he plays for Man Utd and England, that is how he plays . . . all heart, total commitment."
"I loved the reception Beckham got, both the standing ovation and getting booed when he first played the ball. Brilliant!!"[26]

Four days later, David was called on to start a Serie A match at San Siro stadium against Chievo Verona. It turned out to be another match where the Beckham experiment would again face an unexpected circumstance.

SIDELINED

In the 89th minute of a match against Chievo Verona on March 14, with AC Milan en route to a 1–0 win, Beckham suddenly felt a snap. He proceeded to give the ball another kick, then hopped a few times on one leg. He reached down to feel his left ankle, then limped off to the side. Later, inconsolable, holding his head in his hands, Beckham had to be carried out on a stretcher. He knew it the moment it had happened, and his fears were confirmed—he'd ruptured his left Achilles' tendon and would likely be unable to play for the next five to six months. As Leonardo Nascimento de Araújo, Milan's coach, reported, "He felt the muscle begin to come up, which is a typical symptom when you break an Achilles' tendon. This is a real blow."

A day after flying to Turku, Finland, to have an operation on his leg, Dr. Sakari Orava, who performed the surgery, was quoted giving Beckham a positive prognosis, saying that the thirty-four-year-old "will be able to make a full comeback after his rehabilitation is complete."[27] He added,

I think it went quite fine. The prognosis is he needs a rehabilitation for the next few months, and the plaster cast is the next six to eight weeks. I would say that [it will be] maybe four months before he's running, but six months before he's jumping and kicking. I think that he understood it's a serious injury and he's not able to contemplate [the World Cup].[28]

Although the surgery had gone well, when Beckham was carried off the San Siro field, it marked a number of endings for the English midfielder. First, he would be unable to make the roster for the England national team to participate in the 2010 World Cup in South Africa in June. Missing the tournament meant he effectively ended his bid to become the first player for England to appear in four World Cup tournaments. It also put in jeopardy his hopes of reaching the English record of 125 caps. And lastly, it put an end to his playing for AC Milan.

Soccer fans across the globe hoped the injury would not be the end of David Beckham's career.

YOU ARE HERE: CAMP BASTION, HELMAND PROVINCE, AFGHANISTAN

It had been raging nearly ten years, this war in Afghanistan, with troops arriving there shortly after the 9/11 terrorist attacks in the United States. The American and British soldiers stationed at Camp Bastion and Camp Leatherneck were about to get a welcomed break from their daily routine. A break from missing family back home. A break from the unrelenting desert heat. A break from the constant sound of bombs going off in the distance. That's because on the schedule was a morale-boosting visit, the kind arranged where celebrities traveled to the region in support of troops serving tours of duty.

Today the eight thousand soldiers on the military base were going to meet football legend David Beckham.

During his months of recuperation and rehabilitation, Beckham had downtime to fulfill nonathletic obligations and take on other work he might not otherwise have had time for. It had been a long-held desire of his to visit war troops. He was able to make the journey to the Middle East in May in support of U.S. and British forces.[29]

The thirty-five-year-old former England captain arrived at Camp Bastion, Afghanistan, for his two-day visit on an RAF C-17 plane, then set out for Helmand Province, where he was scheduled to meet with troops from the 67 Squadron, 6 Regiment RLC. His visit was kept a secret until the day he arrived.[30]

Beckham, dressed in a T-shirt, fatigues, and combat boots, started the day with a full English breakfast, then participated in a question-and-answer session with troops. Afterward there was lots of autograph signing and picture taking and later he was shown around the base and given a lesson on how to handle weapons. At one point, Beckham hopped into a helicopter and signed a machine gun with this message to the crew: "Stay safe, David Beckham—x 7"

Of course the former England captain could not leave the base without playing a little football. There was no actual football field, but the soldiers created a makeshift pitch in the Afghan dirt and sand. So on a hot afternoon in the Middle East, in a recreation area on Camp Bastion, Beckham had a mini kickabout with the lads from Squadron 67. After his second day, and after visiting a memorial on the site, David praised the bravery of the servicemen he met in Afghanistan.[31]

> I have nothing but admiration for these young men and women, and it makes me very proud to be British. I've wanted to visit Afghanistan for a long time, and I hope that in some small way it helps remind everyone at home what an amazing job they are doing out here in very difficult conditions. I feel very humble.
>
> It really is, like I said, amazing to be around but you feel the love from everybody. It just really is scary work. These guys are the bravest people that I've ever met and it really is, it truly is, an honour to be here.[32]

BACK IN THE SADDLE

Within weeks of traveling to the Middle East, Becks would need to head to South Africa. While his Achilles injury would rob the superstar midfielder from capping his career with a record-setting appearance in a fourth World Cup, he would be joining his fellow England compatriots at the tournament. Shortly after his injury, England coach Fabio Capello had invited Beckham to be a part of his coaching staff, acting as a mediator between the players and management and being a role model for the younger team members.[33]

In South Africa, Beckham arrived with the Three Lions as they first set up training camp. Later, he represented the club from the sidelines as they opened the tournament facing a U.S. squad that featured his Galaxy teammate, Landon Donovan. The match ended in a draw, but England had an awful showing in South Africa, tying its first two matches, and losing the next, then was eliminated in the Round of 16 after a 4–1 loss to Germany.[34]

It had been five months since David Beckham last put on a jersey and played in a soccer match. After his Achilles' injury, the English midfielder was sidelined from football and had time for numerous off-the-field commitments while he recovered. But rehab had gone as scheduled, and Beckham appeared at his first Galaxy training session on August 12.[35]

Finally, on September 11, in a match at the Home Depot Center vs. the Columbus Fire, Beckham made his triumphant return to Major League Soccer. He played in the team's final seven matches, scored his first goal of the season on October 3, with a game-winning free kick, and started all three of the Galaxy's playoff matches.[36] After making his Galaxy comeback, Beckham wrapped up his turbulent year on a high note when he was honored with the BBC Sports Personality of the Year Lifetime Achievement Award.[37]

THE DEBUT OF A NEW NO. 7

The name was elegantly scripted, like the calligraphy on wedding invitations. The tattoo was visible on Beckham's left collarbone. Of course this was not his first-ever tattoo. But it was unique, as it read "Harper," the name of his first daughter, who was born July 10 in Los Angeles. His daughter's name now joined the twenty or so other tattoos that adorned the famous footballer's heavily photographed body, and meant he had inked the names of all his children.[38]

David shared this with his Facebook fans on July 10, 2011:

> I am so proud and excited to announce the birth of our daughter Harper Seven Beckham. She weighed a healthy 7lbs 10oz and arrived at 7.55 this morning, here in LA. Victoria is doing really well and her brothers are delighted to have a baby sister xx.[39]

RE-UNITED

When former Manchester United captain Gary Neville, best friend to David Beckham and best man at his wedding, announced he was retiring after more than twenty years playing for the Reds, the question that appeared immediately in the papers was whether the former United star would return to Old Trafford to play in Neville's testimonial match.

Testimonial matches are put on to honor a player for years of service to a club. Typically other prominent players who were also once members of the team are asked to play, and the match is usually a friendly. The practice has been popular in England for decades, originally including that the money raised in ticket sales would go to the honored player as a way to help supplement his salary. Today most athletes donate those proceeds to charity. Gary Neville came up with United through the youth ranks and was a member of the 1992 FA Youth Cup team. He went on to play in more than six hundred matches for Manchester, highlighted by eight Premier League titles, three FA Cups, and the 1999 treble. He announced his retirement in February 2011, and his testimonial match was scheduled for May 24 in a friendly with Italy's Juventus.[40] To pay tribute to Neville, several former players were scheduled to participate in the match. David Beckham, Nicky Butt, and Ryan Giggs, who, along with Neville, made up the core four from the famed Class of '92 team, would join him once again on the pitch at Old Trafford.

Beckham, who was granted a pass from Los Angeles manager Bruce Arena to miss one Galaxy game, donned a United jersey for the first time in seven years.[41] He was all smiles the entire night, from the sidelines during the pregame warm-up, through the introductions, and finally playing on his home field with his former teammates. David partnered with Gary Neville on defense, and even managed to get in a free kick, in a match that turned out to be mostly fun and frolics. At one point, Beckham even had to restrain—with a bear hug—an ambitious but harmless young fan who ran out on the pitch before he was taken away by security. And no one seemed to really mind that United were beaten, 2–1.[42]

After the game, David spoke with reporters.

> Tonight was all about Gary. He got an amazing send-off from the fans but we all knew, even before tonight, how much they love him and how much he means to this club. He'll always be a part of this club and its history. It was great. I haven't been on a pitch with them for almost 10 years. To be out there again on this field in front of this crowd with Sir Alex Ferguson as manager was a great occasion.[43]

United no. 7 embraced no. 2, his retiring best friend and teammate, near the end of the match, and with the crowd giving him a standing ovation, Beckham walked off the field at Old Trafford one last time.

THREE COUNTRIES, THREE TEAMS, THREE LEAGUE TITLES

With the new year and the new season the Galaxy were primed to continue building on their success from the previous season. The team's management overhaul seemed to have everyone on the same page and after one goal—winning the MLS championship. For David Beckham that meant refocusing his energy toward having a successful campaign with L.A. Perhaps he was inspired, after having been so close to the MLS Cup finals last season when the Galaxy had a heartbreaking loss in the Western Conference final match just months ago. Or maybe it was that he'd started the year training with Premier League team Tottenham.[44] Or it just might have been joy that he was still able to play the game he loved, after returning from what could have been a career-ending injury.

When the Los Angeles Galaxy started their 2011 campaign in March, what the fans saw was a thirty-five-year-old David Beckham who appeared for the first time to be enjoying his experience playing in the United States. Like a man on fire, the English superstar appeared in twenty-six matches of the season, scoring five goals. His fifteen total assists for the year were second best in the league. He was named to his second All-Star Game, earned his first berth on the MLS Best XI, and was named the MLS Comeback Player of the Year.[45]

The final season of David Beckham's five-year Galaxy deal was turning out to be the best year of his MLS career.

The team also played more focused and cohesively during the season, and driven by coach Bruce Arena, dominated most opponents. They were unbeaten in April, then in early May went on a fourteen-game winning streak that put them comfortably atop the Western Conference. They went the entire season without being beaten at the Home Depot Center. The Galaxy claimed its second consecutive Supporter's Shield, the league's recognition for the team with the best regular season record, and advanced to the postseason for the second year in a row. This time, they swept through the playoffs, easily became Western Conference winners, and were set to face the Houston Dynamo in the final.[46]

The MLS Cup championship match on Sunday, November 20, at the Home Depot Center marked the second finals appearance for David Beckham, and he did not want it to end as it did before with a loss. A sellout crowd of more than 30,000 fans were on hand for the finals clash. The wet and cool weather didn't favor either of the teams, as both were flustered by missed scoring opportunities. With the Galaxy offense set to run though Beckham, the midfielder methodically and consistently sent passes over to the Galaxy front line. Finally, late in the second half, Beckham found a surging Robbie Keane with a flick pass. Keane drifted to about twenty-five yards out. Waiting to strike, he spotted Donovan approaching from the left, made the perfect pass, and the sprinting Donovan sent a right-footed blast into the Houston box, to give the Galaxy the 1–0 lead. It was all they needed, and when the whistle blew, L.A. had captured the MLS Cup title, their third in the club's history, and the first for Beckham.[47]

Donovan had celebrated his goal with a fist pump and slide into the corner. After the match and after winning the game's MVP trophy, the Galaxy captain celebrated, embracing David Beckham.

After the match it was revealed that Beckham had played with a strained hamstring. Coach Arena had nothing but praise for his midfielder:[48]

David's a champion. I've been around great athletes and competitors in my life in different sports. This guy is as good as it comes. Unbelievable desire to win. He's a great teammate, a great person. He's done it all in every country he's been in. What more can you say about a guy like this and what he's brought to this organization and this league in five years?[49]

The uniform was different, and so was the country. But winning a championship title, that was something familiar to David Beckham. This was the third league title he'd won playing for three different teams. With the win, Beckham became the second English player to win league titles in three countries.[50]

Beckham had also come to the end of his five-year deal with the Galaxy and there was already speculation about which European club he'd be playing for next. As he took a long, perhaps final trot around the Home Depot Center pitch, draped in the St. George's flag, and accompanied by his three sons, the Galaxy fans applauded their English star. It was the perfect Hollywood ending.

> It's been the most enjoyable time of my career in America over the last year, and this just tops it off. I've said before, I need to sit back and relax and enjoy this moment, and then I'll figure out what I'm going to do next year. I might talk in the past tense sometimes, but that doesn't mean I'm leaving. It's been an amazing five years.[51]

A HARD ROAD TO GLORY

This time there was no confetti, no screaming fans, and no band, but that didn't mean the news was any less exciting. In a press conference on January 19, heavily attended but a rather subdued affair compared to the welcome party of five years ago, the Los Angeles Galaxy announced that their star midfielder, David Beckham, who'd helped the club capture its first MLS Cup title since 2005, had signed a contract extending his stay for another two seasons.

> This was an important decision for me. I had many offers from clubs from around the world. However, I'm still passionate about playing in America and winning trophies with the Galaxy. I've seen firsthand how popular soccer is now in the States and I'm as committed as ever to growing the game here. My family and I are incredibly happy and settled in America and we look forward to spending many more years here.[52]

The details of the two-year extension left Beckham with the option to end the agreement after one year. So after months of speculation as to where the former England captain would be playing next, the Los Angeles Galaxy got ready for the start of the 2012 season and defending their MLS Cup title.

1600 PENNSYLVANIA AVENUE

The call to Galaxy coach Bruce Arena came in the middle of the night. But it was Barack Obama, the president of the United States on the other end, and fortunately it was good news. This was a congratulatory call and invitation to the White House in celebration of the team winning the 2011 MLS Cup.

So on May 15, 2012, members of the Galaxy team and coaching staff, twenty-four in total, were honored in the East Room of the White House in Washington, D.C. In his remarks, President Obama praised the team for combining star power and hard work in capturing their third championship title, and teased David Beckham for his celebrity:

> I'm not going to flatter myself by assuming these cameras are for me. I want to thank the Galaxy for letting me share in the spotlight. The truth is, in America, most professional soccer players have the luxury of being able to walk around without being recognized. But not these guys. This is the Miami Heat of soccer. And together, they represent one of the most talented lineups that MLS has ever seen.
>
> We also have a young up-and-comer on the team, a guy named David Beckham. I have to say I gave David a hard time—I said half his teammates could be his kids. We're getting old, David. Although you're holding up better than me.
>
> Last year, at the age of 36, David had his best year in MLS, leading the team with 15 assists. He did it despite fracturing his spine halfway through the season, injuring his hamstring the week before the championship game. He is tough. In fact, it is a rare man who can be that tough on the field and also have his own line of underwear. David Beckham is that man.[53]

After the presentation, the team participated in a question-and-answer session and soccer clinic with young students on the South Lawn, hosted by First Lady Michelle Obama as part of her Let's Move program.

LONDON 2012—THE GAMES OF THE THIRTIETH OLYMPIAD

Weeks after his White House appearance, Beckham was excused from Galaxy duty to represent his country, fulfilling his commitment as ambassador of the London 2012 Olympic Games. But even as he would get to experience the high of representing his country, he still had to deal with a bit of adversity. It had been announced on June 28, that despite having been short-listed for the provisional squad, David had been cut from the England National team that would be playing in the Olympic Games.[54] It ended his dream of participating in his only Olympics, and of playing them in his hometown. Beckham held no grudge and still carried on with his ambassador duties. He was one of the Olympic Torch bearers, making a dramatic appearance in a speedboat on London's Thames River. And once the games got underway, he was as big a fan as any other, cheering for his fellow countrymen from the sidelines at several events. Though Beckham was unable to fulfill his dream of playing in the Olympics, it didn't stop the proud Englishman from having an excellent Olympic adventure.

END IT LIKE BECKHAM

Shifting gears and countries again, Beckham switched into his Galaxy kit in time to be back in the lineup on August 2 when L.A. played Real Madrid at the Home Depot Center in a World Football Challenge. There were two and a half months left in the regular season and at 10–11-3, L.A. was in fifth place in the Western Conference. Thanks to a once again fully focused Beckham, the midfielder's play—accounting for playing in twenty-four league matches and collecting seven goals and nine assists—helped propel the Galaxy into the playoffs for the fourth consecutive year. L.A. defeated the Seattle Sounders on November 18, and then they were assured of a spot in the MLS Cup Championship game.[55]

Then came the announcement on November 19, that after six years, the Beckham experiment had come to an end in Los Angeles. Major League Soccer's most recognizable athlete announced two weeks before the Galaxy was set to face the Houston Dynamo for the league's championship cup that he would be retiring after the game.

The Los Angeles Galaxy issued this statement from Beckham on November 19, 2012:

> In my time here I have seen the popularity of the game grow every year. I've been fortunate to win trophies, but more important to me has been the fantastic reception I've had from fans in L.A. and across the States. Soccer's potential has no limits in this wonderful country and I want to always be part of growing it. I don't see this as the end of my relationship with the league as my ambition is to be part of the ownership structure in the future.[56]

By all accounts, Beckham's American journey had turned out a success. When it looked as if the English superstar was finally able to give 100 percent to his Galaxy teammates and honor the commitment he made when he originally signed, his story ended on a high note. With his play on the pitch, the Galaxy won. And winning takes care of everything. Once again, the international star, the most photographed footballer in the world, had shown how he overcame adversity. He'd come to the United States to capture the attention of a nation not yet enraptured with the world's beautiful game. And after a rocky start, he put his head down, and used his talent on the field to show what a champion is made of. Reinvented and reinvigorated, he won back the fans' adoration. In 2011, when he could have moved on, he stayed. David Beckham had triumphed on and off the football pitch in his role as ambassador in the MLS. Like the first English settlers who arrived on the shores of America centuries ago, Beckham too, demonstrated his pioneer spirit and sense of adventure. He had the foresight to see the marketing field before him open with tremendous possibilities, tackle any obstacles or opponents that might get in his path, and, keeping his eye on the goal, ultimately reach his target.

In the 2012 MLS final, on December 1, Los Angeles hosted the Houston Dynamo at the Home Depot Center. Storming back from a deficit, the Galaxy scored three second-half goals—two of them on penalty kicks—to beat the Dynamo 3-1. It was a repeat of the previous year's championship game, where L.A. again defeated this same Dynamo team for the title. More active than he'd been during last year's title game when he was hampered by a hamstring injury, Beckham was very involved in play all game long and was involved in several near misses, though he didn't factor in any goals. Fans thanked him with a thunderous ovation as he left the pitch, on a substitution, late in the game. It was an emotional finale for the legendary midfielder, as he added yet another championship title to his storied career.[57]

During the championship celebration Beckham kissed his teammates, his three sons, and took his final bow for the audience. "I'm 37 and I've been able to play in quite a few finals and championship games, and I still love it like I did when I won my first."[58]

STATE OF MAJOR LEAGUE SOCCER—2012

After Beckham lifted his second MLS Cup trophy, and paraded triumphantly around the Home Depot Center, all that was left for the analysts to do was weigh in on whether the Beckham experiment had worked and if it had, to what extent. In terms of the league there was substantial evidence that the Beckham era had been a calculated marketing and financial triumph for the Galaxy and MLS.

- In 2007, there were thirteen MSL teams; by 2012, that number had grown to nineteen.
- Attendance at the end of 2006 MLS season was at an average 15,504; in 2012 it was up to 18,807.

- Soccer-specific stadiums had been built in four MLS markets, and major renovations had been made on several others.
- Beckham's presence helped the Galaxy sign an MLS groundbreaking ten-year agreement with Time Warner Cable Inc. in November 2011 that included broadcast with a Spanish-language network.[59]
- National television contracts with ESPN, NBC Sports, and Univision Communications Inc., kept exposure levels of the Galaxy and MLS at respectable highs.[60]
- TV ratings increased also, but only slightly, by 5 percent in five years.[61]
- The Designated Player Rule (aka the Beckham Rule), first approved in 2007, allowed for an exception in the league's strict salary cap rules. It paved the way for major European talent such as Thierry Henry, Rafa Marquez, and Robbie Keane, who followed Beckham into the league.
- The media landscape has transformed—soccer was the second most popular sport in America among twelve- to twenty-four-year-olds according to an ESPN survey.[62]
- The start of the 2013 season marked the nineteenth, making MLS longer lasting than any professional soccer organization in the United States, including the North American Soccer League.[63]

The hope from MLS commissioner Don Garber was that the significance of the David Beckham legacy would be measured in how it helped the league increase on four fronts: quality of play, level of fan support, local relevance of teams, and the league's value from top to bottom. Garber:

> I don't think anybody would doubt that he has over-delivered on every one of those measures. There's arguably not a soccer fan on this planet that doesn't know the L.A. Galaxy and Major League Soccer, and David played a significant role in helping us make that happen. He was an unbelievable ambassador for the league, for the Galaxy.[64]

Galaxy owner Tim Leiweke agreed: "Seldom does an athlete redefine a sport, and David not only took our franchise to another level but he took our sport to another level. It has been an honor and privilege to be a part of his world, and more importantly, to have him be a part of ours."[65] And Sunil Gulati, president of the United States Soccer Federation, said, "I don't think there's any doubt that David has increased the visibility of MLS and the sport more generally. That very positive impact will be felt for many years."[66]

THE BECKHAM BRAND IN 2012

Not surprisingly, success followed Beckham off the field during his time in the United States as well. Just as he was able to infiltrate the Spanish market while playing with Real Madrid, the soccer superstar had crossed the pond to find the American market equally ready to buy Beckham. Sponsorship deals during his time in the States included fast food giant Burger King, UK supermarket Sainsbury's, and electronics powerhouse Samsung. And in perhaps another stroke of marketing genius, Beckham had formed a partnership with clothing retailer H&M that saw him for the first time launch his own line of underwear, T-shirts, and pajamas. The Bodywear collection was available in eighteen hundred stores worldwide in 2012.[67]

While Beckham had a Beverly Hills address, the soccer superstar didn't really live the boisterous, glamorous Hollywood lifestyle. Neither he nor Victoria were frequent participants of the red-carpet, glitzy event scene. Though they were paparazzi mainstays, the images were more often of one or the other leaving the gym, or heading to dinner, or heading somewhere with their children. David was often at a Lakers game as he was a huge basketball fan and had become friendly with Kobe Bryant. The world's most photographed footballer did share the wealth factor that high-profile athletes do. In 2012, Beckham was ranked the highest-paid footballer, and appeared eighth overall on a *Forbes* magazine list. His reported earnings were $46 million—$9 million in salary and $37 million in endorsements.[68]

When Beckham walked off the field at the Home Depot Center on December 2, he didn't exit as just another athlete winning just another championship. His triumph included reminding the world that Brand Beckham was as relevant in the United States as it was in other parts of the world. He arrived with the intention of bolstering MLS interest in the United States, and to expand his brand here, and he did both, continuing to drive the Beckham-as-famous-footballer-and-cultural-icon narrative that continues to be written. If he had a microphone, walking off the pitch that night would have been the perfect time to drop it.

DONE AND DUSTED

His Galaxy career over, David Beckham was faced with contemplating his future beyond the game as many athletes have done before him. What does a global icon do for a living once playing the sport that made him famous is no longer an option?

The speculations were numerous: Would Beckham pursue ownership of an MLS franchise? Would he push his thirty-seven-year-old body in an attempt to play for yet another team? In yet another country? France? China? Australia? Russia? There was a long list of options. Or would he head back to his native England to suit up for a team not named Manchester United? Would he get into coaching, continue building his empire as an entrepreneur, or turn his attention to charity work?

His statement about remaining committed to MLS, and that his family was happy in Los Angeles pointed to signs that while Beckham's playing days have come to an end, he may not yet be done with his American adventure.

Based on his star power, was there anything he couldn't take on? As 2012 came to a close, and the last images were snapped of the football legend as player in the MLS, the world waited anxiously to find out what would be the next entry in the David Beckham career log.

10

LORD OF THE RINGS

Just outside London's City Hall, a speedboat on the Thames River was about to make history. It was the evening of July 27, 2012, and the night of the Opening Ceremonies of the Summer Olympic Games. The eyes of billions from across the globe were cast on this city on this night to watch England as the host of the pageantry and the performances and to enjoy the uniting spirit of sports.

A camera was fixed on a speedboat out on the water. A torch lit with the Olympic Flame was set inside a clear container attached to the front of the British-built boat. And the driver behind the wheel was none other than footballer David Beckham.

The course of the Torch Relay of the 2012 London Olympic Games took seventy days, was comprised of eight thousand miles, covered the United Kingdom from coast to coast and saw the torch carried by eight thousand torchbearers. But the night of the Opening Ceremonies was saved for the "Who's Who," of the sports world—the athletes known the world over as champions. Who better to highlight the greatest sports show on earth than one of the world's most celebrated football players? Matt Lauer, announcer, NBC News: "And here, it comes. At the wheel is David Beckham, the wildly popular British soccer star, who was born here in the East End, and was so instrumental in getting these games to London."[1]

Escorting the Olympic Torch, Beckham beamed with pride. The London native was dressed immaculately in a black suit, white shirt, and black tie. The speedboat raced up the river, met by hundreds of fans who cheered from the shorelines. Jade Bailey, a Team GB under-17 women's football player, was at the front of the boat, holding up the torch. Electric blue beams illuminated the boat and neon pink colored the vessel's wake. It was a glowing beacon as it glided along in the pitch-black water. Fireworks accompanied the boat and torchbearers, filling the night sky with white sparkles of light. The speedboat sped past the HMS *Belfast*, then sailed under the centuries-old Tower of London Bridge. A camera crew along for the ride filmed the entire route.[2]

In making this trip, David Beckham was also retracing the footsteps of his ancestors, who one hundred years ago had made a journey along the same Thames, and passed under the same Tower of London Bridge. Beckham guided the speedboat to a dock at Stratford, in the East End of London, that was the site of the new Olympic Stadium and the home of the London 2012 Summer Games.

FIRST THE BANG . . .

It started out as merely a passing thought. But it was persistent, like a melody replaying in the subconscious. *"What if? one two. What if?, three four."* It lingered and grew. Details emerged, images appeared, and it wasn't long before the concept began to take on a more concrete form. And once the idea had taken shape it turned into an elaborate plan. Then on Wednesday, July 6, 2005, it became a reality.

The crowd in London's Trafalgar Square was well over one thousand strong. They were waving Union Jacks as they waited for the news. And everyone was hopeful. This was the day the announcement would be made on the host city of the 2012 Summer Olympic Games. The loud and boisterous crowd was ready for a celebration. But when it was time to hear the announcement, the group quieted enough to hear a pin drop.

Six-thousand miles away, in the island country of Singapore, the International Olympic Committee held its 117th session. The purpose of the meeting was to select the host city of the 2012 Summer Olympic Games. In the hall of the Raffles City Convention Centre was the delegation from Great Britain, led by Sebastian Coe, himself a former Olympian. The group, comprised of other former Olympians, athletes, and politicians, included David Beckham. The English footballer, taking a break from playing for Real Madrid, had been invited to participate as an ambassador to help raise the profile of the country, of sports, and to help bring the games to the United Kingdom.[3]

A total of nine cities had started the bidding process to host the 2012 Summer Olympic Games. But by May 18, 2004, that number had been whittled down to five—London, Madrid, Moscow, New York City, and Paris.[4]

Representatives from the five finalist countries were all gathered in Singapore. Madrid was hoping to become only the second city in Spain to host the Olympics after the successful 1992 Summer Games in Barcelona. The Spanish capital had hosted other international sports championships, and they had the backing of former IOC president Juan Samaranch. But their bid did not get far. It was reported that questions of security did in the bid from Madrid, after 191 people were killed in terrorist attacks on March 11, 2004. Moscow had hosted the Summer Olympics of 1980. Its downfall in the end was insufficient housing for tourists, and an old transport system that was unlikely to accommodate extreme levels of traffic. New York City emerged as the city to bid for the games coming to the United States. And while the city boasted experience hosting numerous high-level events, they were never seen as a front-runner. Finally, after early-round eliminations, it came down to a contest between Great Britain and France.

Paris was not only a contender, it was widely regarded as a solid favorite to win the 2012 Olympics. The city had bid for and lost the opportunity to host the 1992 and 2008 games. The Parisian venue plan received a high score from the IOC, with the city's prior experience in hosting successful international sporting events, such as the 1998 FIFA World Cup and the 2003 World Championships in Athletics.[5]

For London, Coe and his team had put together a brilliant and flawless plan. Failed bids from Birmingham and Manchester convinced the British Olympic Committee that London was the best city to host the games. Constructing venues meant a revitalization of a rundown, working-class area in the East End of the city. In its place would be a five-hundred-acre park and an eighty-thousand-seat stadium. The space would also be home to the Olympic Medical Institute, a sports medical and rehabilitation center. World-class sports facilities, like a new swimming center and cycling velodrome, would inspire the next generation of athletes. New and upgraded transportation structures would help link hundreds of thousands.[6] The British delegation's presentation, which included highlighting the legacy the Games would have on the country, as well as young athletes for generations to come, was impressive. And everyone was hopeful.

The moment finally arrived to hear the results. International Olympic Committee president Jacques Rogge was given an envelope, which, slowly, he proceeded to open. Seconds felt like hours as the entire delegation, and likely the whole of England, waited anxiously to learn what the contents revealed.[7]

Rogge: "The International Olympic Committee has the honor of announcing, that the Games of the Thirtieth Olympiad in 2012 are awarded to the city of . . . London."[8]

They burst into cheers and tears—in the convention center in Singapore, and in Trafalgar Square in London. There was lots of hugging and high-fiving as the delegation celebrated after a tremendous presentation and collective effort. There was a lot of work ahead, but there would be plenty of time for that. It was a monumental victory for Great Britain.

Her Majesty the Queen, Elizabeth II, issued a statement from England: "I send my warmest congratulations to you [Seb Coe] and every member of the London 2012 team for winning the bid for the UK. It's really an outstanding achievement to beat such a highly competitive field."[9]

The Red Arrows, a jet squadron from the Royal Air Force, flew over the crowd at Trafalgar Square, filling the skies with a trail of red, white, and blue, as the celebration took on a full, party vibe. Dame Kelly Holmes, double Olympic champion, said in Trafalgar Square:

This is incredible. I'm really emotional and I don't know what I did when they announced "London." This will do wonders for the country. We came from the back and proved we wanted it and this will change the face of Great Britain forever.[10]

And in Singapore, the British Olympic bid committee members rejoiced. Lord Sebastian Coe, London bid team chief:

It is just the most fantastic opportunity to do everything that we've always ever dreamed of in British sport. We now have the chance, over the next seven years, and way beyond that, to change the face of sport and get, what I've always, always wanted—more young people into sport. This was a splendid team performance from two years ago when the team came together and everyone pulled together. We never lost confidence.[11]

For London native David Beckham, the news and the feeling were "amazing." He was born and raised in East London and was familiar with the area where many of the sports events were to be competed. The Olympic complex would be built on the grounds where he learned to play football.

Beckham: "The whole area is going to be transformed. It's not just about the East End—it's not just about London. It's going to transform the whole country. To have the Olympics in London—that's something special."[12]

The British delegation, triumphant and elated, was set to head home buoyed with optimism and pride with the news of its win. But the plans for a victory homecoming, and a celebratory news conference, would have to be put on hold, because within less than twenty-four hours after joy and jubilation, another event would put London in the headlines.[13]

... AND THEN THE BOOM

As daylight broke on the morning of July 7, and the sun rose above Trafalgar Square, citizens of London and all of Great Britain were rejoicing. Smiles were on the faces of Londoners. And as thousands headed to work or school or wherever their day took them, there was an extra bounce in many steps as they beamed with pride of knowing that come 2012, London would be hosting the world and the Summer Olympic Games. It was another, normal morning rush hour on the streets and the public transport system

Calm and routine turned into chaos at 8:50 AM.[14]

A coordinated series of bombs exploded in quick succession on the city's underground public transportation, causing death and massive destruction. The terrorist attacks were made by suicide bombers who all died in the explosions. The train stations hit were Russell Square, Aldgate, and Edgware Road, and the final bomb went off aboard a crowded double-decker bus at Tavistock Square. More than forty people were killed, and more than seven hundred were injured in the disaster.[15]

Prime Minister Tony Blair: "The terrorists will not succeed. Today's bombings will not weaken in any way our resolve to uphold the most deeply held principles of our societies and to defeat those who would impose their fanaticism and extremism on all of us. We shall prevail and they shall not."[16]

One of the explosions was only a few stations away from Trafalgar Square, where just a day ago thousands had gathered for the Olympic news celebration. Beckham:

> I don't think anyone can prepare themselves for the range of emotions our country went through. It was joy, and then just incredible pain and sadness. But we have to go forward and move on. There was fear. But at the end of the day, you can't let them win and you have to live your life. It's like in America for (Sept. 11), with struggle people come together. People will see how strong English people are, especially people in London.[17]

Following the bombings, the International Olympic Committee issued statements of condolences and reiterated its sentiments about the appalling attacks: "It has sadly proved there is no safe haven and that security must remain the priority whenever Olympics are staged. Security is one of the 17 themes of evaluating the Olympics and we have full confidence in the London authorities for a secure Olympic Games."[18]

With the backing of the IOC, and the new-found confidence of a country determined to prove its resilience and ability to overcome adversity, the seven-year countdown to the 2012 Summer Olympic Games had begun.

THIRD TIME IS A CHARM

London made history the moment it won the 2012 Olympic Games bid, as no other city had ever been selected as host three times.

Long before David Beckham, or Wembley Stadium, or even the Olympic Torch Relay, the city of London found itself the proud host of the Games of the Fourth Olympiad in 1908. The games were actually awarded to London by default. They were originally scheduled to be held in Rome, but the untimely eruption of Mount Vesuvius forced them to be relocated. At the time, a newly constructed venue had been built to house the Franco-British Exhibition, and with the existing structure, London was asked to become host of its first Olympic Games.

White City Stadium became the first stadium specifically built for the Olympics. The sixty-eight thousand-seat structure was at the time the largest stadium in the world. It cost £60,000 to construct.[19] Inside was a one-third-mile running track, a concrete cycling track, and a swimming pool. The Games got underway on April 27, with nearly two thousand athletes competing from twenty-two countries. They lasted a total of 187 days, or six months and four days, allowing time for other exhibition events, and were the longest games in modern Olympics history. Britain captured 146 total medals, more than three times any other country, and dominated most events.[20]

By comparison, the 1948 Summer Games saw no such extravagances. While finances didn't distract from the 1908 games, the lack of funding underscored every element of the Games of the Fourteenth Olympiad. The first to be held after World War II, they were christened the "Austerity Games." No new venues were built for the 4,104 athletes from fifty-nine nations who competed.[21] Defeated nations Germany and Japan were not invited to participate. Large portions of the city had been damaged by bombings, unemployment was high, and morale was low. Food rations meant IOC officials would ask all competitors to provide their own meals. Leftover food was donated to hospitals. And because the city was still rebuilding from the destruction of the war, athletes were housed in existing schools, government buildings, and military barracks. But the event went on and helped lift the spirit of the nation.[22] Gwen and Bert Allison, who attended the 1948 Olympics as twenty-two-year-old newlyweds, recalled, "Everyone was pleased that something great happened in England, people had come to see and look forward to what was going to happen. Everyone hoped it would be a great success—and it was."[23] Ron Godden, who fought for England in World War II and later attended the 1948 games:

> It was so unique because of all the troubles we'd had. It was a pleasure to be able to go and do something that you couldn't do for a few years prior to the war. I think it was a lift for everybody because we'd been through such a terrible time. It really did lift the nation. After the war, it was such a release to have something like the Olympic Games. It was a great event, it really was.[24]

"BEIKEHANMU"

David Beckham showed up for official ambassador duty next in 2008, to the delight of millions of his fans in Asia, when he appeared in the closing ceremonies of the Summer Olympic Games in Beijing.

Football fans in Asia, more precisely China and Japan, had long ago fallen zombie-like under the spell of David Beckham since the soccer star's early days with Manchester United.

Beckham—who is known in China as "Beikehanmu"—stars in ad campaigns for Pepsi, Adidas, and Castrol Oil in China, where soccer is hugely popular. Tens of millions of fans follow sixteen teams in the Chinese Super League, and dozens of smaller clubs.[25] The quest for all things Beckham combined with the country's enormous consumer spending power means endless merchandising opportunities for clubs. This was a leading factor in Real Madrid's decision to sign Beckham. While the Spanish club's execs were well aware that Beckham's contribution to Real Madrid's performances on the field would always be eclipsed by the likes of Luis Figo, Zinedine Zidane, Ronaldo, Raul, and Roberto Carlos, they also knew that no one could stack up to him when it came to selling the football club's kits in Asia.

In 2003, when Real Madrid arrived in China to play a series of friendlies, the team was greeted by folk dancers and elephants at the airport. Was the pachyderm parade simply because one David Beckham was the newest member of the Spanish club? Then in 2008, the Los Angeles Galaxy, Beckham's new team, went on a five-game exhibition tour, designed to tap into the superstar's huge popularity in Asia, with stops planned for Hong Kong, Korea, and China. Beckham's return trip to Beijing in August later that same year was not to play football, but to resume his role as ambassador of the London Olympic Games.[26]

In the handover at the closing ceremonies, host nation China welcomed London onto the stage as the site of the next Olympic Games. Beckham rode into the stadium atop one of London's famous red, double-decker buses along with Led Zeppelin guitarist Jimmy Page and pop star Leona Lewis.

The festive finale included hundreds of dancers from the UK and featured Beckham kicking a golden football into the stands as the world shifted its attention to London as host of the 2012 Summer Olympic Games.[27]

KEEP CALM AND CARRY ON

Concrete, metal, and a sea of yellow hard hats greeted David Beckham and Sebastian Coe on November 30, 2010, when they visited the site of the still-under-construction Olympic Stadium. The groundbreaking to transform the neglected wasteland in East London had begun more than three years ago. In its place would stand a green and spacious public park, complete with several new sports venues. The centerpiece, the eighty-thousand-seat stadium, would be the site of the opening and closing ceremonies of the Games as well as host of the majority of the athletic events. Beckham was impressed as he accompanied Coe to the stadium in his first official visit as ambassador of the games. To the disappointment of legions of his female fans, the on-the-scene photos did not include the English hunk wearing a hard hat.[28] Beckham:

> When you drive up to it—it has obviously got that awe about it. The area I know so well is being transformed, the amazing dream is becoming a reality and I have seen first-hand how much hard work has gone into the project. This is great for the East End and for sport.[29]

The stadium project employed five thousand workers from 240 British businesses. It was completed on March 30, 2011, ahead of schedule, and more than a full year ahead of the start of the 2012 games. The park site was renamed the Queen Elizabeth Olympic Park in 2013 in honor of the British monarch.[30]

Fast forward from Beckham's stadium visit to April 18, 2012, and London was at the 100-day mark to the start of the Olympic Games. Events in and around the city marked the occasion.

The OMEGA Countdown Clock originally erected in Trafalgar Square at the 500-day mark, switched to 100 with a small ceremony and a speech by IOC president Jacques Rogge.[31]

An aerial view from Kew Gardens showed a picturesque flowerbed grown specifically in the colors and shape of the five Olympic rings.[32]

Members of the Queen's Guard in their traditional red coats and black hats formed the number 100 at the Horse Guards Parade, soon to be the site of beach volleyball.[33]

First-class stamps issued by the Royal Mail and featuring Olympic sports were available for sale.[34]

The Olympic gold, bronze, and silver medals, designed by British artist David Watkins, were revealed for the first time.[35]

Weeks after the 100-day mark, on May 16, David Beckham would find himself on a plane to Greece, honored to be making the journey to Athens to collect the Olympic Flame.

YOU ARE HERE: VASILEOS KONSTANTINOU AVENUE, ATHENS, GREECE

The element of fire had sacred meaning in ancient Greek culture. Its divine properties meant it was used in many traditional rituals and ceremonies. The ceremony for the lighting of the Olympic Flame, which dates back to the ancient Olympic Games in 776 BC, was derived from a flame that was kept burning during the length of the sporting event.

Those customs and traditions are kept alive today with a ceremony that starts in Olympia, site of the ancient Olympic Games. A flame is ignited there from the sun's rays. This flame then lights the Olympic Torch of the host country. At the end of a seven-day relay with stops in several Greek cities, the torch arrived in Athens, where it was passed on to the Summer Games host in the handover ceremony at the Panathenaic Stadium, site of the first modern Olympic Games in 1896.[36]

The day started with rain, but by late afternoon a rainbow had filled the sky, providing the perfect backdrop for the torch handover ceremony. The flame arrived, carried into the stadium by Greek rowing world champion Christina Giazitzidou, and the world got its first, up-close look at the London 2012 Olympic Torch.[37]

More than six hundred design firms submitted proposals for the 2012 Olympic Torch. British designers Edward Barber and Jay Osgerby, whose firm is based in East London, won the honor. The final torch is two gold-colored, lightweight aluminum skins, punctuated by eight thousand small, laser-cut holes welded together to form a triangular, tapered cone. The torch's three-sided shape is a unique aspect, as traditionally they've been cylindrical. But it became a vision of the designers to incorporate triples into the form after considering 2012 was the third games to be held in London, and the three virtues that comprise the Olympic motto. The eight thousand holes are pretty and pragmatic, as they prevent the flame's heat from going down the torch's handle.[38] Edward Barber and Jay Osgerby:

> As designers, this is quite simply the best project going: to design an icon for the [Olympic] Games. We've wanted to be involved since July 2005 when we were celebrating winning the bid with the rest of the UK. We have worked hard to develop a Torch that celebrates the Relay, and reflects the passion for London and the Olympic Games. We wanted to make the most of pioneering production technologies and to demonstrate the industrial excellence available in the UK— it's a Torch for our time. This is our opportunity to represent the UK, in design terms, and we are incredibly proud to be doing so.[39]

Jay Osgerby:

> For me, designing the Olympic torch has been a highlight, certainly from the perspective of the excitement it generated. The thing about the torch is that it's of interest to most of the nation, so you're being scrutinised by people who don't have a special interest in design.[40]

Edward Barber:

> It could have gone incredibly badly, but thankfully it's been very well received. It's been called a cheese grater, but we can live with that.[41]

Hundreds gathered at the Panathenaic Stadium for the Olympic Torch handover ceremony. Along with the Hellenic Olympic Committee, the International Olympic Committee, and the British Olympic Committee delegation, was the Games' ambassador, David Beckham. There were children singing and the Greek, Olympic, and British flags flying as part of the ceremony. The torch changed hands from one athlete to the next, and was finally used to light the cauldron in the stadium. A ceremonial Greek high priestess then used the flame from the cauldron to light the London Olympic Torch.

For the final act, England's Princess Anne, a member of the International Olympic Committee and former Olympic athlete, took the flame from Spyros

Capralos, the president of the Hellenic Olympic Committee, and London took official possession of the Olympic Torch.

The following day, David Beckham and the British Olympic delegation, traveling on British Airways Flight 2012, touched down in Cornwall, England, to launch the seventy-day Olympic Torch Relay.[42]

A GOLDEN DELIVERY

Princess Anne stepped off the specially painted gold plane and onto the tarmac at the Royal Naval Air Station Culdrose in Cornwall. In her hand, the Princess Royal was carrying precious cargo—a ceremonial lantern in a specially designed cradle that securely held the Olympic Flame. She was joined by Sebastian Coe; Olympics minister Hugh Robertson; Boris Johnson, mayor of London; and Olympic ambassador David Beckham.

At the naval base there was a small group of students and dignitaries to greet the flame. A temporary platform had been erected on the tarmac and in the center was a ceremonial cauldron. After speeches and media interviews, David Beckham had the honor of lighting it. He positioned the Olympic Torch so that it could be ignited by the flame in the lantern. He raised the lit torch to applause, then cautiously used it to light the cauldron.[43]

The next step for the Olympic torch after the brief ceremony would be delivering the flame to the first torchbearer—triple Olympic gold medalist and sailor Ben Ainslee—who would run the first leg of the seventy-day torch relay. The torch would travel eight thousand miles on a journey that stretched across the United Kingdom and six of the British Isles. Landmark stops along the way would include Stonehenge, Mount Snowdon in Wales, Big Ben, the white cliffs of Dover, and Giant's Causeway in Northern Ireland. In total it would be carried by eight thousand torch bearers, 85 percent of whom were local citizens, children, and volunteers.[44] Mayor Boris Johnson:

> What the torch relay does is it democratises the whole Olympic experience. The Olympic flame is a sacred thing. It's not just there for Jacques Rogge [president of the International Olympic Committee] and priestesses and stuff like that. It's there for people in the streets to look at and to be passed from hand to hand. Millions of people are going to be able to watch it go through Britain.[45]

The Olympic Torch was now burning on British soil as the host country of the Games of the Thirtieth Olympiad.[46]

THE UNKINDEST CUT OF ALL

On June 28, one month before the Opening Ceremonies of the Summer Olympic Games, news emerged that would shock and disappoint legions of David Beckham fans as well as millions of his fellow countrymen. It likely felt worse for the footballer himself.

In a phone call from England national football team manager Stuart Pearce, Beckham learned that he had been cut from the final eighteen-man squad that would represent the United Kingdom in the Olympics.

Surprisingly, in his entire twenty-year career, Beckham had never played in the Olympics. But the fault was not because he hadn't been a good enough player. It was that the United Kingdom had not fielded a team in the Games since 1960, long before the international football player was born. The idea of playing in his first Olympic Games, and adding that to all the other accolades of his career, felt like a dream for Beckham. And the fact that the games were being held in his hometown would make it all the more special. He knew that only three players over the age of twenty-three were allowed to play for the eighteen-man team. But Beckham had reason to hope after learning that he'd made Pearce's shortlist of thirty-five players. And Pearce had even flown to the United States to watch the LA Galaxy midfielder's in-match performance.

Then the disappointing news, and hope gave way to despair.[47] Beckham:

> Everyone knows how much playing for my country has always meant to me, so I would have been honored to have been part of this unique Team GB squad. Naturally I am very disappointed, but there will be no bigger supporter of the team than me. And like everyone, I will be hoping they can win the gold. As a Londoner, I will have been really proud to have played a small part in bringing the Olympics to my home town as part of [Sebastian Coe's] team, and I can't wait for the games to begin and enjoy every moment along with the rest of Great Britain.[48]

The decision ignited a debate over whether Beckham should have been on the team based on merit. Or was simply his involvement in helping to secure the games themselves enough to have rewarded him with a spot on the team? But if the decision makers already included three players over the age of twenty-three, weren't the clubs already making exceptions? Ryan Giggs:

> Obviously as a former team-mate and a friend of David I am disappointed for him, but he will take it on the chin and carry on his career. It's one of those things, it was not meant to be.[49]

Stuart Underwood, Beckham's childhood coach:

Surely a man with David's experience in the game, his ability to bring out the best of certainly younger players that would look up to him, he's got to be selected for the squad. I think it's an unbelievable decision and I think the majority of football lovers in the country will think the same. And let's be really honest about it—the GB team are not going to win this tournament. That's definite. David could have been the answer to going in there and getting the best out of these boys and giving them something to take away out of this tournament, and I just cannot understand the decision that's been made.[50]

Gary Lineker:

Terrible shame for Beckham having given so much to the Olympic bid and football. Never thought for a second that David Beckham would be excluded from GB's team. There are arguments for and against DB selection. What I don't understand though, is why string him along by including him in a short list?[51]

Paul McCartney:

I would've thought first choice would be Beckham because of his huge contribution to getting the Olympics. But, you know, some idiot decided otherwise. I feel a bit sorry for the three over-23-year-olds, because we're going to be looking at them and going, "That should've been Beckham." He's a national hero. And it would've been great for him to lead out our British team, but someone somewhere said . . . What did they say? So-and-so's playing better. Like it matters.[52]

Joanne Beckham, Beckham's sister:

Well, what a ***** joke. Disappointed, outraged and very sad.[53]

Sebastian Coe:

David has been an extraordinary supporter—probably our number one supporter—of the Games from the very beginning and is keen to continue his enthusiastic support right to the end. He is from East London and knows how important the Games and sport are to young people. He is a great role model and we are lucky to have such an advocate.[54]

If the news had in fact crushed Beckham, the world would never know. The words, "Get up, and get on with it," uttered by his father when he was a seven-year-old playing football in the park, were never more appropriate. The sting of disappointment never once showed up in his comments or actions in the days following the announcement. He held his head high and maintained an unwavering commitment to his country. David Beckham pressed on with his duties as ambassador of the London 2012 Summer Games. Admirably.

THE OPENING CEREMONIES OF THE 2012 SUMMER OLYMPIC GAMES

The excitement and build up to the games was palpable. So too was the speculation on what exactly would be David Beckham's role. After David had been cut from the eighteen-man squad of the UK's football team, Olympic committee chairman Sebastian Coe hinted that all consideration would be given to have Beckham figure in a prominent role in the opening ceremonies of the games.

On July 27, that role was revealed to the world.

Each torchbearer has the honor of carrying the Olympic Torch on a portion of its journey to eventually light the cauldron that signals the start of the Olympiad. On the evening of the opening ceremonies that honor belonged to David Beckham as he ferried the Olympic Torch in a speedboat along London's Thames River. It's an honor he won't soon forget.

One fan wrote this after watching the event on a YouTube video:

> I honestly believe that David Beckham arriving with the Olympic torch via speed boat, is the coolest thing I have ever seen! The music ["I Heard Wonders," by David Holmes], his sharp suit, his smile, Jade's glance over her shoulder, the blue/pink colours emanating from the rear of the boat and the terrific spectacle of the fireworks, as they pass under Tower Bridge—it just doesn't get any better than that![55]

The speedboat finally arrived at Stratford, to a pier at the new Olympic Stadium. Beckham arrived to meet fellow countryman and five-time Olympic gold medalist Steve Redgrave. The handoff saw Beckham use the torch he delivered to help light the flame of the one Redgrave was carrying, and the torch exchange was made. David Beckham, the lad from East London, England, had completed his part in the proceedings of the 2012 Summer Olympic Games.

SIXTEEN DAYS OF GLORY

It was 7 PM, July 29, and Team GB were on the pitch inside Wembley Stadium. The new ninety-thousand-seat venue, completed in 2007 after the original was demolished, has a sliding roof, and a signature lattice arch that stretches 436 feet above it.[56] There are now 107 steps to collect a winning trophy from the Royal Box. The stadium was one of six used to host Olympic soccer.[57] The Great Britain national team, fielding a team that represented the country for the first time since the 1960 Olympic Games, was well on its way to capturing a win in its second match of the tournament against United Arab Emirates.

Only David Beckham was missing to make this historic picture complete. Except he wasn't. The thirty-seven-year-old former England captain had been omitted from the final team cut, but Beckham held no grudge toward the team he would not be playing for or his country. And though his personal dream of playing in his first Olympics in his hometown London was dashed, in a show of utmost patriotism and professionalism, David showed up as a fan and supporter.

Alongside his oldest son, Brooklyn, and His Royal Highness, Prince William, Beckham took in the football action from the stands at Wembley, cheering and applauding and enjoying the Olympic experience.[58]

Beckham watched from the stands as longtime friend and former Manchester United teammate Ryan Giggs scored the opening goal of the game. Many of Beckham's fans were there too, some even wearing David Beckham masks. Team GB defeated UAE, 3–1, and won two additional matches in the group stage. But the squad was then beaten on penalty shots by South Korea and exited the Olympics in the knockout round.[59]

Football wasn't the only sport on David Beckham's agenda. Like a kid in a candy store, which was in his hometown London, Beckham took full advantage of the sixteen days of the 2012 Summer Olympic Games.

BECKHAM'S OLYMPIC TIME LINE

Wednesday, August 8, Men's, Women's BMX Cycling

Venue—London VeloPark. The newly constructed cycling center in London's East End has a 250-metre track velodrome for speed cycling, a BMX racing track, and mountain bike road course.

Beckham spent a sunny day at the outdoor motocross track with his three sons to check out BMX cycling events. Mariana Pajón of Colombia won the women's final and Maris Strombergs from Latvia took gold in the men's event.

Other celebrity fans in attendance: British prime minister David Cameron.[60]

Wednesday, August 8, Women's Beach Volleyball

Venue—Horse Guards Parade. Tons of sand were hauled into this location, home of the Trooping of the Color event that takes place on the Queen's official birthday each year, to provide fifteen thousand fans with a man-made beach scene to enjoy Olympic volleyball.

Beckham was with all three of his sons again, Brooklyn, Romeo, and Cruz, as the family watched the USA team of Misty May-Treanor and Kerri Walsh Jennings become the first to capture a third consecutive Olympic Gold Medal.

Other celebrity fans in attendance: His Royal Highness, Prince Harry; Team GB's gold medal cyclists Laura Trott and Jason Kenny.[61]

Saturday, August 11, Men's, Women's Athletics

Venue—Olympic Stadium. Beckham returned once again to the venue that was the center stage of the games. The performers from the opening ceremonies were gone, though, replaced with track stars who were quite capable of putting on a show themselves. David and his sons cheered on fellow countryman Mo Farah, who won gold in the 5,000 m race.

Other celebrity fans in attendance: London Mayor Boris Johnson.[62]

Saturday, August 11, Men's Diving, 10 m Platform

Venue—Aquatics Centre. This facility was constructed with two 50 m Olympic-sized swimming pools and a 25 m diving pool. It hosted all of the swimming, diving, and synchronized swimming events.

After taking in the action at the Olympic Stadium, Beckham and his boys raced over to the Aquatics Centre to check out the diving. The Beckham clan cheered on as Great Britain teen sensation, Tom Daley, made a splash, collecting the bronze medal in the 10 m platform final.

Other celebrity fans in attendance: One Direction star Louis Tomlinson.[63]

Sunday, August 12, Men's Basketball

Venue—North Greenwich Arena. The O$_2$ arena, with a capacity of up to twenty thousand, is the second-largest in the UK. Since its opening in 2007, besides basketball, it has hosted numerous musicians and events including Andrea Bocelli, Barbra Streisand, and boxing.

Again, with his three sons in tow, Beckham enjoyed the men's Olympic basketball final. Team USA defeated Spain, 107–100, in a hard-fought contest to take home the gold medal.

Other celebrity fans in attendance: Arnold Schwarzenegger and his son Patrick; Jesse Eisenberg.[64]

ALL'S WELL THAT ENDS WELL

By late afternoon on August 12, the eyes of the world were once again centered on the Olympic Stadium and the games' closing ceremonies. Musicians filled the stage as the performance theme featured a flashback to British music with artists the Who, One Direction, George Michael, Annie Lennox, Liam Gallagher, Muse, and one special performance by a Beckham on the world stage who wasn't named David.[65]

The Spice Girls reunion brought the crowd to its feet. Victoria Beckham, in full Posh Spice–persona, her black hair and black Giles Deacon gown blowing in the wind, belted out "Wannabe" and "Spice Up Your Life" as the quintet reminded fans why the all-girl group had rocked the top of the pop charts for years.[66]

When the British musical tributes ended, the Rio de Janeiro Olympic delegation treated the audience to the sexy samba, a taste of what's to come in four years as the Latin American city hosts the next summer games. Finally the Olympic Torch was extinguished, and London celebrated the end of a historic sporting event.

The games had brought a renewed sense of patriotism to Great Britain's citizens, and the hope of creating a future generation of sport enthusiasts. There were new sports arenas and new housing built, and the revival of an entire area of London. There would be talk of how to translate the temporary labor force into long-term jobs and growth. And the Games' impact will obligatorily be analyzed from a performance, cultural, social, philosophical, and political point of view.

More than 10,500 athletes from 204 National Olympic Committees took part in the Games, with 302 medal events being held. More than twenty-one thousand accredited media representatives communicated the Games to a worldwide audience of four billion people. And a total workforce of two hundred thousand, including more than seventy thousand volunteers, helped make the Games possible. Great Britain collected sixty-five medals at these games, making it their most successful Olympics since 1908.[67]

In the end, none of the numbers mattered to David Beckham. His "hall pass," granted by the Los Angeles Galaxy, had excused him from a handful of Major League Soccer matches and allowed him to attend to his Olympic ambassador duties, ignoring the critics who questioned his loyalty to the team and league. Following his heart and love for his country, was there anywhere else Beckham could have been?

As he proudly watched his wife's performance in the closing ceremonies, he could reflect on his own legacy of the Games. And it was likely one that included the sheer joy he had in participating, at the highest level, in helping to get the games in the first place. There was the excitement of taking part in the many traditional ceremonies surrounding the Olympics. And of course, the thrill of attending the events with his children. For sixteen days, David Beckham made the Games of the Thirtieth Olympiad, in his hometown, London, his playground.

11

LEAVE A LEGACY

Up. Up. And up again. It was something the players did to mark such occasions and David Beckham's teammates were honoring it. They tossed the footballer up into the air, over and over, a spirited gesture that showed their appreciation and was the guys' way of giving him a proper sendoff. It was Beckham's last professional football match.

Dav-eed Beck-ham! Dav-eed Beck-ham!

The fans at Parc des Princes Stadium were giving Beckham a standing ovation and no. 32 applauded back, acknowledging the cheers. His team, Paris Saint-Germain won the game that night, playing the last home match in a season in which it had captured the French Ligue 1 championship title for the first time since 1994. That made Beckham the first English player to win league championships in four countries. Beckham draped himself in England's flag and, along with his three sons, felt the shower of love and confetti as he joined his teammates on the center of the pitch for the trophy presentation. In the stands his wife, as well as his mother and father, looked on.[1] It was an emotional night for everyone. Along with the celebration there was a twinge of sadness, as Beckham had announced his retirement from football only days earlier, hanging up his cleats after an illustrious twenty-one-year career.

When Beckham closed the chapter on his trailblazing endeavor in the United States as a member of the Los Angeles Galaxy, capped with a second MLS Cup, there was enormous speculation as to his next move. Interested parties came from teams as far away as Asia and Australia. The man and the brand were in high demand. On January 31, Beckham signed a five-month contract to play for Paris Saint-Germain, a club in the top-tier French league.[2] At the press conference,

Beckham, impeccably dressed, charmed the media as he answered a barrage of questions. He also revealed that he would be donating his entire salary, a reported $5 million, to a children's charity in Paris.[3]

There was speculation—*quelle suprise!*—that Beckham's acquisition was merely a marketing stunt. But one French publication declared his arrival in the city of lights as the most important event since man walked on the moon.[4] Sales of Beckham's no. 32 PSG shirt had reached the thousands within one week of the superstar's signing, before he had played a match.[5] David's first team session at the Camp des Loges training complex was a media hit—photographers from France, England, and Sweden showed up to watch the midfielder. He jogged while warming up alongside his new teammates, smiled and waved for the TV crews.[6]

Beckham went on to play in fourteen matches for the French club. Then came the sad but true news that the megastar athlete was retiring. At the farewell match, on May 18, Beckham was handed the honorary team captaincy by manager Carlo Ancelotti. After starting the match and showing the 44,983 in attendance the skills he built his career on, with passes that set up two of the team's goals late in the second period, the former Manchester United, Real Madrid, AC Milan, and L.A. Galaxy midfielder got the call. The game came to a complete standstill as one by one his teammates hugged and congratulated him.[7]

As the enormity of the occasion sank in, the lad from Leytonstone who became the world's most popular footballer was visibly shaken.

> I spoke to (coach) Carlo (Ancelotti) before, who told me he would bring me off about 80 minutes. 65 minutes came and all of a sudden I couldn't breathe. I got short of breath and I had a real struggle controlling my emotions. I broke down. It was not something I wanted to do, but I couldn't control it.[8]

FOOT NOTES

The David Beckham story is about love. Love for football, love for family, love for country. It is a story about passion and perfection. About focus, discipline, and devotion. And relevance and reach. It's also about pie and mash and snooker and underwear and tattoos. But mostly it is a story about simple things. Pride and patriotism, dedication and sacrifice, respect and professionalism. For all of those values are at the core of what make up the man, the footballer, the father, the style maven, the global superstar, the working-class lad from East London, David Beckham.

The story is highlighted, of course, with football. Lots of football. The hours of practice as a youth. The impossible dream of playing for a cherished childhood team. The highs after a win and not being able to sleep until nearly dawn the next day. And the lows of knowing your actions cost your team victory. The teammates, the clubs, the countries, the championship titles. All of this shaped the football legend David Beckham and gave a generation of followers delight. Off the football field, Beckham was an ideal role model. His name was never attached to the scandals that so often plague athletes. He remains a decent bloke from the east of London who made good.

And Beckham will always hold a unique place in English football history.

Beckham wasn't born with a magic right foot, but his hard-work ethic and his relentless pursuit of perfection eventually earned him a spot on many lists of football's greatest. As a free-kick specialist, his talent affected the outcome of many matches. And it should be noted, Beckham won everywhere he played.

Equally impressive as his work ethic, and likely because of it, was Beckham's ability to overcome adversity. Many a triumph-over-tragedy ends with the victor reciting, "It doesn't matter how many times you get knocked down, but what's important is that you get back up." Beckham took knee-buckling hits—the horrific backlash from his countrymen after the red card of 1998, the dismissal from his childhood dream team, the cut from the England National squad. But the footballer bounced back every time. He held his head high, kept his nose to the ground and demonstrated great maturity and professionalism. His restraint and strength to not strike back were courageous and admirable. Despite what the media speculated, Beckham always blocked out the distractions and stayed focused on what he loved doing and what he did best—playing football.

Beckham was a consummate patriot. Captaining the England National team for fifty-nine matches, giving everything he had for his country, consistently trying to maintain his position on the team and then emotionally turning over the armband, all point to his pride and devotion to honor his country. It is a sad footnote to his career, though he made enormous contributions to the Three Lions team, that they were never able to capture any titles during his time playing with them.[9]

Those who were not football fans got to enjoy Beckham also, thanks to his handsome face and toned athlete's body. No advertiser is going to pass on a chance to sell sex appeal, and Beckham had it by the tons. Would posters of Michael Jordan or Tiger Woods posing in their underwear have drawn the same kind of stop-in-your-tracks attention? Football was his first brand, but Beckham's body also became his brand, and his brand was admired and adored universally. Brand experts credited Beckham's marketability to everything from his values being those that the everyman can understand, to his association with his wife, Victoria, and his willingness to take risks. It may all boil down to his likeable personality and his looks. Beckham is by all accounts genuinely decent and likeable and ultimately isn't that what makes a person most attractive?

If Beckham were a musician with twenty-one years of work behind him, the cast of the TV show *Glee* would surely feature his greatest hits in an episode. If he were an ice cream flavor, Baskin-Robbins would bump their wonderful total selection to thirty-two. If he were a book, the midnight-release parties his title would attract would have to start hours earlier. The most-photographed footballer on the planet, the most-searched sports term on Google in 2003 and 2004,[10] and the most popular athlete in the world bears the telltale signs of a true cultural icon.

By definition, the oft overused term has several meanings. People who are considered icons are revered or idolized. They are easily recognized. They influence, they are inspirational, and they make a difference. Some are known by one name, and some are often imitated. Pop culture icons that come to mind are Jackie O, Frank Sinatra, Bono, Oprah, and Muhammad Ali.

Ellis Cashmore, a professor of culture, media, and sport at Staffordshire University in the United Kingdom, believes Beckham embodies many of these criteria. Cashmore, who wrote the book, *Beckham*, as well as several others on sport and pop culture, defines the megastar as a unique type of icon:

> Nothing that he did or said made him an icon. He played decent soccer, he appeared with his wife and he was discussed. We attribute meaning to people and we attributed him with so much meaning that we made him into an icon. Icons are a symbol of something, they stand for something. What does David Beckham stand for? He stands for anything we want him to. He means so many things to different people. *We* built the icon.[11]

With his goals ingrained in memory and his face imprinted in the subconscious, David Beckham is an icon of his generation.

IN 140 CHARACTERS OR LESS

Beckham the player graced the football pitch for the last time in 2013, but Beckham the global superstar continues to make his mark in history. The Twittersphere blew up the minute Beckham announced his retirement from football, with comments from those in the sports industry, celebrities, politicians, and the star's gazillion followers from around the globe. Hashtags that day included #Beckhamretires, #ThankYouDavidBeckham, #joyofbecks, #GiveThatManAKnighthood, and #End it Like Beckham.

A minute sample of love from his fans:

"Six club. Twenty titles win. Twenty years. 111 goals in 641 appearence. 500 haircuts."

"Maestro! #ForeverUnited"

"i love manchester united because of him. the legendary number 7. the freekick specialist, the great passer."

"So much more than just a footballer, champion!"

"se retira un grande un hombre de las mejores pegadas gracias por todo bechkam"

"Watching your hero leave is honestly the saddest thing."

"Merci pour tout David Beckham et bonne retraite sportive."

"#thankyoudavidbeckham Not only for your joyful football memories but also for adding glamour in it by turning b'ful girls into Footy fans:D"

"#thankyoudavidbeckham por ser el mejor en tiros libres de la historia y parte de una de las mejores épocas del Real Madrid."

"Gutted Beckham is retiring. He is a brilliant role model for the sport."

"Not only a great athlete, also a great role model and man to be inspired by #ThankYouDavidBeckham"

"#thankyoudavidbeckham tu grandeza nunca sera comparada, una leyenda que siempre recordaremos gracias sir david beckham!!"

"David Beckham has done extraordinary work to grow soccer in the u.s."[12]

CHEERS

Those in the football world were equally moved when news emerged that Beckham's illustrious career was over. Gary Neville, former Manchester United and England teammate:

When you think back on the way football has changed over the last 22 years, he has probably been the most influential player in that time out of England in terms of transforming football. He has transported England around the world and that's something he was aware of and wanted to do. Every clothing garment he wore, every hairstyle was followed. Not just in football.[13]

Paul Scholes, former Manchester United and England teammate:

It's a sad day but hopefully David is happy with what he's done. From the start you knew the quality he had and the professionalism. His range of passing and his free-kicks were brilliant and that was no accident—he was out there practising all day long.[14]

Phil Neville, former Manchester United and England teammate:

David Beckham—what an unbelievable career—4 titles in 4 countries over 100 caps for Eng and the best ambassador this country has had![15]

Andrei Kanchelskis, former Manchester United teammate:

He is a big name off the pitch, he is fashionable, maybe he will work as a model. He is a nice personality, a nice football player and I am very pleased I played alongside him. I wish him all the best.[16]

Bruce Arena, Beckham's former Los Angeles Galaxy coach:

He adds an incredible intensity. He brought the focus to players each and every game. He taught our young players the little things you need to do to win games. He was an important part of the LA Galaxy being champions. I've never seen a player with his ability.[17]

Wayne Rooney, Manchester United forward and former England teammate:

Just heard that David Beckham has retired. What a career, but most of all what a great person. Good luck for the future Becks![18]

Sven-Goran Eriksson, former England National team manager:

He's a fantastic footballer, fantastic man and probably the world's biggest sports personality. I don't think there is any other football player more popular than him. He was a very, very good captain.[19]

Eric Harrison, Beckham's United youth academy coach:

There's nobody in the world when they see a boy at 12, who can say he's going to go to such great heights as David. But I saw a very talented player—one absolutely in love with football. The hard work was the catalyst. He never had a lot of pace but in terms of stamina, running and work-rate, he was probably one of the best I've worked with.[20]

Sepp Blatter, FIFA president:

David grew up as a football-loving child and achieved his dreams, and unquestionably inspired millions of boys and girls to try and do the same. Whatever he chooses to do next I'm sure he'll approach with the same dedication and good grace he displayed the last 21 years.[21]

Beckham's wife Victoria posted a sweet and candid photo of the couple on a vacation, then revealed to *Glamour* magazine that she was looking forward to having her husband around more with her and the children: "That will be really nice. We've spent a lot of time apart, because he's been working and I've been working, but the future's very exciting. He's got lots of great things up his sleeve, so we're looking forward to the future for sure."[22]

YOU ARE HERE: TONJI UNIVERSITY, SHANGHAI, CHINA

Outside the gates of the football field nearly one thousand young fans stood waiting. Some had been there for hours, climbing over cars and railings and trying to get as high as they could, all for a glimpse of their hero, David Beckham. The megastar footballer, recently appointed ambassador to the Chinese Super League, had scheduled a visit this afternoon to Tonji University in Shanghai to meet with fans and practice with the school's football team. But soon after Beckham stepped onto the school's track there was chaos. Tons of overexcited students and autograph-seeking fans surged toward the former England captain, past a wall of security, and the ensuing melee left several people injured.[23]

Beckham was quickly escorted back into his car and the event had to be canceled. He later sent well wishes to those who were injured from his Facebook page. This was Beckham's second trip to China in 2013 since being named an ambassador to help raise the profile of football in the world's most populous country.[24]

The Chinese Super League is the latest incarnation of top-tiered professional football in China. Formed in 2004, the league was comprised of sixteen teams competing in a thirty-game season. Football has a long history in China, with the country receiving FIFA sanctioning in 1924. But the league's strength is not on par with European powerhouses, and fans of the game are more apt to follow foreign teams and players. Team China's only World Cup appearance was in 2002.[25]

In 2012, the league was hit by a major scandal when two high-ranking officials, a referee, and several former players were convicted of taking bribes and were sentenced to prison. Then in early 2013, CFA officials found fifty-eight people guilty of being involved with match fixing. With such a muddied reputation, some wondered why Beckham would want to be associated with the league, while others questioned the real likelihood of his participation making any kind of difference.[26] Zhu He Yuan, China Super League deputy general:

> Obviously everyone pays attention to Chinese football, we know that it is going through a rough time, but we are working very, very hard. We invited David Beckham to inspire kids to participate in the game and to inspire more people to watch the game and from his last two trips we have achieved this goal.[27]

In discussing Beckham's deal, Jeff Slack, IMG's senior vice president of football, described it as historic, comparing it to the state invitation Muhammad Ali once received from the Chinese government. Slack also stated Beckham was the only footballer considered because he was the best choice:

> David is the perfect guy, because of how good he is at this, and how genuine and involved he is, and how interested he is in it. But he's also an incredible football player. It wasn't an advertising campaign, let's go find someone, here's five guys—there was one guy. If it hadn't been David, we wouldn't have done this with anyone.[28]

During Beckham's first trip in March, the global star attended a welcoming press conference and then went on to visit three Chinese football clubs as he began his role to grow the game at the grassroots level and engage a new generation of supporters in a country of 1.3 billion. Beckham:

> I'm here as an ambassador. I'm here as a person who's trying to raise the profile of the game here and to be part of something that could be very special in the future. I've enjoyed the soccer academies that I've given around the world over the years. The education of football to children is very important to me. I want to do everything I can to help the young children of China become professional footballers one day.[29]

MAN OF THE HOUR

An alarm goes off, daylight replaces the darkness of sleep, and the morning get-the-kids-off-to-school routine begins. Outfits—is it going to rain today?

Breakfast—my cereal's all gone! Books—don't forget your math homework. Then David Beckham loads up the SUV and the proud stay-at-home dad gets set to drop his children off to school. After years of playing football and traveling and business commitments, the celebrated athlete, global pitchman, and style icon can play the most important role he'll ever have: Dad. And Beckham will gladly tell anyone, his children are his greatest accomplishment: "My children without doubt are what I'm most proud of. It's as simple as that. They are by far the biggest achievements in my life. They're beautiful, they're healthy and they're good kids too."[30]

The paparazzi had been aggressively trying for years to get images of the Beckham children, and now that David was able to spend more time with them, they finally got their wish. Images of the family at Disneyland, at events at the children's schools and even outings to restaurants were quickly posted on the Internet. Beckham was also in the stands or on the sideline while his sons were practicing football, or in the case of his eldest, Brooklyn, trying to make an academy. And the devoted husband continued to support Victoria, with whom he celebrated fourteen years of marriage in 2013 by attending events around her burgeoning design career.

RARE AIR

Ex-athletes don't just fall out of love with their sport the minute they retire. It is something they've been living, sleeping, and breathing for decades. To ease the transition into the nonplaying life, many are intent to stay involved in some aspect of the game. David Beckham's way back into soccer was arranged for him when he signed with the Galaxy back in 2007. A provision in the contract gave him the option to buy a new major league soccer franchise for a discounted price of $25 million.[31] He now decided to exercise that option: "I'm passionate about staying in football and being an owner of a team is something I'm passionate about."[32]

After making several trips to Miami, Florida, speculation spiked that it would be the newest expansion city. Beckham had even been in talks with the NBA's Miami Heat star LeBron James to become an investor.[33] If the deal happens, and if it is in Miami, a David Beckham-backed franchise would be part of the league's plan to expand to twenty-four teams by 2020.[34] His investment came at a time when there seemed to be a trend of American backers buying English football clubs. Once again, Beckham bucked convention and tradition, and wrote his own rules.

In late December 2013, the Miami-Dade County commissioner's office approved the support of finding a stadium location, with reports claiming the international star was looking at property on the city's downtown waterfront.[35] Knowing the marketing power Beckham has, the MLS has wholeheartedly approved a prospective deal. Don Garber, MLS commissioner:

> We are very excited about the opportunity of David putting together an ownership group and finalizing a stadium site in downtown Miami so that we could end up having what we hope would be our 22nd team in a city that's one of the largest in the country and has a strong and passionate soccer fan base.

The discounted ownership proviso came with a December 31, 2013, expiration date, and as the year wound down, it did not appear near finalization. Luckily for the multimillionaire footballer, funds are not likely to be an issue.

In forming a business partnership with major league soccer, Beckham would get to stay involved in his beloved football, and with his name still in the sports pages, his fans and followers would continue to get glimpses into the life of the legend.

BOTH FEET ON THE GROUND

Now that David Beckham the footballer exists only in the history books, sportswriters, historians, sociologists, and bloggers reflect on how he will be remembered. Professor Ellis Cashmore, who specializes in culture and sports, believes one of Beckham's lasting legacies has little to do with sports, but is the connection he's had with the notion of manhood and masculinity. Cashmore:

> People don't necessarily think that immediately, well, he didn't change our ideas of manhood. But I think he was quite a key figure in that process. He changed the perception of the question what it means to be a man. It doesn't mean that you have to be this hard-drinking, two-fisted, macho kind of guy. You can be gentle; you can take care of yourself; you can be a metrosexual; you can be a happy family man; you can take care of your children and be a loving, tender person and still be a legitimate man. We now have a multiplicity of what it means to be a man. Everyone's notions of manhood changed almost imperceptibly. There was no game-changing moment. I think Beckham has been the catalyst of the changes in masculinity.[36]

Journalists from around the globe paid homage to Beckham's career with a bounty of superlatives. Kevin Palmer, ESPNFC.com:

Making the most of your talents is all any sportsman can aim for in his career, and on that score, Beckham deserves top marks. He has also been a fine role model for his millions of admirers around the world. In an era when so many of his fellow sportsmen fall short in that category, this national treasure should be cherished as one of the all-time greats.[37]

Enrico Franceschini, *La Repubblica*:

Football is losing its last superstar. Perhaps the only one, because there are plenty of champions, but only one David Beckham.[38]

Phil McNulty, BBC.com:

As a player it can be argued Beckham never fell into the bracket of the greats. He never possessed serious pace but a magnificent passing range, allied to dead-ball brilliance and his relentless professionalism and work ethic made him an outstanding player. He was a master of dictating tempo and was blessed with natural football intelligence. He was always at pains to stress that, despite the A-list lifestyle, for him it was all about football and he takes his leave as one of the most decorated individuals to have graced the game.[39]

Jere Longman and Sam Borden, NYTimes.com:

Beckham was not merely an athlete; he was an international brand that smartly fused a handsomeness that bordered on beauty with athleticism, marketing savvy and an eager embrace of the role of pop idol. He was as likely to appear in *Vogue* as in *Sports Illustrated*. He was as popular appearing in underwear advertisements as in a soccer uniform. He was appreciated by working-class fans and was also an icon to gay fans.[40]

Spain's *MARCA*:

Elegance and London "glamour" are losing one of their main exponents. Countless precise shots and magical free kicks, all accomplished with the particular aesthetic quality of Beckham's game.[41]

Iain Macintosh, ESPNFC.com:

Beckham was not, by some distance, the greatest footballer ever to play for England. Nor was he the greatest English player of his generation. He was a man who, in spite of everything that life, the game and 21st-century culture had to throw at him, achieved everything that he could in his professional career.[42]

Jonathan Wilson, *Sports Illustrated*:

Beckham occupies an odd place in the English football consciousness, a player of clear gifts who, because his ability never quite matched his celebrity, seems doomed always to be underrated by a certain section of the soccer-following public. In a sense he became the symbol of the changing nature of soccer in England, from grubby game of the terraces to polished global spectacle.[43]

Hungary's *Nemzeti Sport*:

He was the king of free-kicks, who sweated blood for victory if he had to. Off the pitch, he became a style icon, an exemplary family man and a unique superstar.[44]

The David Beckham journey is far from complete, and his legacy is still being shaped. The man, the footballer, the brand is still being photographed, still being discussed and still being written about, even as he is now an ex-athlete. The intense curiosity about him has yet to wane. It is a testament to the global superstar's continuous staying power. After twenty-one years, more than five hundred total matches and two hundred-plus career goals, his faithful fans remain.

After his retirement, David Beckham summed up his career and how he hopes to be remembered:

I just want people to see me as a hardworking footballer, someone that's passionate about the game, someone that—every time I stepped on the pitch—I've given everything that I have, because that's how I feel. That's how I look back on it and hope people will see me."[45]

It has been an incredible, fascinating and emotional journey. I have learned a lot, not least about myself. The challenges have not always been easy; sometimes they have been almost overwhelming. But I learned to dig deep and to trust in myself. These are important lessons that I will always be grateful for. They made me who I am.[46]

If you had told me as a young boy I would have played for and won trophies with my boyhood club Manchester United, proudly captained and played for my country over one hundred times and lined up for some of the biggest clubs in the world, I would have told you it was a fantasy. I'm fortunate to have realized those dreams.[47]

Somewhere in the United States, Africa, China, the Philippines, Ireland, Denmark, Japan, Canada, Afghanistan, Greece, Thailand, England, there's a young girl practicing kicking a football who hopes to one day grow up to be just like her hero David Beckham.

APPENDIX A
TOTAL CAREER STATS

Team	Season	Matches Played	Goals Scored
Preston North End (England)	1991–1992	5	2
Total:	**Seasons, 1**	**Matches, 5**	**Goals, 2**
Manchester United (England)	1992–1993	1	0
	1994–1995	10	1
	1995–1996	40	8
	1996–1997	49	12
	1997–1998	50	11
	1998–1999	55	9
	1999–2000	48	8
	2000–2001	46	9
	2001–2002	43	16
	2002–2003	52	11
Total:	**Seasons, 10**	**Matches, 394**	**Goals, 85**
Real Madrid (Spain)	2003–2004	31	4
	2004–2005	44	5
	2005–2006	38	4
	2006–2007	46	7
Total:	**Seasons, 4**	**Matches, 159**	**Goals, 20**
LA Galaxy (US)	2007	5	0
	2008	25	5
	2009	11	2
	2010	7	2
	2011	26	2
	2012	24	7
Total:	**Seasons, 6**	**Matches, 98**	**Goals, 18**

(continued)

Team	Season	Matches Played	Goals Scored
AC Milan (Italy)	2008–2009	20	2
	2009–2010	13	0
Total:	**Seasons, 2**	**Matches, 33**	**Goals, 2**
Paris Saint-Germain (France)	2012–2013	14	0
Total:	**Seasons, 1**	**Matches, 14**	**Goals, 0**
England (National Team)	1996	3	0
	1997	9	0
	1998	8	1
	1999	7	0
	2000	10	0
	2001	10	5
	2002	9	3
	2003	9	4
	2004	12	2
	2005	9	1
	2006	8	1
	2007	5	0
	2008	8	0
	2009	8	0
Total:	**Years, 14**	**Matches, 115**	**Goals, 17**

APPENDIX B
CAREER MILESTONES

1991   At age sixteen, Beckham joins the Manchester United training academy.

1992   *May*: Won the FA Youth Cup as part of the Manchester United youth side with Ryan Giggs, Gary Neville, and Nicky Butt.

September: Made his debut for the Manchester United first team as a substitute for Andrei Kanchelskis in a League Cup match against Brighton & Hove Albion.

1993   *January*: Signed his first professional contract with Manchester United.

1994   *November*: Made his first starting appearance against Galatasaray and scored both his first Manchester United and UEFA Champions League goal.

1995   *February*: Begins a five-game loan to Preston North End FC for first-team experience.

April: Made his first English Premier League appearance for Manchester United.

August: Scored his first EPL goal against Aston Villa in the first match of the season.

1996   *May*: Won his first FA Cup and EPL title with Manchester United.

August: Scored from the halfway line with a fifty-five-yard lob against Wimbledon on the first day of the Premiership football season.

September: Made his England National team debut against Moldova.

1997   *May*: Beckham takes the no. 7 shirt for Manchester United after Eric Cantona retires.

1998   *June*: Scored his first World Cup goal from a free kick in an England 2–0 victory over Colombia.

June: A kick to Argentina's Diego Simeone in the second-round World Cup match gets him a red card and a sendoff.

1999   Wins Sir Matt Busby Player of the Year Award.

June: Was part of the Manchester United squad that completed a treble of Premiership, FA Cup, and Champions League trophies.

2000   Named FIFA World Football Player of the Year runner-up.

November: Named by Peter Taylor as England captain for a friendly against Italy.

2001   Named FIFA World Football Player of the Year runner-up.

October: His free kick in injury time draws the match against Greece and secures England's qualification for the 2002 World Cup.

December: Voted BBC's 2001 Sport Personality of the Year.

2002   *June*: A metatarsal injury hampers Beckham's performance in the 2002 European Championships and England loses to Brazil in the quarterfinals.

2003   Named England Player of the Year.

April: Beckham's 1996 Wimbledon goal is awarded the Premiership Goal of the decade.

May: Wins his sixth Premiership trophy with Manchester United.

June: Leaves Manchester United and signs with Real Madrid for $41 million.

August: Scores a goal with Real Madrid in a 3–0 victory over RCD Mallorca in his Bernabéu Stadium debut.

November: Receives an Officer of the Order of the British Empire (OBE) from Queen Elizabeth II.

2004   Wins an ESPY for Best Male Soccer Player.

March: Named to FIFA 100, a list of the 100 greatest living players chosen by Pelé.

June: Misses his third penalty shot in a row for England in the quarterfinal penalty shoot-out against Portugal, as his team is eliminated from the European Championships.

2005   *January 10*: Appointed UNICEF Goodwill Ambassador with a focus on the program Sport for Development.

2006   *June*: With a goal in the England vs. Ecuador match at the 2006 World Cup, becomes the first England player to score at three World Cups.

July: After England is knocked out of the World Cup in the quarter-finals, Beckham stands down as England captain after six years and fifty-eight matches.

August: Dropped from England squad.

2007   *January*: Signs on with the Los Angeles Galaxy to join Major League Soccer in the United States.

May: Gets recalled to play for England; plays first match one month later facing Brazil at Wembley Stadium.

June: Wins La Liga title with Real Madrid.

July: Plays his first game with the Los Angeles Galaxy.

August: Scores his first MLS goal in a match with D.C. United.

2008   Wins an ESPY for Best MLS Player.

Inducted into the English Football Hall of Fame

March: Earns his 100th cap against France in Paris.

2009   *January*: Joins Italian club AC Milan on loan.

March: Becomes the all-time outfield player appearance record holder on March 28 when he surpasses Bobby Moore's total of 108 caps.

October: Plays his 115th, and last, England National team match at Wembley Stadium against Belarus.

2010   *January*: Starts second loan to AC Milan.

March: Tears his left Achilles tendon during an AC Milan match and is forced to miss the World Cup in South Africa.

June: Travels to South Africa with England National team as a mediator on manager Fabio Capello's staff.

December: Received BBC Sports Personality of the Year Lifetime Achievement Award.

2011   Wins MLS Comeback Player of the Year.

November: Wins first MLS Cup.

2012   *January*: Signs two-year contract extension with the Galaxy.

June: Left out of Team GB's squad for the London 2012 Olympic Games.

December: Wins second MLS Cup.

2013 *January*: Signs five-month contract with Paris Saint-Germain and donates salary to a local children's charity.

March: Appointed global ambassador for the Chinese Super League.

May: Announces that he will retire from professional soccer at the end of his season with PSG.

May: Wins Ligue 1 title with PSG and becomes first Englishman to win league titles in four different countries.

May 18: Plays final career match in a win with PSG at Parc des Princes.

APPENDIX C
BECKHAM BY
THE NUMBERS

1   Number of BBC Sports Lifetime Achievement Awards, which he won in 2010.
1   Number of orders of chivalry awarded to Beckham, an Order of the British Empire (OBE), by Queen Elizabeth II, received in 2003.
2   Total Major League Soccer off-season loans. Both were to AC Milan, in 2009 and 2010.
3   MLS All-Star appearances, 2008, 2011, and 2012.
4   Countries in which Beckham won the league title—in England, Spain, the United States, and France. He is the only Englishman to accomplish this feat.
6   The number of Premier League titles Beckham won with Manchester United.
7   The number Beckham wore at Manchester United and with England.
9   Times Beckham was sent off during his career, once for United, four times for Real Madrid, once for LA Galaxy, once for PSG, and twice for England.
10 Estimated millions of Beckham jerseys sold throughout his career.
17 Total goals for England. He is the only Englishman to score at three World Cups, against Colombia in 1998, Argentina in 2002, and Ecuador in 2006.
19 Major trophies won by Beckham during his senior career.
23 Beckham's shirt number at Real Madrid and at the Los Angeles Galaxy in honor of basketball player Michael Jordan, who wore the same number.
47 Number of times Beckham appeared on the cover of Spain's sports newspaper, MARCA.

59   The number of times Beckham wore the armband as captain for England, the fourth-highest total ever.

107   Champions League games played. He was the first Englishman to play in more than 100.

111   Beckham goals in 641 league and Champions League games during his club career.

115   Caps for England, the most by any outfield player. Only Peter Shilton has played more times for England.

147   Total Beckham assists in league games during his career.

157   Number of countries that showed the 2012 MLS Cup final, the last match Beckham played with the Los Angeles Galaxy.

231   Percentage increase in worldwide MLS merchandise sales between his first game in 2007 and his last game five years later.

700   Approximate number of accredited media members on July 13, 2007, when Beckham was officially introduced as a Los Angeles Galaxy player.

837   Total number of matches played in Beckham's career.

18,807   Average MLS attendance in 2012, Beckham's final season in the league.

NOTES

CHAPTER 1

1. "David Beckham Receives 100th Cap Award," *MLS Development*, May 28, 2008, http://mlsdevelopment.typepad.com/mls_expansion_and_develop/2008/05/david-beckham-r.html.

2. Tim de Lisle, "The Height of Ambition," *Guardian*, March 13, 2006, http://www.guardian.co.uk/artanddesign/2006/mar/14/architecture.communities.

3. Bill Bateson and Albert Sewell, *News of the World Football Annual 1992–93* (Invincible Press, Australia, 1992).

4. "Wembley's Greatest Events (1923–2010)," *Wembley*, http://greatestevent.wembleystadium.com/.

5. Nick Harris, "Magnificent Monument to Vision of One Man," *Independent*, October 6, 2000, http://www.independent.co.uk/sport/football/news-and-comment/magnificent-monument-to-vision-of-one-man-637502.html.

6. Chuck Culpepper, "Beckham, Working-Class Boy to Man U," *Los Angeles Times*, July 9, 2007, http://articles.latimes.com/2007/jul/09/sports/sp-beckham9.

7. "Ancestry of David Beckham," *Genealogist William Addams Reitwiesner*, http://www.wargs.com/other/beckham.html.

8. "The Leysdown Tragedy—4 August 1912," *Scouting*, http://www.scouting.org.za/capewest/heritage/scar/Scar0030_LeysdownTragedy.pdf.

9. "Boy Scout Disaster, Leysdown," *Genealogy—Glenys Puxty*, http://freepages.genealogy.rootsweb.ancestry.com/~puxty/scouts_disaster.htm.

10. "The Leysdown Tragedy—4 August 1912."

11. Ros Wynne Jones, "A Twist of Fate: David Beckham's Great Grandfather Saved from Thames Disaster," *Daily Mirror*, August 4, 2012, http://www.mirror.co.uk/news/uk-news/david-beckham-story-of-his-great-grandfather-1224493#ixzz2ppPWID2H;

Leysdown Disaster: Drowned Scouts Honoured 100 Years On," *BBC News*, August 4, 2012, http://www.bbc.co.uk/news/uk-england-kent-19096670.

12. "Ancestry of David Beckham."

13. Paul Harris, "David Beckham's Childhood House Fails to Sell Despite Celebrity Connection," *Daily Mail*, May 11, 2009, http://www.dailymail.co.uk/tvshowbiz/article-1180582/David-Beckhams-childhood-house-fails-sell-despite-celebrity-connection.html#ixzz2Y5dW6EK4.

14. Aline Nassif, "On Sale at £1m, the Terrace House Where Becks Grew Up," *Standard*, November 17, 2008, http://www.standard.co.uk/news/on-sale-at-1m-the-terrace-house-where-becks-grew-up-6871363.html.

15. "The Parish and Borough of Chingford," *British History Online*, http://www.british-history.ac.uk/report.aspx?compid=42713#n13.

16. David Young, president of the Chingford Historical Society, e-mail message to author, May 1, 2013.

17. "Chingford History," *A Vision of Britain through Time*, http://www.visionofbritain.org.uk/unit/10236514.

18. "Museums in Essex," http://www.museumsinessex.org/museum.php?id=40.

19. "Top 100 1975," *UK-Charts*, http://www.uk-charts.top-source.info/top-100-1975.shtml.

20. "The *New York Times* Best Seller List," *Hawes*, May 11, 1975, http://www.hawes.com/1975/1975-05-11.pdf.

21. Jon Swaine, "UK Recession: Life in Britain in 1980," *Telegraph*, January 23, 2009, http://www.telegraph.co.uk/finance/recession/4323171/UK-recession-Life-in-Britain-in-1980.html.

22. "The Real Cost of Motoring," *BBC Business*, updated: June 4, 2004, http://news.bbc.co.uk/2/hi/business/3776913.stm; Adam Hill, "The Cost of Living: 1971," *Guardian*, June 17, 2011, http://www.theguardian.com/worklifeuk/cost-of-living-1971-today.

23. David Beckham with Tom Watt, *Both Feet on the Ground: An Autobiography* (New York: It Books, 2004), 85–89.

24. James Reginato, "American Idols," *W*, August 2007, http://www.wmagazine.com/celebrities/2007/08/beckhams_steven_klein?currentPage=2.

25. Beckham, *Both Feet on the Ground*, 85–89.

26. Stephen Moyes and Fiona Cummins, "My David," *Free Library*, September 17, 2005, http://www.thefreelibrary.com/MY+DAVID+By+Ted+Beckham%3B+ON+DAVID..+I'd+love+to+go+to+Madrid.+It's...-a0136277592.

27. James Wallis, "World Football: Ranking the Top 25 Free-Kick Specialists on the Planet," *Bleacher Report*, April 13, 2011, http://bleacherreport.com/articles/657257-world-football-ranking-the-top-25-free-kick-specialists-on-the-planet/page/2.

28. "How to Bend It Like Beckham: Physics Students Calculate Perfect Soccer Ball Kicking Formula," *Science Daily*, June 29, 2012, http://www.sciencedaily.com/releases/2012/06/120629120328.htm.

29. Billy Baker, "Bending It Like Beckham Takes Practice, Physics," *Boston.com*, August 6, 2007, http://www.boston.com/news/science/articles/2007/08/06/bending_it_like_beckham_takes_practice_physics/?page=full.

30. Beckham, *Both Feet on the Ground*, 9.

31. Graham Nickless, "Beckham: The Star Discovered in the Small Ads," *Free Library*, January 4, 1998, http://www.thefreelibrary.com/Beckham%3a+the+star+discovered+in+the+small+ads.-a060658591.

32. "Football Programmes & Sports Memorabilia," *Football Zone*, http://www.footballzone.co.uk/All-Football-Teams-Programmes/C-Teams/Mixed-C-Teams/Cowley-Youth-V-Ridgeway-Rovers-1987-Includes-Young-David-Beckham.html.

33. Nickless, "Beckham: The Star Discovered in the Small Ads."

34. Peter White, "Football: The Coach's View: Stuart Underwood, the Youth Coach Who Discovered Beckham 20 Years Ago," *Free Library*, August 3, 2003, http://www.thefreelibrary.com/FOOTBALL%3A+The+Coach's+View%3A+Stuart+Underwood+The+youth+coach+who...-a0106200282.

35. Ian Marshall, chairman Ridgeway Rovers, e-mail message to author, January 18, 2014.

36. "Sir Bobby: A Survivor's Story," *Manchester United*, June 2, 2003, http://www.manutd.com/en/News-And-Features/Munich-Remembered/2013/Feb/Sir-Bobby-A-survivor's-story.aspx.

37. Bobby Charlton Soccer and Sports Academy, http://www.bcssa.co.uk/.

38. Beckham, *Both Feet on the Ground*, 27.

39. Beckham, *Both Feet on the Ground*, 27–30.

40. "Historia," *FC Barcelona*, http://www.fcbarcelona.es/club/historia.

41. "La Masia History," *FC Barcelona*, http://www.fcbarcelona.es/club/historia.

42. "Los cinco fichajes del Barcelona que nunca fueron," *Goal.com*, June 8, 2012, http://www.goal.com/es/news/21/fichajes/2012/06/08/3157782/los-cinco-fichajes-del-barcelona-que-nunca-fueron.

43. Terry Venables, "I Knew from the First Time I Saw Him That David Beckham Would Be Something Special," *Sun*, May 18, 2013, http://www.thesun.co.uk/sol/homepage/sport/football/4932253/Terry-Venables-I-knew-David-Beckham-would-be-star.html.

44. "Scouting Mission," *BBC News*, retrieved December 12, 2008, http://news.bbc.co.uk/sport2/hi/football/teams/c/chelsea/4988100.stm.

45. "What Do Top Scouts Look for in a Player?" *SoccerAgent.net*, www.socceragent.net/footballscout_manu.php.

46. "Want to Be a Football Pro?" *BBC Sport*, September 14, 2009, http://news.bbc.co.uk/sport2/hi/football/get_involved/4202488.stm.

47. "David Beckham—a Football Great and a Canary for a Week!" *Kit Carson Football.com*, http://www.kitcarsonfootball.com/news/david-beckham-a-football-great-and-a-canary-for-a-week.

48. Edmund Tobin, "Waltham Abbey: Planning Go-Ahead for Care Home," *Guardian*, September 1, 2008, http://www.guardian-series.co.uk/news/3635740. WALTHAM_ABBEY__Planning_go_ahead_for_care_home/.

49. Andrew Morton, *Posh & Becks* (New York: Gallery Books, 2007), 43.

50. "Alex Ferguson," *Manchester United*, http://www.manutd.com/en/Players-And-Staff/Managers/Alex-Ferguson.aspx.

51. "Manchester United's Secret Move to Appoint Sir Alex Ferguson," *BBC Sport Football*, November 6, 2011, http://www.bbc.co.uk/sport/0/football/15611208.

52. "Martin Edwards Reveals How He Appointed Sir Alex Ferguson," *Sky Sports*, May 4, 2013, http://www1.skysports.com/watch/tv-shows/footballers-football-show/news/8618183/martin-edwards-reveals-how-he-appointed-sir-alex-ferguson.

53. "Beckham Admits: I Owe It ALL to Fergie," *Mirror Football Blog*, March 11, 2011, http://www.mirrorfootball.co.uk/opinion/blogs/mirror-football-blog/David-Beckham-exclusive-interview-I-owe-it-all-to-Alex-Ferguson-the-Manchester-United-and-England-hero-tells-Mirror-Oliver-Holt-as-Fergie-celebrates-25-years-as-Old-Trafford-boss-article826397.html.

54. Beckham, *Both Feet on the Ground*, 31.

CHAPTER 2

1. David Beckham with Tom Watt, *Both Feet on the Ground: An Autobiography* (New York: It Books, 2004), 35–40.

2. Gwen Russell, *Arise Sir David Beckham: The Biography of Britain's Greatest Footballer* (London: John Blake, 2007), 10.

3. *Beckham—The Real David Beckham*, directed by Ian Denyer (2000; London: 3DD Entertainment, 2000), DVD, YouTube video at http://www.youtube.com/watch?v=r_4-Zg5s97w.

4. James McCarthy, *Manchester United: Born Winners* (Warwickshire, UK: Coda Books, 2011).

5. "Dallas Cup History and Previous Champions," *Dallas Cup*, http://www.dallas-cup.com/about/history/index_E.html.

6. Steve Davis, "Flashback: When Retiring Soccer icon David Beckham was just a 13-year-old in a Dallas Pickup Truck," *Dallas News*, May 16, 2013, http://www.dallasnews.com/sports/more-sports/headlines/20130516-flashback-when-retiring-soccer-icon-david-beckham-was-just-a-13-year-old-in-a-dallas-pickup-truck.ece.

7. Benedict Moore-Bridger and Paul Fielder, "Becks' Sorrow as Walthamstow Goes to the Dogs for Final Time," *Standard*, August 15, 2008, http://www.standard.co.uk/news/becks-sorrow-as-walthamstow-goes-to-the-dogs-for-final-time-6816917.html.

8. Chuck Culpepper, "Beckham, Working-Class Boy to Man U," *Los Angeles Times*, July 9, 2007, http://articles.latimes.com/2007/jul/09/sports/sp-beckham9.

9. Tom Dunmore, "Youth Development in England," *Pitch Invasion*, May 20, 2008, http://pitchinvasion.net/blog/2008/05/20/youth-development-in-england/.

10. "St George's Park Centre Of Excellence Officially Opened," *BBC Sport*, October 9, 2012, http://www.bbc.com/sport/0/football/19881116.

11. Beckham, *Both Feet on the Ground*, 119.

12. Jim Whitte and Andy Mitten, *The Rough Guide to Manchester United, 2003/04 Season* (London: DK Publishing, 2004), 389.

13. Whitte, *The Rough Guide to Manchester United*, 389.

14. "Brand Finance Football 50," 2013, http://www.brandfinance.com/images/upload/brandfinance_football_50_2013_new_opt.pdf.

15. Beckham, *Both Feet on the Ground*, 35–40.

16. Paul Campbell, "David Beckham: Product of Sir Alex Ferguson's School of Hard Graft," *Guardian*, May 17, 2013, http://www.theguardian.com/football/blog/2013/may/17/david-beckham-alex-ferguson-manchester-united.

17. Campbell, "David Beckham: Product of Sir Alex Ferguson's School of Hard Graft."

18. "Legends, Gary Neville," *Man Utd.com*, http://www.manutd.com/en/players-and-staff/legends/gary-neville.aspx.

19. "Nicky Butt, Manchester United player," *About Man Utd*.com, http://www.aboutmanutd.com/man-u-players/nicky-butt.html.

20. "Players & Staff, Ryan Giggs," *Man Utd.com*, http://www.manutd.com/en/Players-And-Staff/First-Team/Ryan-Giggs.aspx.

21. Grant Cameron, BBC sports broadcaster who has covered the Northern Ireland Milk Cup since its inception in 1983, e-mail to author, October 18, 2013.

22. "An Exclusive (+ Excellent) Overview of Manchester United in the Northern Ireland Milk Cup for Red News by Gary Fowler," *Red News*, September 14, 2011, http://www.rednews.co.uk/forum/showthread.php/108753-38-An-exclusive-(-excellent)-overview-of-Manchester-United-in-the-Northern-Ireland-Milk-Cup-for-Red-News-by-Gary-Fowler; Heart of Midlothian FC Youth Program 1991.

23. "Where Are They Now—Eric Harrison," *Football League*, February 17, 2011, http://www.football-league.co.uk/features/20110217/where-are-they-now-eric-harrison_2293307_2295509.

24. Beckham, *Both Feet on the Ground*, 58.

25. Nick Rostron-Pike, "Harrison Looks Back on David Beckham's Career," *Talk-Sport*, May 16, 2013, http://talksport.com/radio/drivetime/130516/harrison-looks-back-david-beckhams-career-197730.

26. "FA Youth Cup History," *FA.com*, http://nav.thefa.com/sitecore/content/TheFA/Home/Competitions/FACompetitions/TheFAYouthCup/History/FAYouthCupHistory.

27. Paul Rowles, "Different Mentality from Youth Players Nowadays," *Stretty News*, posted July 21, 2012, http://strettynews.com/different-mentality-from-youth-players-nowadays/.

28. "Manchester United History, Busby's Babes (1950s)," *About Man Utd.com,* http://www.aboutmanutd.com/man-u-history/busby-babes.html.

29. "Manchester United History, Busby's Babes (1950s)."

30. Stuart Mathieson, "Manchester United Youth History Chronicled," *Manchester Evening News,* December 1, 2012, http://www.manchestereveningnews.co.uk/sport/football/football-news/manchester-uniteds-youth-history-chronicled-698111.

31. "Interview with the Authors," *Sons of United,* April 5, 2013, http://www.sonsof united.com.

32. "Interview with the Authors."

33. "FA Youth Cup History."

34. Adam Marshall, "On This Day: Class of '92," *Manchester United,* May 15, 2012, http://www.manutd.com/en/News-And-Features/Features/2012/May/manchester-united-fa-youth-cup-final-1992-on-this-day.aspx; "Man United's Class of 92 Reunited for New Documentary," *Inside Soccer World,* November 5, 2013, http://www.insideworldsoccer.com/2013/11/manchester-united-class-92-documentary-movie.html; "PFA Awards 2013 PFA Special Merit Award—Manchester United Class of 92," *YouTube,* posted, April 29, 2013, http://www.youtube.com/watch?v=FGhT8LKiBO0.

35. David Meek, "Long Wait Over as Glory Days Return," *Manchester Evening News,* May 15, 1992.

36. Meek, "Long Wait Over as Glory Days Return."

37. Adam Bate, "Our Best Player," *Sky Sports,* Last Updated: November 21, 2013, http://www1.skysports.com/news/18232/9042966/.

38. Gary Neville, "Gary Neville: Can I Give My All to Management? Probably Not," *Guardian,* March 6, 2010, http://www.theguardian.com/football/2010/mar/07/gary-neville-manchester-united-interview.

39. Beckham, *Both Feet on the Ground,* 199.

40. "Man United's Class of 92 Reunited for New Documentary."

41. "PFA Awards 2013 PFA Special Merit Award—Manchester United Class of 92."

42. "PFA Awards 2013 PFA Special Merit Award—Manchester United Class of 92."

43. "David Beckham Reveals Release of Documentary about Man United's 'Class of '92,'" *Bleacher Report,* November 4, 2013, http://bleacherreport.com/articles/1837181-david-beckham-reveals-release-of-documentary-about-man-uniteds-class-of-92.

44. "PFA Awards 2013 PFA Special Merit Award—Manchester United Class of 92."

45. *Class of '92* trailer, *YouTube,* http://www.youtube.com/watch?v=z3KSaxgppXg.

46. Liam Prenderville, "Watch Manchester United Stars Ryan Giggs, Nicky Butt and Phil Neville Preview Upcoming *Class of 92* film," *Mirror,* November, 26, 2013, http://www.mirror.co.uk/sport/football/news/class-92-manchester-united-stars-2852369#ixzz2pqb5SDq5.

47. "Behind the Scenes of the Class of '92," *Goal.com,* November 21, 2013, http://www.goal.com/en-us/slideshow/5751/3/title/behind-the-scenes-of-the-class-of-92?ICID=OP.

48. Martin Lipton, "Alex Ferguson Lavishes Praise on 'Fergie's Fledglings' Generation at Manchester United in New Autobiography," *Daily Mirror*, October 22, 2013, http://www.mirror.co.uk/sport/football/news/alex-ferguson-lavishes-praise-fergies-2481966#ixzz2sO89SKs6.

49. Paul Hayward, "United Again: Me, Jack and the Meaning of Brotherly Love," *Observer*, January 10, 2009, http://www.theguardian.com/football/2009/jan/11/manchester-united-bobby-charlton.

50. Louise Taylor, "Manchester United's Most Influential Eric Speaks—No, Not That One, Follow Louise Taylor," *Guardian*, February 14, 2010, http://www.theguardian.com/football/2010/feb/14/eric-harrison-manchester-united-champions-league.

51. "FA Youth Cup History," *FA.com*, http://nav.thefa.com/sitecore/content/TheFA/Home/Competitions/FACompetitions/TheFAYouthCup/History/FAYouthCupHistory.

52. "Why Beckham Was at Bottom of Class of '92," *Manchester Evening News*, May 21, 2013, http://www.manchestereveningnews.co.uk/sport/football/football-news/beckham-bottom-class-92-3902119.

53. "17-Year-Old David Beckham Giggles Way through Media Training Interview," *YouTube*, published August 1, 2013, http://www.youtube.com/watch?v=glncXTp3ezU.

CHAPTER 3

1. John Vinicombe, "Albion 1, Manchester Utd 1," *Evening Argus*, September 24, 1992.

2. "David Beckham, Manchester United Player," *About Man Utd.*, http://www.aboutmanutd.com/man-u-players/david-beckham.html.

3. "1992/93 Brighton v Manchester United, Coca Cola Cup 2nd Round 1st Leg," *YouTube*, http://www.youtube.com/watch?v=k25nPEMBvYw.

4. David Beckham with Tom Watt, *Both Feet on the Ground: An Autobiography* (New York: It Books, 2004), 13.

5. "Old Trafford, The Theatre of Dreams," *Manchester United*, http://www.manutd.com/en/Visit-Old-Trafford/Virtual-Tour.aspx?section={0341FBBA-96FA-42BB-896B-0D15ABAFA643}; "Manchester United Old Trafford: The Old Trafford Story," *About Man Utd.*, http://www.aboutmanutd.com/man-u-old-trafford/old-trafford.html.

6. "David Beckham, Manchester United Player."

7. David Lacey, "Babes Go Out with a Hollow Flourish," *Guardian*, December 8, 1994.

8. Samuel Luckhurst, "Manchester United v Galatasaray: When David Beckham Scored His First Reds Goal (video)," *Huffington Post UK*, September 19, 2012,

http://www.huffingtonpost.co.uk/2012/09/19/manchester-united-v-galatasaray-david-beckham-first-goal_n_1895927.html.

9. "Man Utd Boss Moyes Pays Tribute to Ex-Preston Prodigy Beckham," *Tribal Football*, May 17, 2013, http://www.tribalfootball.com/articles/man-utd-boss-moyes-pays-tribute-ex-preston-prodigy-beckham-3958159#.UfQYD9zD9dg.

10. "Celebrating the Life and Career of One of English Football's Most Legendary Players, Preston North End's Sir Tom Finney," *Sir Tom Finney*, http://sirtomfinney.com/.

11. Oliver Wheeler, "Becks—The 1994/95 Season," *P.NEFC.net*, May 17, 2013, http://www.pnefc.net/news/article/becks-the-199495-season170513-825983.aspx.

12. "Preston North End Club Match Record: 1995," *Home of Football Statistics and History*, http://www.11v11.com/teams/preston-north-end/tab/matches/season/1995.

13. "Man Utd Boss Moyes."

14. Joe Bernstein, "What Was England Legend Finney's Role in the Making of Football Icon?" *Daily Mail*, May 18, 2013, http://www.dailymail.co.uk/sport/football/article-2326776/David-Beckham-retires--Sir-Tom-Finneys-role-making-icon.html.

15. Tom Adams, "Fergie's Fledglings Flourish," *ESP.NFC.com*, February 4, 2011, http://espnfc.com/columns/story/_/id/875600/rewind-to-1996:-fergie's-fledglings-flourish-at-manchester-united?cc=5901.

16. Adams, "Fergie's Fledglings Flourish."

17. Beckham, *Both Feet on the Ground*, 89.

18. "Man Utd v Chelsea: Past Encounters," *Daily Mail*, last updated May 18, 2007, http://www.dailymail.co.uk/sport/football/article-455727/Man-Utd-v-Chelsea-Past-encounters.html#ixzz2pstMhUXD.

19. Paul Henderson, "When GQ Met Eric Cantona," *British GQ*, July 5, 2011, http://www.gq-magazine.co.uk/entertainment/articles/2011-07/05/gq-sport-eric-cantona-interview-manchester-united-football/page/2.

20. "Last Time at Wembley—FA Cup Final 1996," *This Is Anfield*, February 25, 2012, http://www.thisisanfield.com/2012/02/last-time-at-wembley-fa-cup-final-1996/; Jonathan Birchnall, "English Football's Two Greatest Rivals Are Set to Go Head to Head at Anfield on Saturday for What Will Be Their 17th Meeting in the Game's Oldest Competition," *Goal.com*, January 27, 2012, http://www.goal.com/en-india/news/2292/editorials/2012/01/27/2868923/cream-suits-cantona-and-the-classic-liverpool-vs-manchester.

21. Paul Collins, "Call Him Goaldenballs! Sportsmail Recalls Retiring Beckham's 10 Greatest Strikes," *Daily Mail*, May 16, 2013, Video: http://www.dailymail.co.uk/sport/football/article-2325583/David-Beckham-retires-Best-goals-VIDEO.html.

22. Anton Stanley, "Neil Sullivan on Conceding THAT David Beckham Wonder Goal," *TalkSport.com*, May 16, 2013, video: http://talksport.com/radio/drivetime/130516/neil-sullivan-conceding-david-beckham-wonder-goal-197734#HpR5LRgkmdVpdF82.99.

23. David Beckham, with photography by Dean Freeman, *Beckham: My World* (London: Hodder and Stoughton, 2000), 53–56.

24. "Argentina Kicks Out England," *CNN Sports Illustrated*, June 30, 1998, http:// sportsillustrated.cnn.com/soccer/world/events/1998/worldcup/news/1998/06/30/ argentina_update/.

25. David Hill, "Beckham," *Independent*, August 15, 1998, http://www.indepen dent.co.uk/life-style/beckham-1171687.html.

26. "Beckham vs. Diego Simeone," *World Cup Fails*, May 20, 2010, http://www .worldcupfails.com/2010/05/david-beckham-vs-diego-simeone.html; "Argentina Kicks Out England."

27. "History of the Premier League," *PremierLeague.com*, http://www.premier league.com/content/premierleague/en-gb/about/history.html.

28. Andrew Jordan, "The Treble Looms Large!" A Look Back at the 1999 Man Utd Treble," *Bleacher Report*, April 24, 2009, http://bleacherreport.com/articles/161417- the-treble-looms-large-a-lookback-at-the-1999-man-utd-treble.

29. "Man United v Tottenham 1998/99," *YouTube*, uploaded on May 14, 2009, http://www.youtube.com/watch?v=GoLZoWGtcQU.

30. "Glorious United Crowned Champions," *BBC News*, May 27, 1999, http:// news.bbc.co.uk/2/hi/sport/football/fa_carling_premiership/345445.stm.

31. "The Football Association," www.thefa.com.

32. "Manchester United Player Profiles," *BBC News*, May 20, 1999, http://news .bbc.co.uk/2/hi/sport/football/fa_cup/348822.stm.

33. "Double Joy for Man United," *BBC News*, May 22, 1999, http://news.bbc.co .uk/2/hi/sport/football/fa_cup/350192.stm.

34. "Sir Bobby: A Survivor's Story, Man United," *Man Utd.com*, June 2, 2013, http://www.manutd.com/en/News-And-Features/Munich-Remembered/2013/Feb/ Sir-Bobby-A-survivor's-story.aspx.

35. "1966 FIFA World Cup England," *FIFA.com*, http://www.fifa.com/world cup/archive/edition=26/results/matches/match=1633/report.html.

36. "Miracle Triple Play," *Sports Illustrated*, May 30, 1999, http://sportsillustrated .cnn.com/soccer/world/1999/champions_league/.

37. Beckham, *Both Feet on the Ground*, 26–27.

38. "History 1998–99: Man United 2–1 Bayern," *UEFA.com*, http://www.uefa.com/ uefachampionsleague/season=1998/matches/round=1214/match=56379/index.html.

39. Martin Thorpe, "Solskjaer Takes Treble Chance," *Guardian*, May 26, 1999, http://www.guardian.co.uk/football/1999/may/26/newsstory.sport.

40. Rob Hughes, "Pele Offers Final Accolade," *Sunday Times* (RedWeb3), May 27, 1999, http://homepage.eircom.net/~redweb3/home/9899/reports/articles/ becks2.html.

41. "An Archive of the Manchester United 1999 Treble Season," *Manchester United*, http://www.manutdtreble.com/quotes.htm.

42. Thorpe, "Solskjaer Takes Treble Chance."

43. "History 1998–99: Man United 2–1 Bayern."

44. David Beckham, *David Beckham* (London: Headline, 2013), 108.

45. "Solskjaer Answers United's Prayers," *UEFA.com*, May 26, 1999, http://www .uefa.com/uefachampionsleague/season=1998/overview/index.html#199899+solskjær+ answers+uniteds+prayers.

46. "United Crowned Kings of Europe," *BBC News*, May 27, 1999, http://news.bbc .co.uk/2/hi/sport/football/353842.stm.

47. "50 Great Sporting Moments: Manchester United Win the Treble, 1999," *Sunday Times*, *RedWeb3*, May 30, 1999, http://homepage.eircom.net/~redweb3/ home/9899/reports/articles/europe28.html.

48. "Manchester United FC 2-1 FC Bayern München: Post-Match Reaction," *UEFA.com*, May 26, 1999, http://red11.org/mufc/images/99/ecfinal/pdf/uefa.pdf.

49. "An Archive of the Manchester United 1999 Treble Season," *Manchester United*.

50. Ben Smith, "Class of '92 on Sir Alex Ferguson, Leaving Man Utd—and Each Other," *BBC Sport*, December 2, 2013, http://www.bbc.com/sport/0/foot ball/25184865.

51. "An Archive of the Manchester United 1999 Treble Season," *Manchester United*.

52. "Manchester United FC 2-1 FC Bayern München: Post-Match Reaction," *UEFA.com*.

53. "An Archive of the Manchester United 1999 Treble Season."

54. "50 Great Sporting Moments."

55. Beckham, *David Beckham*, 108.

56. "David Beckham, Biography," *People.com*, http://www.people.com/people/ david_beckham/biography/.

57. Ciar Byrne, "Gossip Inflated £1m Beckham Wedding Deal," *Guardian*, March 9, 2004, http://www.theguardian.com/media/2004/mar/09/pressandpublishing4.

58. "Elton John, Biography," *IMDb*, http://www.imdb.com/name/nm0005056/bio.

59. "Branded Like Beckham," *Economist*, July 3, 2003, http://www.economist.com/ node/1900131?zid=319&ah=17af09b0281b01505c226b1e574f5cc1.

60. Sam Wallace, "Beckham's Open Wound," *Telegraph*, February 18, 2003, http:// www.telegraph.co.uk/sport/football/2396426/Beckhams-open-wound.html.

61. "Beckham Axed by Ferguson," *BBC Sport*, Sunday, February 20, 2000, http:// news.bbc.co.uk/2/hi/sport/football/fa_carling_premiership/647603.stm.

62. Tom Adams, "Fergie Gives Beckham the Boot," *ESPNSoccer.net*, October 21, 2010, http://espnfc.com/columns/story?id=833712&sec=england&root=england &cc=5901.

63. Adams, "Fergie Gives Beckham the Boot."

64. Franklin Foer, "Bye, Bye, Becks," *Slate*, June 18, 2003, http://www.slate.com/ articles/sports/sports_nut/2003/06/bye_bye_becks.html.

65. "Becks Fury at Flying Boot," *Daily Mail*, http://www.dailymail.co.uk/news/ article-161942/Becks-fury-flying-boot.html#ixzz2a5mTE8JO; "Sir Alex Refuses to Apologise for Becks' Injury," *Daily Mail*, http://www.dailymail.co.uk/news/article-163284/ Sir-Alex-refuses-apologise-Becks-injury.html#ixzz2a5mjLlQ3; "David Beckham Biog-

raphy," *Biography Channel*, http://www.thebiographychannel.co.uk/biographies/david-beckham.html.

66. Stuart Roach, "Will Becks Give Man Utd the Boot?" *BBC Sport*, February 18, 2003, http://news.bbc.co.uk/sport2/hi/football/teams/m/man_utd/2775269.stm.

67. Beckham, *Both Feet on the Ground*, 319-20.

68. "Beckham Forgives Ferguson," *BBC Sport*, February, 19, 2003, http://news.bbc.co.uk/sport2/hi/football/teams/m/man_utd/2778353.stm.

69. Roach, "Will Becks Give Man Utd the Boot?"

70. "Beckham's Transfer as It Happened," *BBC Sport*, June 16, 2003, http://news.bbc.co.uk/go/pr/fr/-/sport2/hi/football/teams/m/man_utd/2977997.stm.

71. Beckham, *Both Feet on the Ground*, 319-43.

72. "Real Big News," *Sports Illustrated*, June 17, 2003, http://sportsillustrated.cnn.com/soccer/news/2003/06/17/beckham_madrid_ap/.

73. "Real Big News."

74. "David Beckham's Career in Numbers," *BBC News*, May 17, 2013, http://www.bbc.co.uk/news/uk-22555991.

75. "Legends Profile, David Beckham," *Manchester United*, http://www.manutd.com/en/Players-And-Staff/Legends/David-Beckham.aspx?pageNo=3; "David Beckham's Career in Numbers."

76. *David Beckham—A Footballer's Story*, directed by Damon Thomas (London: Century Films, 2006), YouTube video at http://www.youtube.com/watch?v=r78aN0JKpzM.

CHAPTER 4

1. "Gill Whyte Comes to the Spice Girls Not to Criticise but to Applaud," *NME*, September 2, 1998, http://www.nme.com/reviews/spice-girls/190#JKAqL6sf5x2X30BY.99; "Spice Girls Live at Wembley Stadium DVD Rip Part 1," YouTube video at http://www.youtube.com/watch?v=hFiOyLAMbXc.

2. "Gill Whyte Comes to the Spice Girls."

3. "Spice Girls Timeline, 1993," *Spice Girls*, http://www.thespicegirls.com/facts/timeline.

4. "Victoria Beckham: Biography," *People.com*, http://www.people.com/people/victoria_beckham/.

5. "Spice Girls Timeline, 1993," *Spice Girls*.

6. "Spice Girls Timeline, 1993," *Spice Girls*.

7. "Spice Girls, Biography, 1993," *Spice Girls*, http://www.thespicegirls.com/facts/biography

8. Sterling Wong, "Are Adele, Mumford and Sons Sign of a New British Invasion?" Music, Celebrity, Artist News, *MTV*, retrieved September 1, 2011, http://www.mtv.com/news/articles/1661905/adele-mumford-and-sons-british-invasion.jhtml.

9. James Reginato, "American Idols," *W*, August 2007, http://www.wmagazine.com/people/celebrities/2007/08/beckhams_steven_klein/.

10. David Beckham with Tom Watt. *Both Feet on the Ground: An Autobiography* (New York: It Books, 2004), 88.

11. From a *Guardian* condensed version of Victoria Beckham, *Learning to Fly: The Autobiography* (New York: Penguin Global, 2005), http://www.theguardian.com/books/2001/oct/06/digestedread.

12. "Victoria Beckham opens up about high school bullying," *3 News*, December 7, 2011, http://www.3news.co.nz/Victoria-Beckham-opens-up-about-high-school-bullying/tabid/418/articleID/235570/Default.aspx.

13. "Victoria Beckham," *People.com*, http://www.people.com/people/victoria_beckham/biography/.

14. Beckham, *Learning to Fly*, 170.

15. James Reginato, "American Idols."

16. Beckham, *Learning to Fly*, condensed version.

17. Beckham, *Learning to Fly*, 204.

18. "Posh and Becks: A Match Made In A-List Heaven," *Hello!*, November 8, 2010, http://www.hellomagazine.com/celebrities/gallery/201010214359/victoria-beckham/david/love-story/2/.

19. Joey Baily, "Great Love Stories No. 14, David & Victoria Beckham," *This Is Glamorous*, November 7, 2012, http://www.thisisglamorous.com/2012/07/great-love-stories-14-david-beckham.html.

20. "David Beckham, Biography," *People.com*, http://www.people.com/people/david_beckham/biography/.

21. Baily, "Great Love Stories No. 14."

22. "David Beckham, Biography," *People.com*.

23. Louise Oswald, "Beckham's Tears of Joy for New Baby; Posh's News Lifts Depression over World Cup Disaster," *Free Library*, August 23, 1998, http://www.thefreelibrary.com/BECKHAM'S+TEARS+OF+JOY+FOR+NEW+BABY%3B+Posh's+news+lifts+depression...-a060635702.

24. David Beckham, with photography by Dean Freeman, *Beckham: My World* (London: Hodder and Stoughton, 2000), 34–35.

25. Andrew Morton, *Posh & Becks* (New York: Gallery Books, 2007), 87.

26. "Brooklyn Beckham Scores First Goal at Old Trafford in 2001," *Daily Mail*, http://www.dailymail.co.uk/video/video-1060301/Brooklyn-Beckham-scores-goal-Old-Trafford.html.

27. Tom Sykes, "Brooklyn Beckham Tests for Chelsea," *Yahoo!*, January 25, 2013, http://news.yahoo.com/brooklyn-beckham-tests-chelsea-094500697--politics.html.

28. Sykes, "Brooklyn Beckham Tests for Chelsea."

29. "Luttellstowncastle," http://www.luttrellstowncastle.com/.

30. Beckham, *Both Feet on the Ground*, 181.

31. Katherine E. Krohn, *Vera Wang: Enduring Style* (Minneapolis, MN: Twenty-First Century Books, 2008), 60.

32. "Throwback Thursdays: Victoria Beckham's Wedding," *Vera Wang*, May 31, 2012, http://www.verawang.com/veraunveiled/2012/05/throwback-thursdays-victoria-beckhams-wedding/.

33. Ashley Lutz, "The 12 Most Expensive Celebrity Wedding Gowns of All Time," *Business Insider*, September 12, 2012, http://www.businessinsider.com/the-most-expensive-celebrity-wedding-dresses-2012-9.

34. *OK! Magazine*, July 1999.

35. Morton, *Posh & Becks*, 87.

36. *OK! Magazine*, July 1999.

37. "David Beckham, Biography," *People.com*; Ciar Byrne, "Gossip Inflated £1m Beckham Wedding Deal," *Guardian*, March 9, 2004, http://www.theguardian.com/media/2004/mar/09/pressandpublishing4.

38. *OK! Magazine*, July 1999.

39. Beckham, *Both Feet on the Ground*, 181.

40. "David Beckham, Biography," *People.com*.

41. "David Beckham Says Becoming a Father Has Made Him Selfless," *I'm Not Obsessed*, September 19, 2009, http://www.imnotobsessed.com/blog/2009/09/19/david-beckham-says-becoming-a-father-has-made-him-selfless/#vJ0vUcYL3YZ4i4pw.99.

42. Lucy Waterlow, "Romeo Beckham Helps Burberry Notch Up 13% Hike in Sales after 'Exceptional' Response to Spring/Summer Collection," *Daily Mail*, July 10, 2013, http://www.dailymail.co.uk/femail/article-2359418/Romeo-Beckham-helps-Burberry-notch-13-hike-sales-exceptional-response-spring-summer-collection.html#ixzz2lWicJrM9.

43. "David Beckham, Biography," *People.com*.

44. Brenda Rodriguez, "David Beckham Answers Your Questions," *About.com*, July 29, 2009, http://marriage.about.com/gi/o.htm?zi=1/XJ&zTi=1&sdn=marriage&cdn=people&tm=99&f=10; Sarah Gilbert, "Victoria "Posh Spice" Beckham Gives Birth to Son Cruz," *Parent Dish*, February 20, 2005, http://www.parentdish.com/2005/02/20/victoria-posh-spice-beckham-gives-birth-to-son-cruz/.

45. Sam Rigby, "David Beckham: 'I Don't Regret Any of My 32 Tattoos,'" *Digital Spy*, May 12, 2013, http://www.digitalspy.com/celebrity/news/a480787/david-beckham-i-dont-regret-any-of-my-32-tattoos.html#ixzz2qyK4xsen.

46. Michael Easter, "David Beckham Is About to Change the Way You Think about Your 'Best' Years," *Men's Health*, http://www.menshealth.com/celebrity-fitness/david-beckham.

47. Kate Stanhope, "Photos: Meet David and Victoria Beckham's New Daughter Harper Seven," *TV Guide*, July 17, 2011, http://www.tvguide.com/news/harper-seven-beckham-photos-1035415.aspx.

48. "Victoria Beckham," *Twitter*, July 14, 2011, https://twitter.com/victoria beckham/status/91566655724994561.

49. Zach Johnson, "David Beckham: Daughter Harper Plays Soccer, Carries Handbags," *US Weekly*, October 2, 2012, http://www.usmagazine.com/celebrity-moms/news/david-beckham-daughter-harper-plays-soccer-carries-handbags-2012210#ixzz2qxxwtaFD.

50. "David Beckham Says Having a Daughter Is 'Amazing,'" *CTV News*, July 15, 2011, http://www.ctvnews.ca/david-beckham-says-having-a-daughter-is-amazing-1.670657#ixzz2pyROjhxA.

51. "Victoria and David Beckham Appear Together in Steamy New Armani Underwear Campaign—Pictures," *Mirror*, July 2, 2009, http://www.mirror.co.uk/3am/celebrity-news/victoria-and-david-beckham-appear-together-403966#ixzz2qyZSlbCQ.

52. Ron Hagwood, "Soccer Studs David Beckham and Christiano Ronaldo Have a 'Model-Off,'" *Sun Sentinel*, October 9, 2009, http://articles.sun-sentinel.com/2009-10-09/features/0910100065_1_armani-jeans-underwear-david-beckham; Hilary Alexander, "The Beckhams strip off again for Giorgio Armani," *Telegraph*, July 2, 2009, http://fashion.telegraph.co.uk/columns/hilary-alexander/TMG5722930/The-Beckhams-Strip-Off-Again-for-Giorgio-Armani.html; Amy Odell, "Victoria and David Beckham Writhe in Armani Underwear Together," *New York*, July 2, 2009, http://nymag.com/thecut/2009/07/victoria_and_david_beckham_wri.html.

53. Hagwood, "Soccer Studs."

54. Olivia Holbrow, "Who's Who Victoria Beckham," *Vogue*, February 7, 2012, http://www.vogue.co.uk/spy/biographies/victoria-beckham.

55. Holbrow, "Who's Who Victoria Beckham."

56. Holbrow, "Who's Who Victoria Beckham."

57. "Victoria and David Beckham Named as 'Perfect Married Couple,'" *Telegraph*, July 4, 2009, http://www.telegraph.co.uk/sport/football/players/david-beckham/5736097/Victoria-and-David-Beckham-named-as-perfect-married-couple.html.

58. Baily, "Great Love Stories No. 14."

59. "Posh and Becks: A Match Made in A-List Heaven."

CHAPTER 5

1. "Centurion Beckham Picks Up UEFA Gong at Wembley alongside Charlton and Shilton," *Daily Mail*, June 2, 2012, http://www.dailymail.co.uk/sport/football/article-2153766/David-Beckham-collects-UEFA-award-100-caps-Wembley-alongside-Sir-Bobby-Robson.html#ixzz2aRgiAw8z.

2. "Moldova 0 England 3, 1998 World Cup Qualifying Game—Group 2, Republican Stadium, Kishinev, Moldova—Sunday 1 September 1996," *England FC*, http://www.englandfc.com/reports/report_mol_v_eng96.html.

3. "David Robert Joseph Beckham," *England Football Online*, page last updated May 16, 2013, http://www.englandfootballonline.com/TeamPlyrsBios/PlayersB/Bio-BeckhamDRJ.html.

4. "The History of The FA," *FA.com*, http://www.thefa.com/england; "England National Football Team."

5. Josh Williams, "Beckham Begins Remarkable England Journey," *ESPN .com*, September 6, 2012, http://www.espn.co.uk/football/sport/story/168506 .html#RgOWhrf38YomVGxC.99.

6. David Beckham with Tom Watt, *Both Feet on the Ground: An Autobiography* (New York: It Books, 2004), 120.

7. Adam Shergold, "Gazza, Becks and Andy Hinchcliffe . . . What happened to the Glenn Hoddle England Team That Visited Moldova in 1996?" *Daily Mail*, September 6, 2012, http://www.dailymail.co.uk/sport/football/article-2199157/Moldova-v-England-David-Beckhams-debut-1996.html#ixzz2aRtusEHq.

8. *Anglia Football Online*, page last updated September 11, 2013, http://www .englandfootballonline.com/Opp/OppMol.html.

9. "World Cup 1998, Statistics," *Planet World Cup*, http://www.planetworldcup .com/CUPS/1998/wc98statistics.html.

10. David Beckham, with photography by Dean Freeman, *Beckham: My World* (London: Hodder and Stoughton, 2000), 53–58.

11. Beckham, *Beckham: My World*, 53–56; Argentina Kicks Out England," *CNN Sports Illustrated*, June 30, 1998, http://sportsillustrated.cnn.com/soccer/world/events/1998/worldcup/news/1998/06/30/argentina_update/.

12. David Hill, "Beckham," *Independent*, August 15, 1998, http://www.independent.co.uk/life-style/beckham-1171687.html.

13. "Beckham vs. Diego Simeone," *World Cup Fails*, May 20, 2010, http://www .worldcupfails.com/2010/05/david-beckham-vs-diego-simeone.html; "Beckham Says Fergie Strength Revived His Career," *Football.co.uk*, October 26, 2013, http://www .football.co.uk/manchester_united/beckham_says_fergie_strength_revived_his_career_rss4461001.shtml.

14. *Beckham—The REAL David Beckham*, directed by Ian Denyer (2000, London: 3DD Entertainment, 2000), DVD, YouTube video at http://www.youtube.com/watch?v=r_4-Zg5s97w).

15. "Beckham's Darkest Hour," *UEFA.com*, July 12, 2002, http://web.archive.org/web/20060112062436/http://en.uefa.com/news/newsId=27844,printer.htmx.

16. Beckham, *Beckham: My World*, 58.

17. "Beckham's Darkest Hour," *UEFA.com*.

18. Gwen Russell, *Arise Sir David Beckham: Footballer, Celebrity, Legend—The Biography of Britain's Best Loved Sporting Icon* (London: John Blake Publishing, 2011).

19. Hill, "Beckham"; Beckham, *Both Feet on the Ground*, 128.

20. Grant Wahl, *The Beckham Experiment* (New York: Three Rivers Press, 2010), 30.

21. "Deportes, David Beckham El fútbol tiene un rey inglés," *La Nacion.com*, July 18, 1999; http://www.lanacion.com.ar/211698-david-beckham-br-el-futbol-tiene-un-rey-ingles.

22. "Simeone Admits Faking World Cup Injury," *BBC News*, March 2, 1999, http://news.bbc.co.uk/2/hi/sport/football/288889.stm.

23. "Manchester United vs Internazionale—3 Mar 1999," *About ManUtd*, http://www.aboutmanutd.com/man-u-matches/03-03-1999-internazionale.html.

24. Bill Thornton, "Huckin Crazy Red," *Red Web*, http://www.redweb.zen.co.uk/news/.

25. Beckham, *Both Feet on the Ground*, 149.

26. Beckham, *Beckham: My World*, 77.

27. "The Rise of Captain Beckham, Saturday," *BBC Sport*, October 6, 2001, http://news.bbc.co.uk/sport2/hi/football/world_cup_2002/1583402.stm.

28. Colin Malam, "Brilliant Beckham Averts Greek Tragedy," *Telegraph*, October 6, 2001, http://www.telegraph.co.uk/sport/football/teams/england/3014197/Brilliant-Beckham-averts-Greek-tragedy.html.

29. David Beckham, *David Beckham* (London: Headline, 2013), 24–25.

30. "Beckham Saves England," *BBC Sport*, October 6, 2001, http://news.bbc.co.uk/sport2/hi/football/world_cup_2002/1583482.stm.

31. "Beckham's Joy at BBC award," *BBC Sport*, December 10, 2001, http://news.bbc.co.uk/sport2/hi/in_depth/2000/sports_personality/1701054.stm.

32. "England's Sweet Revenge," *BBC Sport*, June 7, 2002, http://news.bbc.co.uk/sport3/worldcup2002/hi/matches_wallchart/argentina_v_england/default.stm.

33. "England 0–0 Portugal, Saturday," *BBC Sport*, July 1, 2006, http://news.bbc.co.uk/sport2/hi/football/world_cup_2006/4991618.stm.

34. Alan Cowell, "After Loss, Beckham Resigns as England's Captain," *New York Times*, July 2, 2006, http://www.nytimes.com/2006/07/02/sports/soccer/03englandcnd.html?fta=y&_r=0.

35. "David Beckham Resigns as England Captain," *Beckham Zone*, July 2, 2006, http://beckhamzone.blogspot.com/2006/07/david-beckham-resigns-as-england.html.

36. "Tearful Beckham Quits as England Captain," *AP for ESPN*, July 6, 2006, http://espnfc.com/news/story?id=373083&cc=5901; "David Beckham Resigns as England Captain," *Beckham Zone*.

37. "Tearful Beckham Quits as England Captain."

38. *David Beckham: New Beginnings*, directed by Gary Brooks (2007, United Kingdom: 19 Television), YouTube video at http://www.youtube.com/watch?v=xDwZU4h7jd8).

39. "Bio Beckham DRJ," *England Football Online*, page last updated May 16, 2013, http://www.englandfootballonline.com/TeamPlyrsBios/PlayersB/BioBeckhamDRJ.html.

40. "Beckham Achieves Century Landmark," *BBC Sport*, updated March 26, 2008, http://news.bbc.co.uk/sport2/hi/football/internationals/7315475.stm.

41. V. S. Luck, *From Twelve to One* (Google ebook, AuthorHouse, 2011), 46.

42. Greg Thomas, "Don't Bag Beckham; France v England Sven Says 100 Caps Must Not Be the End," *Daily Record*, March 26, 2008, http://www.thefreelibrary.com/ DON'T+BAG+BECKHAM%3B+FRANCE+v+ENGLAND+Sven+says+100+caps+ must+not+be...-a0177046714.

43. "Beckham Achieves Century Landmark."

44. Tom Wells and Lynsey Haywood, "Beckham: The Boy Ton Good," *Sun*, March 26, 2008, http://www.thesun.co.uk/sol/homepage/news/960666/David-Beckham-The-boy-ton-good-100-England-caps.html#ixzz2YDovkeT7.

45. "David Beckham Intends to Enjoy His 100th England Cap to the Full," *Sun*, March 25, 2008, http://www.thesun.co.uk/sol/homepage/sport/football/955327/ David-Beckham-intends-to-enjoy-his-100th-England-cap-to-the-full.html.

46. "David Beckham Celebrates with Posh in Paris," *Now Daily*, March 28, 2008, http://www.nowmagazine.co.uk/celebrity-news/250873/david-beckham-celebrates-with-posh-in-paris#HCMAH2zRFGfQjsSA.99.

47. Shaun Custis, "Beckham Is the All Mighty," *Sun*, March 25, 2008, http://www .thesun.co.uk/sol/homepage/sport/football/955327/David-Beckham-intends-to-enjoy-his-100th-England-cap-to-the-full.html.

48. Wells and Haywood, "Beckham: The Boy Ton Good"; "David Beckham makes 100 caps for England," *Telegraph*, March 25, 2008, http://www.telegraph .co.uk/sport/football/teams/england/2295456/David-Beckham-makes-100-caps-for-England.html.

49. Dave Wood, "David Beckham Stretchered Off in Milan Victory: World Cup Fear for England Midfielder," *Daily Mail*, updated March 14, 2010, http://www.daily mail.co.uk/sport/football/article-1257934/David-Beckham-stretchered-Milan-victory-World-Cup-fear-England-midfielder.html.

50. "Catching Up with David Beckham: The Soccer Star Discusses His Career, His Kids and His Future," *ABC News.com*, April 26, 2010, http://abcnews.go.com/ GMA/video/catching-david-beckham-10476229?&clipId=10476229&playlistId=-1&cid=siteplayer.

51. Steve Alexander, "Dr Sakari Orava Confirms David Beckham Will Make a Full Recovery from Achilles Tendon Injury," *Goal.com*, March 15, 2010, http://www.goal .com/en/news/9/england/2010/03/15/1834650/dr-sakari-orava-confirms-david-beckham-will-make-a-full-recovery-.

52. "David Beckham," *Facebook*, March 16, 2010, https://www.facebook.com/Beck ham/posts/393702594714.

53. Oliver Harvey, "I Want David in South Africa Because He's an Ambassador for Football, Sport and England," *Sun*, March 23, 2010, http://www.thesun.co.uk/sol/ homepage/features/2900642/Capello-I-want-David-in-South-Africa-he-is-an-ambassa-dor-for-football-sport-and-England.html.

54. James Pearce, "Beckham Impresses in South Africa," *BBC.com*, June 16, 2010, http://www.bbc.co.uk/blogs/jamespearce/2010/06/beckham_impresses_in_south_afr .html.

55. "2010 FIFA World Cup South Africa, Teams, England," *FIFA.com*, http://www.fifa.com/tournaments/archive/worldcup/southafrica2010/teams/team=43942/index.html.

56. Sarah Bull, "'Victoria, You're an Inspiration to Me': Posh Reduced to Tears as She Watches David Beckham Accept the Lifetime Achievement Award," *Daily Mail*, December 20, 2010, http://www.dailymail.co.uk/tvshowbiz/article-1340001/Sports-Personality-Year-2010-David-Beckham-supported-wife-Victoria-sons.html#ixzz2G0izSAOH.

57. "David Beckham Wins Lifetime Achievement Award," *BBC Sport*, page last updated December 19, 2010, http://news.bbc.co.uk/sport2/hi/tv_and_radio/sports_personality_of_the_year/9303339.stm.

58. "David Beckham," *England Football Online*, http://www.englandfootballonline.com/TeamPlyrsBios/PlayersB/BioBeckhamDRJ.html.

59. Bill Chappell, "David Beckham Retires from Soccer, Ending Storied Career," *NPR*, May 16, 2013, http://www.npr.org/blogs/thetwo-way/2013/05/16/184469614/david-beckham-retires-from-soccer-ending-storied-career.

60. Bull, "'Victoria, You're an Inspiration to Me.'"

CHAPTER 6

1. David Beckham with Tom Watt, *Both Feet on the Ground: An Autobiography* (New York: It Books, 2004), 299; "The Most Hated Man in Britain," *People*, June 30, 1998, http://www.people.com/people/david_beckham/biography/.

2. David Beckham, with photography by Dean Freeman, *Beckham: My World* (London: Hodder and Stoughton, 2000), 85.

3. Beckham, *Beckham: My World*, 85.

4. "Nine Held over Beckham Kidnap Plot," *BBC News*, November 3, 2002, http://news.bbc.co.uk/2/hi/uk_news/england/2392211.stm.

5. Stephen Silverman, "Passages: Police Foil Posh Kidnap Plot," *People*, November 4, 2002, http://www.people.com/people/article/0,26334,624980,00.html; Beckham, *Both Feet on the Ground*, 318.

6. Ciar Byrne, "Gossip Inflated £1m Beckham Wedding Deal," *Guardian*, March 9, 2004, http://www.theguardian.com/media/2004/mar/09/pressandpublishing4.

7. "SFX 'Surprised' by Beckham Split Claim," *ESPNFC.com*, October 14, 2003, http://espnfc.com/news/story?id=280361&cc=5901.

8. Simon Donohue, "My Year with the Beckhams," *Manchester Evening News*, 2001.

9. Jessica Vince, "A History of Victoria Beckham Documentaries in Honour of her Skype Collaboration," *Grazia Daily*, January 29, 2014, http://www.graziadaily.co.uk/fashion/news/the-best-victoria-beckham-documentaries.

10. Kate Stanton, "David and Victoria Beckham Sell 'Beckingham Palace' for $19 million," *UPI.com*, October 6, 2013, http://www.upi.com/blog/2013/10/06/David-and-Victoria-Beckham-sell-Beckingham-Palace-for-19-million/3761381111412/#ixzz 2rG0x5yzh.

11. Kim Peiffer, "Victoria Beckham: David's 'Romantic'—Also, Tidy," *People.com*, October 31, 2007, http://www.people.com/people/article/0,,20155984,00.html.

12. *David Beckham—A Footballer's Story*, directed by Damon Thomas (London: Century Films, 2006), YouTube video at http://www.youtube.com/watch?v=r78aN0JKpzM).

13. Andrew Anthony, "In Pursuit of Goldenballs," *Observer*, October 2, 2004, http://www.theguardian.com/books/2004/oct/03/sportandleisure.sport.

14. "David Beckham Shows Letterman GRUESOME Surgery Picture (Video)," *Huffington Post*, July 4, 2010, http://www.huffingtonpost.com/2010/05/04/david-beckham-shows-lette_n_562419.html.

15. "David Beckham's Hidden Camera Fun!" YouTube video at http://www.youtube.com/watch?v=In9XbjyCbnY.

16. "'Bend It' Like Beckham (CBS News)," YouTube video at http://www.youtube.com/watch?v=0N6G8XlyCMM.

17. "Sesame Street: David Beckham: Persistent," YouTube video at http://www.youtube.com/watch?v=Vq4wrPL1o4s.

18. *Bend It Like Beckham*, directed by Gurinda Chadha (2002; USA: Fox Searchlight, 2003), DVD.

19. "David Beckham Biography," *People.com*, http://www.people.com/people/david_beckham/.

20. Judith Woods, "A Royal Coup de Theatre," *Telegraph*, April 3, 2012, http://www.telegraph.co.uk/news/uknews/theroyalfamily/9180950/A-royal-coup-de-theatre-at-Madame-Tussauds.html.

21. "Beckham's Goal Relived," *BBC Sport*, March 22, 2002, http://news.bbc.co.uk/sport2/hi/football/world_cup_2002/1887946.stm.

22. "David Beckham, Biography," *People.com*.

23. "David Beckham: New Commission of Footballer David Beckham," *National Portrait Gallery*, http://www.npg.org.uk/about/press/david-beckham.php.

24. "Art: Oh Come Let Us Adore Him," *Waldemar Januszczak*, April 25, 2004, http://www.waldemar.tv/2004/04/art-oh-come-let-us-adore-him/.

25. "Art: Oh Come Let Us Adore Him."

26. "David Beckham Sleeping," YouTube video at http://www.youtube.com/watch?v=z0UEuuYuNDo.

27. "David Beckham: New Commission of Footballer David Beckham."

28. Beckham, *Both Feet on the Ground*, 289.

29. Beckham, *Both Feet on the Ground*, 289.

30. "United for Unicef," *Manchester United*, http://www.mufoundation.org/en/Charities/UnitedForUnicef2.aspx; "David Beckham, Goodwill Ambassador," *Unicef*, http://www.unicef.org/people/people_47871.html.

31. "David Beckham Joins Team UNICEF," *Unicef*, January 12, 2005, http://www.unicef.org/emerg/disasterinasia/index_24809.html.

32. "David Beckham in the Philippines and Visits Sick Children," *Daily Mail*, December 2, 2011, http://www.dailymail.co.uk/sport/football/article-2069093/David-Beckham-Philippines-visits-sick-children.html.

33. David Garfinkel, "Going for a Sarong: Mirrorman Puts New Beckham Skirt to the Test," *Daily Mirror*, June 5, 1998, http://www.thefreelibrary.com/GOING+FOR+A+SARONG%3B+Mirrorman+puts+new+Beckham+skirt+to+the+test.-a060672350.

34. Beckham, *Beckham: My World*, 93.

35. "Brand It Like Beckham," *Time*, June 23, 2003, http://content.time.com/time/world/article/0,8599,460400,00.html.

36. Jonathan Petre, "Rosary Is Not Just a Fashion Item," *Telegraph*, October 23, 2004, http://www.telegraph.co.uk/news/1474839/Rosary-is-not-just-a-fashion-item-explains-Church.html.

37. "David Beckham and Me: The Underwear Interview," *Mr. Blasberg*, March 27, 2012, http://www.mrblasberg.com/2012/03/27/david-beckham-and-me-the-underwear-interview/.

38. "Magazine Covers," *Lucy Who*, http://magazine-covers.lucywho.com/; David Beckham Magazine Covers," *Who's Dated Who?*, http://www.whosdatedwho.com/tpx_2873/david-beckham/magazinecovers.

39. "Magazine First for David Beckham," *Daily Mail*, http://www.dailymail.co.uk/tvshowbiz/article-111069/Magazine-David-Beckham.html.

40. "Beckham First Man to Grace *Elle* Magazine Cover," *Express Tribune*, May 31, 2012, http://tribune.com.pk/story/386834/beckham-first-man-to-grace-elle-magazine-cover/.

41. *Beckham—The REAL David Beckham*, directed by Ian Denyer (2000; London: 3DD Entertainment, 2000), DVD, YouTube video at http://www.youtube.com/watch?v=Q0mA8AejOWw).

42. "Branded Like Beckham, Brand It Like Beckham," *Economist*, July 3, 2003, http://www.economist.com/node/1900131?zid=319&ah=17af09b0281b01505c226b1e574f5cc1.

43. David Coad, *The Metrosexual: Gender, Sexuality, and Sport* (Albany: State University of New York Press, 2009), 183–89.

44. James Masters, "Beckham: The Man Who Broke Football's Gay Taboo?" *CNN*, May 17, http://edition.cnn.com/2013/05/17/sport/football/football-david-beckham-gay-icon-fashion/.

45. Quoted in Masters, "Beckham: The Man Who Broke Football's Gay Taboo?"

46. Quoted in Masters, "Beckham: The Man Who Broke Football's Gay Taboo?"

47. Beckham, *Beckham: My World*, 36.

48. Robert Klemko, "Colin Kaepernick's Parents Upset at Criticism of Son's Tattoos," *USA Today Sports*, November 30, 2012, http://www.usatoday.com/story/sports/nfl/2012/11/29/49ers-colin-kaepernick-tattoo-criticism-sporting-news/1736671/.

49. Sam Rigby, "David Beckham: 'I Don't Regret Any of My 32 Tattoos'" *Digital Spy*, May 12, 2013, http://www.digitalspy.com/celebrity/news/a480787/david-beckham-i-dont-regret-any-of-my-32-tattoos.html#ixzz2rR9JE3lR.

50. "Beckham Signs New Contract," *BBC Sport*, May 12, 2002, http://news.bbc.co.uk/sport3/worldcup2002/hi/team_pages/england/newsid_1976000/1976699.stm.

51. John Norman, "Bergkamp's Legacy Has Opened the Image Rights Floodgates," *SportsPro*, February 25, 2011, http://www.sportspromedia.com/guest_blog/bergkamps_legacy_has_opened_the_image_rights_floodgates/.

52. Michael Hirschorn, "Will America Buy David Beckham?" *Details*, http://www.details.com/celebrities-entertainment/cover-stars/200702/soccer-star-david-beckham-invades-america#ixzz2rRB1YWJS.

53. Aidan Radnedge, "Why David Beckham Owes Much to Simon Fuller," *Metro*, May 16, 2013, http://metro.co.uk/2013/05/16/why-david-beckham-owes-much-to-simon-fuller-3766602/.

54. "David Beckham Biography," *People.com*, http://www.people.com/people/david_beckham/biography/.

55. Gordon MacMillan, "Beckham Gets His Own Logo as He Signs New Adidas Deal," *BrandRepublic.com*, March 4, 2004, http://www.brandrepublic.com/news/204009/.

56. "Beckham Extends Contract and Gets Own Logo," *Adidas Group*, March 3, 2004, http://www.adidas-group.com/en/media/news-archive/press-releases/2004/beckham-extends-contract-and-gets-own-logo/.

57. Tim Newcomb, "The 2012 Super Bowl, by the Numbers," *Time*, February 2, 2012, http://newsfeed.time.com/2012/02/02/the-2012-super-bowl-by-the-numbers/.

58. "H&M—HM/David Beckham—2012 Super Bowl Commercials @ NFL," *NFL.com*, February 5, 2012, http://www.nfl.com/videos/nfl-super-bowl-commercials/09000d5d8268e196/HM-David-Beckham.

59. "Our History," *H&M*, http://about.hm.com/en/About/facts-about-hm/people-and-history/history.html#cm-menu.

60. "David Beckham and Me: The Underwear Interview."

61. "Launch of David Beckham Bodywear for H&M in London," *H&M*, February 2, 2012, http://about.hm.com/en/news/newsroom.html.

62. Saya Weissman, "H&M's Super Bowl David Beckham Ad on Top," *Digiday*, February 6, 2012, http://www.digiday.com/social/hms-super-bowl-david-beckham-ad-on-top-thanks-to-the-ladies/; Sam Laird, "Brand or Celeb? Social Media Shows Who Super Bowl Ads Helped Most," *Mashable*, February 6, 2012, http://mashable.com/2012/02/06/brand-or-celeb-social-media-shows-who-super-bowl-ads-helped-most/.

63. "H&M Hennes & Mauritz Ab, Nine-Month Report," December 1, 2011–August 31, 2012, http://about.hm.com/content/dam/hm/about/documents/en/cision/1799854_en.pdf, 2.

64. "Man Utd Icon Beckham Going to Madrid in $41 Million Deal," *Sports Illustrated*, June 17, 2003, http://sportsillustrated.cnn.com/soccer/news/2003/06/17/beckham_madrid_ap/.

65. Kurt Badenhausen, "David Beckham Departs MLS after Earning $255 Million," *Forbes*, November 30, 2012, http://www.forbes.com/sites/kurtbadenhausen/2012/11/30/david-beckham-departs-mls-after-earning-255-million/.

66. "David Beckham Joins PSG, Will Donate Salary to Charity," *Sports Illustrated*, posted January 31, 2013, http://sportsillustrated.cnn.com/soccer/news/20130131/david-beckham-sign-french-club.ap/#ixzz2rSfJc2Sc.

67. Ben Priechenfried, "David Beckham Paid Himself $23 Million Last Year, Accounts Show," *Bloomberg News*, October 8, 2013, http://www.bloomberg.com/news/2013-10-08/david-beckham-paid-himself-23-million-last-year-accounts-show.html.

68. Kurt Badenhausen, "Mayweather Tops List of the World's 100 Highest-Paid Athletes," *Forbes.com*, June 18, 2012, http://www.forbes.com/pictures/mli45igdi/8-david-beckham/#gallerycontent.

69. "David Beckham Tops Richest Footballers List," *Sky.com*, March 12, 2013, http://news.sky.com/story/1062882/david-beckham-tops-richest-footballers-list.

70. Philip Beresford, "Football Is the Real Winner of 2012 Gold," *Sunday Times*, April 28, 2013, http://www.thesundaytimes.co.uk/sto/business/BusinessRichList/article1251420.ece.

71. "David Beckham Receives Award for Charity Work," *Global Gift Foundation*, http://globalgiftfoundation.org/2013/david-beckham-receives-award-for-charity-work/.

72. Chloe Hamilton and Sian Boyle, "Victoria and David Beckham Have a Clear-Out, Donating Thousands of Pounds' Worth of Clothes to London Charity for Philippines Fund," *London Evening Standard*, November 22, 2013, http://www.standard.co.uk/news/london/victoria-and-david-beckham-have-a-clearout-donating-thousands-of-pounds-worth-of-clothes-to-london-charity-for-philippines-fund-8956605.html.

73. Amit Katwala, "David Beckham—'I Never Wanted to Be Famous,'" *Talk Sport*, December 5, 2013, http://talksport.com/football/david-beckham-i-never-wanted-to-be-famous-13120570716#QVqWZG8g96IzQmII.99http://talksport.com/football/david-beckham-i-never-wanted-be-famous-13120570716#8Z9XUebPIrtISrP0.99.

CHAPTER 7

1. Beckham, David, with Tom Watt, *Both Feet on the Ground: An Autobiography* (New York: It Books, 2004), 355–56.

2. Raquel Fornieles, "Beckham llegó blanco y radiante," *AS*, July 2, 2003, http://masdeporte.as.com/masdeporte/2003/07/02/polideportivo/1057119282_850215.html.

3. Henry Winter, "Beckham So Stylishly Past First Hurdle," *Telegraph*, July 2, 2003, http://www.telegraph.co.uk/sport/football/european/2406996/Beckham-so-stylishly-past-first-hurdle.html; David Millward, "Beckham Enters Spanish Arena 'Fit as a Bull,'" *Telegraph*, July 2, 2003, http://www.telegraph.co.uk/news/worldnews/europe/spain/1434587/Beckham-enters-Spanish-arena-fit-as-a-bull.html.

4. "Beckham's Transfer as It Happened," *BBC Sport*, June 16, 2003, http://news.bbc.co.uk/go/pr/fr/-/sport2/hi/football/teams/m/man_utd/2977997.stm.

5. "Man Utd Icon Beckham Going to Madrid in $41 Million Deal," *Sports Illustrated*, June 17, 2003, http://sportsillustrated.cnn.com/soccer/news/2003/06/17/beckham_madrid_ap/.

6. "Beckham Gets No 23 Real Shirt," *Daily Mail*, http://www.dailymail.co.uk/news/article-187014/Beckham-gets-No-23-Real-shirt.html#ixzz2o2PR3ytc.

7. "Friendship Match," *RealMadrid.DK*, August 5, 2003, http://www.realmadrid.dk/fixtures/game/?id=160.

8. "Marketing Madrid," *Sports Illustrated*, August 11, 2003, http://sportsillustrated.cnn.com/soccer/news/2003/08/11/real_home/.

9. Beckham, *Both Feet on the Ground*, 89.

10. "Spain," *FIFA.com*, http://www.fifa.com/associations/association=esp/index.html.

11. Jimmy Burns, *La Roja: How Soccer Conquered Spain and How Spanish Soccer Conquered the World* (New York: Nation Books, 2012); Jack Graul, "La Roja—by Jimmy Burns," *ESPNFC.com*, August 28, 2012, http://espnfc.com/feature/_/id/1144718/la-roja:-how-soccer-conquered-spain-and-spain-conquered-the-world-?src=mobile&cc=5901.

12. Matthew Futterman, "They Reign in Spain," *Wall Street Journal*, updated July 12, 2010, http://online.wsj.com/news/articles/SB10001424052748703580104575361241625333012.

13. Sergio Dominguez, "The Rise of Spanish Sport," *Arts London*, page last updated May 10, 2010, http://www.artslondonnews.co.uk/20100705-spanish-sport-nadal-alonso-gasol.

14. "History," *Real Madrid.com*, http://www.realmadrid.com/cs/Satellite/en/1193041516534/Historia/Club.htm.

15. Rik Sharma, "Bayern Conquered Europe and Have Now Knocked Man United off Their Perch as the World's Most Valuable Football Brand . . . but Which Other English Sides Are in the Top 10?" *Daily Mail*, May 29, 2013, http://www.dailymail.co.uk/sport/football/article-2332596/Bayern-Munich-overtake-Manchester-United-world-footballs-valuable-brand.html.

16. Burns, *La Roja*.

17. Pedro Cesca, "Remembering the Age of Galácticos," *Managing Madrid*, June 29, 2013, http://www.managingmadrid.com/2013/6/29/4477126/real-madrid-galacticos-white-angels-john-carlin-david-beckham.

18. John Carlin, *White Angels: Beckham, Real Madrid and the New Football* (London: Bloomsbury Publishing PLC., 2004).

19. Enrique Ortego, "Los debuts de los galácticos," *MARCA.com*, September 14, 2013, http://www.marca.com/2013/09/14/futbol/equipos/real_madrid/1379161279 .html.

20. "The Honours System," https://www.gov.uk/honours/overview.

21. *David Beckham: New Beginnings*, directed by Gary Brooks (2007, United Kingdom: 19 Television), YouTube video at http://www.youtube.com/watch?v=vVHrcy_iFZE).

22. "OBE My Biggest Honour Yet—Beckham," *ESP.NFC.com*, November 27, 2003, http://espnfc.com/print?id=284396&type=story.

23. Sonia Elks, "Beckham 'to Be Snubbed for Knighthood,'" *London Times*, last updated December 29, 2013, http://www.thetimes.co.uk/tto/life/celebrity/article3960 235.ece.

24. Beckham, *Both Feet on the Ground*, 397.

25. "David Beckham Academy," YouTube video at http://www.youtube.com/ watch?v=tHsuDkDHXM0.

26. "The David Beckham Academy," *Soccer Training Info*, http://www.soccer-training-info.com/david_beckham_academy.asp.

27. *Beckham—The REAL David Beckham*, directed by Ian Denyer (2000; London: 3DD Entertainment, 2000), DVD, YouTube video at http://www.youtube.com/ watch?v=Q0mA8AejOWw).

28. Nick Green, "Beckham Soccer Academy Shut Down," *Daily Breeze*, February 7, 2010, http://www.dailybreeze.com/general-news/20100208/beckham-soccer-academy-shut-down.

29. Beckham, *Both Feet on the Ground*, 416–21.

30. Sid Lowe, "Axed Beckham Nears Exit Door at Real Madrid," *Guardian*, January 10, 2007, http://www.theguardian.com/football/2007/jan/11/newsstory.european football1.

31. "Uncertainty over Beckham's Future at Real Madrid," *International Herald Tribune*, January 10, 2007, http://www.nytimes.com/2007/01/10/sports/10i ht-web.0110beckham.4162244.html?_r=1&.

32. Oliver Marre, "The Man with Stars in His Eyes," *Observer*, January 14, 2007, http://www.guardian.co.uk/media/2007/jan/14/broadcasting.pop.

33. Grant Wahl, "The Americanization of David Beckham," *Sports Illustrated*, July 16, 2007, 52–56.

34. "Capello: "Beckham no volverá a jugar más," *El País.com*, January 13, 2007, http://deportes.elpais.com/deportes/2007/01/13/actualidad/1168676515_850215.html.

35. Wahl, "The Americanization of David Beckham."

36. *David Beckham: New Beginnings*.

37. "Beckham Scores in Return to Starting Lineup," *ESP.NFC.com*, February 10, 2007, http://espnfc.com/news/story?id=407888&cc=5901.

38. *David Beckham: New Beginnings.*

39. Sid Lowe, "David Beckham Was One of the Most Popular Players at Real Madrid," *Guardian*, May 16, 2013, http://www.theguardian.com/football/blog/2013/may/16/david-beckham-real-madrid-retires.

40. "Guillem Balague on Beckham's Time at Real Madrid," *talkSPORT*, May 16, 2013, https://soundcloud.com/talksport/guillem-balague-on-beckhams.

41. "Zinedine Zidane Congratulates David Beckham on Award," *BBC Sport*, page last updated December 18, 2010, http://news.bbc.co.uk/sport2/hi/football/9300784.stm.

42. "Sus portadas en MARCA," *MARCA.com*, http://archivo.marca.com/reportajes/07/01/11/adiosbeckham/portadas.html.

43. "Beckham Limps off Field in Final Game with Real Madrid," *ESPNFC.com*, June 17, 2007, http://espnfc.com/news/story?id=439478&cc=5901.

44. Paul Maidment, "Becks and Bucks," *Forbes*, Retrieved August 14, 2008, http://www.forbes.com/forbeslife/sports/2007/07/07/beckham-soccer-marketing-face-markets-cx_pm_0707autofacescan01.html.

45. *David Beckham: New Beginnings.*

CHAPTER 8

1. "Robert Mora," http://www.robertmora.com/about.

2. "Behind-the-Scenes: LA Galaxy Head Shot Photoshoot," YouTube video at http://www.youtube.com/watch?v=1t6P-BVLqbk.

3. "Adidas Reveals New Look for LA Galaxy as David Beckham Prepares for his MLS Debut," *PR NewsWire*, July 11, 2007, http://www.prnewswire.com/news-releases/adidas-reveals-new-look-for-la-galaxy-as-david-beckham-prepares-for-his-mls-debut-52724877.html.

4. Grant Wahl, *The Beckham Experiment* (New York: Three Rivers Press, 2010), 42.

5. Kevin Wicks, "Yes, It's True: David Beckham's Coming to America!" *BBC America*, January 13, 2007, http://www.bbcamerica.com/anglophenia/2007/01/yes-its-true-david-beckhams-coming-to-america/.

6. Beth Harris, "David Beckham Set to Invade America," *Washington Post*, January 12, 2007, http://www.washingtonpost.com/wp-dyn/content/article/2007/01/12/AR2007011200894.html.

7. "Beckham Will Play for MLS' L.A. Galaxy in $250M deal," *SI.com*, January 11, 2007, http://sportsillustrated.cnn.com/2007/soccer/01/11/beckham.mls/.

8. "Preparen la fiesta," *ESPN Deportes*, Actualizado el 12 de enero de 2007, http://espndeportes.espn.go.com/news/story?id=519046&s=gen&type=story&src=mobile.

9. "David Beckham, the New Star in L.A.'s Galaxy," *NPR*, January 12, 2007, http://www.npr.org/templates/story/story.php?storyId=6840325.

10. Michael Hirschorn, "Will America Buy David Beckham?" *Details*, February 2007, http://www.details.com/celebrities-entertainment/cover-stars/200702/soccer-star-david-beckham-invades-america#ixzz2rd1xrrl0.

11. "Beckham's Gonna Be Big," *Edmonton Journal*, June 21, 2007, http://www.canada.com/edmontonjournal/news/sports/story.html?id=56ca734b-306e-4bba-b80e-9f530ebaabce&k=72978.

12. Beth Harris, "David Beckham to Play for L.A. Galaxy," *Associated Press*, January 11, 2007, http://www.washingtonpost.com/wp-dyn/content/article/2007/01/11/AR2007011102221_pf.html.

13. Jack Bell, "David Beckham Is Coming to America," *New York Times*, January 11, 2007, http://www.nytimes.com/2007/01/11/sports/soccer/12beckham.html?_r=0.

14. Bell, "David Beckham Is Coming to America."

15. Grant Wahl, "Anatomy of a Blockbuster," *SI.com*, January 17, 2007, http://sportsillustrated.cnn.com/2007/writers/grant_wahl/01/17/beckham.qa/2.html.

16. Mike Penner, "Beckham to U.S.? Galaxy Can Dream," *Los Angeles Times*, June 3, 2005, http://articles.latimes.com/2005/jun/03/sports/sp-soccer3.

17. Wahl, "Anatomy of a Blockbuster."

18. Rich Thomaselli, "Herbalife Brand to Appear on Beckham's Jersey," *AdAge*, March 23, 2007, http://adage.com/article/news/herbalife-brand-beckham-s-jersey/115737/.

19. Harris, "David Beckham to Play for L.A. Galaxy."

20. "Beckham Sells 250,000 No 23 Shirts in the US," *Daily Mail*, http://www.dailymail.co.uk/sport/football/article-467960/Beckham-Sells-250-000-No-23-shirts-US.html#ixzz2re63VQoF.

21. Wahl, *The Beckham Experiment*, 45.

22. "MLS Attendance Second Best in History," *Soccer America Daily*, October 30, 2007, http://www.socceramerica.com/article/24198/mls-attendance-second-best-in-history.html.

23. Rick Horrow and Karla Swatek, "Fall Sports a Windfall for Advertisers," *Bloomberg Businessweek*, November 5, 2009, http://www.businessweek.com/stories/2009-11-05/fall-sports-a-windfall-for-advertisersbusinessweek-business-news-stock-market-and-financial-advice.

24. "Television: TeleFutura to Broadcast MLS and CONCACAF games in 2007," *SoccerAmerica.com*, May 19, 2006, http://www.socceramerica.com/article/3676/television-telefutura-to-broadcast-mls-and-concac.html.

25. Trevor Steven, "Trevor Steven: Only David Could Match My Record Hat-Trick of Titles!" *Daily Mail*, November 21, 2011, http://www.dailymail.co.uk/sport/football/article-2064464/Trevor-Steven-Only-David-Beckham-match-record.html#ixzz2sC41V01Y.

26. David Benady, "Becksploitation," *Marketing Weekly*, January 18, 2007, http://www.marketingweek.co.uk/becksploitation/2054718.article.

27. James Reginato, "American Idols," *W*, August 2007, http://www.wmagazine.com/celebrities/2007/08/beckhams_steven_klein_s#slide=1.

28. "*W* Is Acquired as Part of Fairchild Publications," *CondeNast.com*, http://www.condenast.com/about-us/heritage#/1999-w-acquired-part-fairchild-publications.

29. Oliver Marre, "Profile: Steven Klein, The Man Who Shapes Fame," *Observer*, July 14, 2007, http://www.guardian.co.uk/lifeandstyle/2007/jul/15/fashion.photography.

30. Mark Lamport-Stokes, "Beckham Arrives in L.A. to Start American Adventure," *Reuters*, July 13, 2007, http://www.reuters.com/article/2007/07/13/us-soccer-beckham-arrival-idUSN1224907120070713.

31. Wahl, *The Beckham Experiment*, 9.

32. *ESPN Presents David Beckham's LA Story* (2007, ESPN video), http://www.mlssoccer.com/blog/mls-insider/2012/03/15/espn-presents-david-beckhams-la-story.

33. "Beckham earning big bucks to pitch, not kick," *NBCNews.com*, January 12, 2007, http://www.nbcnews.com/id/16599439/#.Uucja9Io5dg.

34. Paul Doyle, "MLS and Beckham: It's about Celebrity," *Hartford Courant*, July 20, 2007, http://articles.courant.com/2007-07-20/sports/0707200107_1_beckham-s-debut-david-beckham-north-american-soccer-league/1.

35. Grant Wahl, "The Americanization of David Beckham," *Sports Illustrated*, July 10, 2007, http://sportsillustrated.cnn.com/2007/writers/grant_wahl/07/10/beckham0716/.

36. "Q&A: Sunil Gulati," *US National Soccer Players*, August 22, 2007, http://www.ussoccerplayers.com/2007/08/qa-sunil-gulati.html.

37. Rachel Brown, "Fans, Media Crush Welcome Beckham to Galaxy," *CNN.com*, July 13, 2007, http://www.cnn.com/2007/SHOWBIZ/07/13/beckham.galaxy/index.html.

38. Clemente Lisi, "It's Beck to the Future," *New York Post*, January 12, 2007, http://nypost.com/2007/01/12/its-beck-to-the-future/.

39. Andrew Gumbel, "The Ultimate Product Placement," *LA Weekly*, February 7, 2007, http://www.laweekly.com/2007-02-08/news/the-ultimate-product-placement/.

40. Gumbel, "The Ultimate Product Placement."

41. *ESPN Presents David Beckham's LA Story.*

42. Andrew Scurr, "Becks Ready for LA Challenge," *Sky Sports*, http://www1.skysports.com/football/news/12003/2609780/becks-ready-for-la-challenge.

43. *ESPN Presents David Beckham's LA Story.*

44. "Los Angeles 0–1 Chelsea," *ESPNFC.com*, July 21, 2007, http://soccernet.espn.go.com/report?id=221516&cc=5901.

45. "David Beckham Debut—LA Galaxy vs Chelsea 7/21," YouTubevideo at http://www.youtube.com/watch?v=PTRwWyEuaTU.

46. Paul Smith, "LA Galaxy 0–1 Chelsea," *Mirror*, July 22, 2007, http://www.mirror.co.uk/sport/football/la-galaxy-0-1-chelsea-713197#ixzz2rkEfx7qh.

47. "Celebs Step Out for David Beckham's L.A. Soccer Debut," *People*, July 22, 2007, http://www.people.com/people/article/0,,20047654,00.html.

48. "Beckham Makes MLS Debut as Galaxy Fall," *ESPNFC.com*, August 9, 2007, http://espnfc.com/us/en/report/215310/report.html?soccernet=true&cc=5901.

49. Christine Brennan, "Beckham or Not, U.S. Soccer Interest Near Nil," *USA Today*, August 22, 2007, http://usatoday30.usatoday.com/sports/columnist/brennan/2007-08-22-soccer-column_N.htm.

50. Courtney Rubin, "David Beckham Scores His First Galaxy Goal," *People.com*, updated August 16, 2007, http://www.people.com/people/article/0,,20051984,00.html.

51. "Beckham draws 66,000 as Galaxy lose thriller," *ESPNFC.com*, August 18, 2007, http://espnfc.com/us/en/report/215316/report.html?soccernet=true&cc=5901.

52. "Beckham's Season in Jeopardy," *New York Times*, August 31, 2007, http://www.nytimes.com/2007/08/31/sports/soccer/31sportsbriefs-beckham.html?_r=0.

53. "Beckham Ruled Out of England Games," *CNN.com*, August 31, 2007, http://edition.cnn.com/2007/SPORT/football/08/31/us.beckham/index.html?eref=edition_sport&utm_source=feedburner&utm_medium=feed&utm_campaign=Feed%3A+rss%2Fedition_sport+(RSS%3A+Sport).

54. "David Beckham," *LA Galaxy*, http://www.lagalaxy.com/players/david-beckham.

55. "Photos: The Life and Times of David Beckham," *Today.com*, http://www.today.com/id/25050341#.UuiIOD0o5dg.

56. "Beckham Advertising Blitz About to Begin," *ABC Money.co.uk*, June 24, 2007, http://abcmoney.co.uk/news/25200792540.htm.

57. "New ESPN David Beckham Galaxy Commercial," YouTube video at http://www.youtube.com/watch?v=NrQjFuklUuw.

58. Wahl, *The Beckham Experiment*, 25.

59. Christopher Weber, "Beckhams Get Starry Welcome-to-L.A. Party," *USA Today*, July 23, 2007, http://usatoday30.usatoday.com/life/people/2007-07-23-beckham-party_N.htm.

60. "Meet the Beckhams' New Neighbors," *Today.com*, updated July 17, 2007, http://www.today.com/id/19817433/ns/today-today_entertainment/t/meet-beckhams-new-neighbors/#.Uo4w0dKsim4.

61. Pete Norman, "Victoria Beckham: 'Loving Our New House,'" *People.com*, August 14, 2007, http://www.people.com/people/article/0,,20051543,00.html.

62. "Spice Girls Set Date to Reveal Plans," *Washington Post*, June 22, 2007, http://www.washingtonpost.com/wp-dyn/content/article/2007/06/22/AR2007062200691.html.

63. "Bio Beckham DRJ," *England Football Online*, page last updated May 16, 2013, http://www.englandfootballonline.com/TeamPlyrsBios/PlayersB/BioBeckhamDRJ.html.

64. Jonathan Stevenson, "England 2–3 Croatia," *BBC Sport*, November 21, 2007, http://news.bbc.co.uk/sport2/hi/football/internationals/7103110.stm.

65. "BBC Sport-Football," November 21, 2007, http://news.bbc.co.uk/player/sol/newsid_7100000/newsid_7106700/7106749.stm?bw=nb&mp=wm&news=1&ms3=6&ms_javascript=true&bbcws=2.

66. "David Beckham," *2011 LA Galaxy Media Guide*, http://pressbox.mlssoc-cer.com/sites/g/files/g211536/f/2011%20LA%20Galaxy%20Media%20Guide.pdf, 54–55.

67. "Galaxy's Beckham Leads Fan Voting for All-Star Clash against West Ham," *Daily Mail*, last updated June 11, 2008, http://www.dailymail.co.uk/sport/football/article-1025777/Galaxys-Beckham-leads-fan-voting-All-Star-clash-West-Ham.html.

68. Ridge Mahoney, "MLS All-Stars Put Reputation on Line," *Soccer America Daily*, July 24, 2008, http://www.socceramerica.com/article/27458/mls-all-stars-put-reputation-on-line.html.

69. "MLS All-Star Game 2008," *MLSSOCCER.com*, http://www.mlssoccer.com/history/allstar/2008.

70. "David Beckham Inspires MLS All-Stars to Victory over West Ham United," *Telegraph*, July 25, 2008, http://www.telegraph.co.uk/sport/football/teams/west-ham/2458972/David-Beckham-inspires-MLS-All-Stars-to-victory-over-West-Ham-United.html.

71. "Galaxy's Beckham Leads Fan Voting."

72. "David Beckham, Leona Lewis and Boris Johnson in Beijing Olympic Handover to London 2012," *Daily Telegraph*, August 14, 2008, http://www.telegraph.co.uk/sport/olympics/2556245/David-Beckham-Leona-Lewis-and-Boris-Johnson-in-Beijing-Olympic-handover-to-London-2012.html.

73. Read Madlen, "Stocks Plunge on Service Sector Weakness," *Yahoo! Finance*, February 5, 2008, http://web.archive.org/web/20080208145814/http://biz.yahoo.com/ap/080205/wall_street.html.

74. "Case Study: The Collapse of Lehman Brothers," *Investopedia*, April 2, 2009, http://www.investopedia.com/articles/economics/09/lehman-brothers-collapse.asp.

75. "U.S. Stocks Hammered after House Rejects Rescue," *MarketWatch*, September 29, 2008, http://www.marketwatch.com/story/us-stocks-slide-dow-plunges-777-points-as-bailout-bill-fails-2008929164700.

76. "Beckham to Join AC Milan on Short-Term Loan," *USA Today*, updated October 30, 2008, http://usatoday30.usatoday.com/sports/soccer/2008-10-30-beckham-milan_N.htm.

77. Jamie Jackson, "I Am Committed to LA Galaxy, Insists Beckham," *Observer*, October 25, 2008, http://www.guardian.co.uk/football/2008/oct/26/serieafootball-acmilan-david-beckham.

78. "Club History," A.C. Milan, http://www.acmilan.com/en/club/history.

79. Wahl, *The Beckham Experiment*, 280.

80. Tony Forrest, "Picture Special: David Beckham Officially Unveiled in Milan," *Daily Mail*, updated December 20, 2008, http://www.dailymail.co.uk/sport/football/article-1098991/Picture-special-David-Beckham-officially-unveiled-Milan.html #ixzz2sJNmDKE7.

81. "Beckham to San Siro: Forza Milan!" *Milanisti*, December 22, 2008, http://milanistacalcio.blogspot.com/.

CHAPTER 9

1. "David Beckham: I Want to Leave LA Galaxy and End Football Career with AC Milan," *Telegraph*, February 4, 2009, http://www.telegraph.co.uk/sport/football/players/david-beckham/4518028/David-Beckham-I-want-to-end-career-with-AC-Milan.html.

2. Mark Zeigler, "Beckham Gets Cold Shoulder in L.A. Return," *San Diego Union Tribune*, July 20, 2009, http://www.utsandiego.com/news/2009/jul/20/1s20galaxy233840-beckham-gets-cold-shoulder-l-retu/?sports.

3. "Beckham Booed by Furious Fans," *BBC News*, page last updated July 20, 2009, http://news.bbc.co.uk/2/hi/8159287.stm.

4. "David Beckham," *2011 LA Galaxy Media Guide*, http://pressbox.mlssoccer.com/sites/g/files/g211536/f/2011%20LA%20Galaxy%20Media%20Guide.pdf, 53.

5. Helene Elliott, "David Beckham Doesn't Get a Royal Welcome," *Los Angeles Times*, July 20, 2009, http://articles.latimes.com/2009/jul/20/sports/sp-elliott-galaxy20; Matt Marrone, "David Beckham Confronts Angry Fans in Ugly Return to L.A. Galaxy," *Daily News*, July 20, 2009, http://www.nydailynews.com/sports/more-sports/david-beckham-confronts-angry-fans-ugly-return-galaxy-article-1.428652#ixzz2s7MK7hWA.

6. Neil Ashton, "Beckham Set to Start His First Game for AC Milan after Impressing Ancelotti," *Daily Mail*, updated January 11, 2009, http://www.dailymail.co.uk/sport/football/article-1112124/Beckham-set-start-game-AC-Milan-impressing-Ancelotti.html.

7. "Mixed Reviews in Italy for Beckham's Milan Debut," *Soccer America Daily*, January 12, 2009, http://www.socceramerica.com/article/30529/mixed-reviews-in-italy-for-beckhams-milan-debut.html.

8. "The History of the San Siro Stadium," *AC Milan*, http://www.acmilan.com/en/stadium.

9. "AC Milan 1–0 Fiorentina," *ESPN.FC.com*, January 17, 2009, http://espnfc.com/us/en/report/251477/report.html?soccernet=true&cc=5901.

10. "Beckham Scores First Goal for AC Milan," *ESPN.FC.com*, January 25, 2009, http://soccernet.espn.go.com/news/story?id=612673&&cc=5901.

11. "Beckham Torn Between Lure of AC Milan or Completing American Dream at Galaxy," *Daily Mail*, updated January 28, 2009, http://www.dailymail.co.uk/sport/football/article-1130476/Beckham-torn-lure-AC-Milan-completing-American-dream-Galaxy.html.

12. "Beckham: Milan 'Special,' MLS 'Frustrating,'" *Soccer America Daily*, January 28, 2009, http://www.socceramerica.com/article/30774/beckham-milan-special-mls-frustrating.html.

13. Michael Lewis, "David Beckham Leans to A.C. Milan," *Daily News*, January 28, 2009, http://www.nydailynews.com/sports/more-sports/david-beckham-leans-milan-article-1.420629#ixzz2s7idKhpf.

14. Costa Alberto, "Corriere della Sera, Archivo, Beckham," *Corriere della Sera*, January 28, 2009, http://archiviostorico.corriere.it/2009/gennaio/28/Beckham_co_9_090128089.shtml; "Beckham: Milan 'Special,' MLS 'Frustrating.'"

15. Grant Wahl, *The Beckham Experiment* (New York: Three Rivers Press, 2010), 282–84.

16. "David Beckham," *2011 LA Galaxy Media Guide*, 54–55.

17. "Bruce Arena—General Manager/Head Coach," *LA Galaxy*, http://www.la galaxy.com/club/coaches.

18. Jeffrey Marcus, "The Donovan-Beckham Feud," *New York Times*, July 2, 2009, http://goal.blogs.nytimes.com/2009/07/02/the-donovan-beckham-feud/?_r=0.

19. Wahl, *The Beckham Experiment*, 280.

20. "Alexi Lalas: David Beckham Will Be Booed by LA Galaxy Fans," *Goal.com*, March 10, 2009, http://www.goal.com/en-us/news/1110/major-league-soccer/2009/03/10/1148911/alexi-lalas-david-beckham-will-be-booed-by-la-galaxy-fans.

21. "Bruce Arena—General Manager/Head Coach."

22. Wahl, *The Beckham Experiment*, 284.

23. "AC Milan 5-2 Genoa," *ESPN.com*, January 6, 2010, http://espnfc.com/us/en/gamecast/278309/gamecast.html?soccernet=true&cc=5901.

24. "Rooney Double Rocks San Siro," *ESPN.com*, February 6, 2010, http://espnfc.com/us/en/report/285584/report.html?soccernet=true&cc=5901.

25. "Old Trafford Fans Salute Beckham on Return," *CBC Sports*, March 10, 2010, http://www.cbc.ca/sports/soccer/old-trafford-fans-salute-beckham-on-return-1.921944.

26. Phil McNulty, "Beckham Shows True Colours," *BBC*, March 11 2010, http://www.bbc.co.uk/blogs/philmcnulty/2010/03/beckham_shows_true_colours.html.

27. Matt Lawton, "David Beckham in Tears as Cruel Achilles Injury in AC Milan Win Wrecks World Cup Dream," *Daily Mail*, updated March 15, 2010, http://www.dailymail.co.uk/sport/football/article-1257985/David-Beckham-Achilles-injury-AC-Milan-win-wrecks-World-Cup-dream.html.

28. Steve Alexander, "Dr Sakari Orava Confirms David Beckham Will Make a Full Recovery from Achilles Tendon Injury," *Goal.com*, March 15, 2010, http://www.goal.com/en/news/9/england/2010/03/15/1834650/dr-sakari-orava-confirms-david-beckham-will-make-a-full-recovery-.

29. "David Beckham Meets U.S. Troops in Afghanistan," *MLSSOCCER.com*, May 26, 2010, http://m.mlssoccer.com/news/article/david-beckham-meets-us-troops-afghanistan.

30. "David Beckham in Afghanistan," *Guardian*, May 22, 2010, http://www.guardian.co.uk/football/gallery/2010/may/22/david-beckham-afghanistan.

31. "David Beckham in Afghanistan," YouTube video at http://www.youtube.com/watch?v=HrqcctfQQRA.

32. "David Beckham Buoys British Troops in Afghanistan," *CNN*, May 24, 2010, http://www.cnn.com/2010/WORLD/asiapcf/05/22/afghanista.britain.visit/.

33. Oliver Harvey, "I Want David in South Africa Because He's an Ambassador for Football, Sport and England," *Sun*, March 23, 2010, http://www.thesun.co.uk/sol/homepage/features/2900642/Capello-I-want-David-in-South-Africa-he-is-an-ambassador-for-football-sport-and-England.html.

34. "2010 FIFA World Cup South Africa, Teams, England," *FIFA.com*, http://www.fifa.com/tournaments/archive/worldcup/southafrica2010/teams/team=43942/index.html.

35. "David Beckham First Training Session Photos," *LA Galaxy*, August 12, 2010, http://thelagalaxy.blogspot.com/2010/08/david-beckham-first-training-session.html.

36. "David Beckham," *2011 LA Galaxy Media Guide*, 54–55.

37. Owen Gibson, "BBC Sports Personality of the Year Recognises Lesser Known Faces," *Guardian*, December 17, 2010, http://www.guardian.co.uk/sport/2010/dec/18/bbc-sports-personality-year.

38. "Victoria Beckham Gives Husband David Beckham a Tattoo Voucher for His Birthday," *Hello!*, August 27, 2013, http://www.hellomagazine.com/celebrities/2013082714294/david-beckham-tattoo-voucher-victoria-beckham/.

39. "David Beckham," *Facebook*, July 10, 2011, https://www.facebook.com/Beckham/posts/10150227700591571.

40. "Gary Neville," *About Man Utd*, http://www.aboutmanutd.com/man-u-players/gary-neville.html; "Beckham Returns for Neville farewell," *Fox Soccer*, updated May 24, 2011, http://msn.foxsports.com/foxsoccer/soccer/story/david-beckham-manchester-united-gary-neville-testimonial-juevntus-052411.

41. "Beckham Returns for Neville Farewell."

42. Chris Wright, "Man Utd 1–2 Juventus: Gary Neville's Testimonial—Phil Calls Gary a 'Knob,' David Beckham Tackles Pitch Invader (Video & Photos)," *Who Ate All the Pies*, May 25, 2011, [http://www.whoateallthepies.tv/man_utd/72683/man-utd-1-2-juventus-gary-nevilles-testimonial-phil-calls-gary-a-knob-david-beckham-tackles-pitch-invader-video-photos.html.

43. "Anything for My Best Friend: David Beckham Turns Out for Manchester United in Gary Neville's Testimonial Match," *Daily Mail*, May 25, 2011, http://www.dailymail.co.uk/tvshowbiz/article-1390528/David-Beckham-turns-Manchester-United-Gary-Nevilles-testimonial-match.html#ixzz2s8YghwJS.

44. David Beckham Starts Training with Tottenham Hotspur," *Guardian*, January 11, 2011, http://www.theguardian.com/football/2011/jan/11/david-beckham-tottenham-hotspur.

45. "David Beckham, Profile," *LA Galaxy*, http://www.lagalaxy.com/players/david-beckham.

46. Nick Firchau, "MLS Cup Recap: Donovan, LA topple Houston 1–0 for title," *MLSSOCCER.com*, November 20, 2011, http://www.mlssoccer.com/news/article/2011/11/20/mls-cup-recap-donovan-la-topple-houston-1-0-title.

47. Kevin Baxter, "MLS Cup: Galaxy Defeats Dynamo, 1–0, to Win Championship," *Los Angeles Times*, November 20, 2011, http://latimesblogs.latimes.com/sports_blog/2011/11/mls-cup-galaxy-defeats-dynamo-1-0-to-win-championship.html.

48. John Godfrey, "Galaxy Win Title in What May Have Been Beckham's M.L.S. Finale," *New York Times*, November 21, 2011, http://www.nytimes.com/2011/11/21/sports/soccer/soccer-galaxy-beats-dynamo-to-win-mls-cup.html?_r=0.

49. "Dynamo 0, Galaxy 1," *ESP.NFC.com*, Nov. 20, 2011, http://espnfc.com/us/en/report/314397/report.html?soccernet=true&cc=5901.

50. Trevor Steven, "Trevor Steven: Only David Could Match My Record Hat-Trick of titles!" *Daily Mail*, November 21, 2011, http://www.dailymail.co.uk/sport/football/article-2064464/Trevor-Steven-Only-David-Beckham-match-record.html#ixzz2sC41V01Y.

51. "Dynamo 0, Galaxy 1."

52. "LA Galaxy Re-Sign David Beckham," *LA Galaxy*, January 18, 2012, http://www.lagalaxy.com/news/2012/01/la-galaxy-re-sign-david-beckham.

53. "Remarks by the President Honoring the 2011 MLS Cup Champion L.A. Galaxy," *White House*, May 15, 2012, http://www.whitehouse.gov/photos-and-video/video/2012/05/15/president-obama-honors-2011-mls-cup-champion-la-galaxy#transcript.

54. Melissa Rohlin, "David Beckham Doesn't Make Britain's Olympic team," *Los Angeles Times*, http://www.latimes.com/sports/sportsnow/la-david-beckham-doesnt-make-englands-olympic-team-20120628,0,6601351.story#axzz2daUw8uKv.

55. "2012 Season Recap," *MLSSOCCER.com*, http://www.mlssoccer.com/history/season/2012.

56. "David Beckham to Play His Final Game for the LA Galaxy in MLS Cup 2012," *LA Galaxy*, November 19, 2012, http://www.lagalaxy.com/news/2012/11/david-beckham-play-his-final-game-la-galaxy-mls-cup-2012.

57. "MLS Cup 2012," *MLSSOCCER.com*, http://www.mlssoccer.com/history/mlscup/2012.

58. Steve Fallon, "David Beckham Signs Off LA Galaxy Life with 'Old Feeling' of Winning," *Independent*, December 3, 2012, http://www.independent.co.uk/sport/football/news-and-comment/david-beckham-signs-off-la-galaxy-life-with-old-feeling-of-winning-8374381.html.

59. Erik Matuszewski, "Beckham to End U.S. Career in MLS Cup, Seeks Challenge," *Bloomberg*, November 20, 2012, http://www.bloomberg.com/news/2012-11-20/beckham-will-play-last-game-for-los-angeles-galaxy-in-mls-cup.html.

60. Matuszewski, "Beckham to End U.S. Career."

61. Ronald Blum, "Beckham Leaves MLS Much Better for His Six-Year Stay," *South China Morning Post*, Sunday, December 9, 2012, http://www.scmp.com/sport/soccer/article/1100825/beckham-leaves-mls-much-better-his-six-year-stay.

62. Jeremiah Oshan, "Soccer's Popularity among American Youth Obviously Good News for MLS," *SB Nation*, March 3, 2012, http://www.sbnation.com/soccer/2012/3/3/2842696/soccer-popularity-american-youth-mls.

63. "By the Numbers . . . North American Soccer League vs Major League Soccer," *US Soccer Players*, February 11, 2013, http://www.ussoccerplayers.com/2013/02/by-the-numbers-north-american-soccer-league-vs-major-league-soccer.html.

64. Kevin Baxter, "David Beckham Bids a Final Goodbye to Galaxy Play," *Los Angeles Times*, November 28, 2012, http://articles.latimes.com/2012/nov/28/sports/la-sp-david-beckham-20121129.

65. Arash Markazi, "Beckham Down to His Final L.A. Game," *ESPNLosAngeles.com*, updated November 20, 2012, http://espn.go.com/los-angeles/soccer/story/_/id/8654146/david-beckham-says-mls-cup-last-game-los-angeles-galaxy.

66. "David Beckham: He Came, He Sold, He Conquered the USA," *USA Today*, December 2, 2012, http://www.usatoday.com/story/sports/mls/2012/12/02/david-beckham-future-major-league-soccer/1741355/.

67. "Launch of David Beckham Bodywear for H&M in London," *H&M*, February 2, 2012.

68. Kurt Badenhausen, "Mayweather Tops List of the World's 100 Highest-Paid Athletes," *Forbes.com*, June 18, 2012, http://www.forbes.com/pictures/mli45igdi/8-david-beckham/#gallerycontent.

CHAPTER 10

1. "Live: London 2012 Olympics Opening Ceremonies," *USAToday.com*, updated July 28, 2012, http://usatoday30.usatoday.com/sports/olympics/story/2012-07-27/london-2012-olympics-opening-ceremonies-live-blog/56537222/1.

2. Melissa Rohlin, "David Beckham Practiced Driving Speedboat before Opening Ceremony," *Los Angeles Times*, August 2, 2012, http://articles.latimes.com/2012/aug/02/sports/la-sp-sn-david-beckham-speed-boat-opening-ceremony-20120802.

3. "Report of the IOC Evaluation Commission for the Games of the XXX Olympiad in 2012."

4. "Candidature Procedure for the 2012 Olympic Games," *Olympic.org*, April 16, 2007, http://web.archive.org/web/20070416051240/http://www.olympic.org/uk/news/events/117_session/candidature_uk.asp.

5. "Report of the IOC Evaluation Commission for the Games of the XXX Olympiad in 2012."

6. London 2012," *International Olympic Committee*, http://www.olympic.org/london-2012-summer-olympics.

7. Andrew Fraser, "One Great Day in Singapore," *BBC Sport*, July 6, 2005, http://news.bbc.co.uk/go/pr/fr/-/sport2/hi/other_sports/olympics_2012/4657685.stm.

8. "Olympic Reporters' Log," *BBC Sport*, last updated Wednesday, July 6, 2005, http://news.bbc.co.uk/sport2/hi/other_sports/olympics_2012/4654201.stm.

9. "Olympic Reporters' Log."

10. "Olympic Reporters' Log."

11. "Olympic Reporters' Log."

12. "Olympic Reporters' Log."

13. "London Beats Paris to 2012 Games," *BBC Sport*, July 6, 2005, http://news.bbc.co.uk/go/pr/fr/-/sport2/hi/front_page/4655555.stm.

14. Michael Ray, "London Bombings of 2005," *Britannica*, http://www.britannica.com/EBchecked/topic/1696348/London-bombings-of-2005.

15. "7/7 London Bombings," *911memorial.org*, http://www.911memorial.org/77-london-bombings; "2005: Bomb Attacks on London," *BBC News*, July 7, 2005, http://news.bbc.co.uk/onthisday/hi/dates/stories/july/7/newsid_4942000/4942238.stm.

16. Alan Cowell, "After Coordinated Bombs, London Is Stunned, Bloodied and Stoic," *New York Times*, July 7, 2005, http://www.nytimes.com/2005/07/07/international/europe/07cnd-explosion.html?pagewanted=all&_r=0.

17. David Haugh, "Beckham's Fame Bends around the Globe," *Chicago Tribune*, July 13, 2005, http://staugustine.com/stories/071305/spo_3201035.shtml.

18. "IOC Support after London Attacks," *BBC Sport*, July 8, 2005, http://news.bbc.co.uk/sport2/hi/front_page/4659781.stm.

19. Frank C. Zarnowski, "A Look at Olympic Costs," http://library.la84.org/SportsLibrary/JOH/JOHv1n1/JOHv1n1f.pdf.

20. "The Official Report of the Organising Committee for the XIV Olympiad, London, British Olympic Council, 1908," http://library.la84.org/6oic/OfficialReports/1948/OR1948part1.pdf.

21. "Team GB History 1948," *London 2012 Olympic Games, Team GB Media Guide*, 46–47.

22. "London Olympics 1908 & 1948," *BBC London*, June 24, 2005, http://web.archive.org/web/20061010154104/http://www.bbc.co.uk/london/content/articles/2005/06/24/olympics_history_feature.shtml.

23. Sajel Karena and Marco Inzinga, "From Wasteland into Olympic Wonderland," *BBC Local London*, last updated July 26, 2010, http://news.bbc.co.uk/local/london/hi/people_and_places/2012/newsid_8846000/8846766.stm.

24. Catherine Donohoe and Laura Foster, "Londoners Memories of the 1948 Olympic Games," *BBC Local London*, last updated July 23, 2010, http://news.bbc.co.uk/local/london/hi/people_and_places/2012/newsid_8846000/8846766.stm.

25. Melissa Cheung, "Beckham 'Branded' in China," *CBS News.com*, July 25, 2003, http://www.cbsnews.com/news/beckham-branded-in-china/.

26. "Ecstatic Chinese Fans Cheer Arrival Real Madrid," *People's Daily Online*, last updated July 25, 2003, http://english.peopledaily.com.cn/200307/25/eng20030725_120968.shtml.

27. "David Beckham, Leona Lewis and Boris Johnson in Beijing Olympic Handover to London 2012," *Daily Telegraph*, August 14, 2008, http://www.telegraph.co.uk/sport/olympics/2556245/David-Beckham-Leona-Lewis-and-Boris-Johnson-in-Beijing-Olympic-handover-to-London-2012.html.

28. "An Olympic Effort: 80,000-Seat Stadium Is Declared Finished," *Daily Mail*, updated March 30, 2011, http://www.dailymail.co.uk/news/article-1371267/London-2012-Olympics-Great-Britain-breaks-world-record-Stadium-completion.html #ixzz2ec4UIdOs.

29. "David Beckham in Awe of London 2012 Olympic Park," *SportsFeatures.com*, November 29, 2010, http://www.sportsfeatures.com/presspoint/pressrelease/51854/david-beckham-in-awe-of-london-2012-olympic-park.

30. "Bring It On!" *Daily Mail*, November 30, 2010, http://www.dailymail.co.uk/tvshowbiz/article-1334134/David-Beckham-visits-Olympic-Stadium-England-2018-World-Cup-bid.html; "Beckham Visits London 2012 Olympic Park," *Xinhua*, November 30, 2010, http://news.xinhuanet.com/english2010/sports/2010-11/30/c_13627912.htm.

31. "London 2012: Trafalgar Square, Ceremony for a Year to Go," *Daily Mail*, July 21, 2012, http://www.dailymail.co.uk/sport/olympics/article-2019393/London-2012-Olympics-One-year-celebrations-start.html.

32. Bonnie Ford, "100 Days Out: Keep Calm and Carry On," *ESPN.com*, April, 18, 2012, http://espn.go.com/blog/olympics/post/_/id/2511/100-days-out-keep-calm-and-carry-on.

33. "Olympic Oak Trees Planted," *ITV*, April 18, 2012, http://www.itv.com/news/update/2012-04-18/olympic-oak-trees-planted/.

34. "Year-to-Go Olympic Stamps Unveiled by Royal Mail," *BBC News London*, July 21, 2011, http://www.bbc.co.uk/news/uk-england-london-14244890.

35. "London 2012: Olympic Motto Revealed as 100-Day Countdown Begins," *BBC*, April 18, 2012, http://www.bbc.co.uk/news/uk-17741213#story_continues_1.

36. "Ancient Olympic Games," *International Olympic Committee*, http://www.olympic.org/ancient-olympic-games?tab=history.

37. Paul Owen, "Olympic Flame Handover from Greece to London," *Guardian*, May 17, 2012, http://www.theguardian.com/sport/london-2012-olympics-blog/2012/may/17/olympic-flame-handover-from-greece-to-london-live-coverage.

38. "London 2012 offers first look at Olympic Torch design," *London 2012 Press Office*, June 8, 2011.

39. "London 2012 Olympics: Torch Designers Edward Barber and Jay Osgerby Explain the Aspect of the Iconic Object," *Telegraph*, May 19, 2012, http://www.telegraph.co.uk/sport/olympics/torch-relay/9270187/London-2012-Olympics-torch-designers-Edward-Barber-and-Jay-Osgerby-explain-the-aspect-of-the-iconic-object.html.

40. "Edward Barber and Jay Osgerby," *Design Curial*, October 3, 2011, http://www.designcurial.com/opinion/edward-barber-and-jay-osgerby18141822.

41. "Edward Barber and Jay Osgerby."

42. Michael Hirst, "London 2012: Olympic Flame Handed Over to UK in Athens," *BBC News*, May 2012, http://www.bbc.co.uk/news/world-europe-18085399.

43. Danica Kirka, "Olympic Flame Arrives in Britain," *NBC Sports*, updated May 18, 2012, http://m.nbcsports.com/content/olympic-flame-arrives-britain.

44. "Olympic Torch Route," *Guardian*, www.guardian.co.uk/torch-relay.

45. Owen, "Olympic Flame Handover from Greece to London."

46. Danica Kirka, "Olympic Torch Relay: David Beckham Welcomes Flame to Britain Ahead of 2012 London Games," *BBC*, May 18, 2012, http://www.bbc.co.uk/news/uk-18124460.

47. Trevor Huggins, "End It Like Beckham: Soccer Star Cut from Britain's Olympic Team," *Minneapolis Star Tribune*, June 28, 2012, http://www.startribune.com/sports/160663075.html.

48. Melissa Rohlin, "David Beckham Doesn't Make Britain's Olympic Team," *Los Angeles Times*, http://www.latimes.com/sports/sportsnow/la-david-beckham-doesnt-make-englands-olympic-team-20120628,0,6601351.story#axzz2daUw8uKv.

49. "Giggs Disappointed over Beckham Snub," *ESPN.com*, June 30, 2012, http://espnfc.com/news/story/_/id/1120260/giggs-disappointed-over-beckham-olympic-snub?cc=5901.

50. "David Beckham's Childhood Coach Reacts via Skype to Controversial Decision," *10 Group*, accessed September 15, 2013, http://the10group.isebox.net/skype-beckham-misses-squad/beckham-s-first-coach-reacts-to-david-missing-out-on-the-olympics/.

51. Laurie Hanna, "Goldenballs-Up: Anger at Olympic Ambassador Beckham's Snub by Team GB," *Mirror*, last modified June 28, 2012, http://www.mirror.co.uk/news/uk-news/david-beckham-olympics-football-snub-944630#ixzz2dZVVx300; "Beckham Left Out of Olympic Football Squad," *Sky Sports*, June 29, 2012, http://news.sky.com/story/953708/beckham-left-out-of-olympic-football-squad; Jonathan McEvoy and Charles Sale, "Beckham Agony at Olympic Snub: Coe Keen Hand Role to Former England Star," *Daily Mail*, June 28, 2012, http://www.dailymail.co.uk/sport/olympics/article-2165930/David-Beckham-London-2012-Olympics-Team-GB-squad.html#ixzz2q24IDXpt.

52. Ian Stewart Palmer, "Paul McCartney Says 'Idiot' Left Beckham Off Olympic Team," *FTB Pro*, last modified July 26, 2012, http://www.ftbpro.com/posts/ian.stewart.palmer/38827/paul-mccartney-says-idiot-left-beckham-off-olympic-team.

53. Hanna, "Goldenballs-Up: Anger at Olympic Ambassador Beckham's Snub by Team GB."

54. Huggins, "End It Like Beckham."

55. "Olympic Torch Passes Tower Bridge (with David Beckham On Board)," YouTube video at http://www.youtube.com/watch?v=vNskw9VNMxc&feature=related.

56. "Wembley Stadium, London, United Kingdom," *Designbuild-Network*, http://www.designbuild-network.com/projects/wembley.

57. "Football," *London 2012 Olympic Games, Team GB Media Guide*, 122–23.

58. J. J. Anisiobi, "No Hard Feelings Then: Patriotic David Beckham Watches Team GB's Victory against the UAE with Son Brooklyn and Prince William," *Daily Mail*, July 30, 2012, http://www.dailymail.co.uk/tvshowbiz/article-2180959/David-Beckham-supports-Team-GB-watches-sweep-aside-UAE-son-Brooklyn-Prince-William.html.

59. Anisiobi, "No Hard Feelings Then."

60. Paul Vale, "London 2012: David Cameron and David Beckham Enjoy BMX Final," *Huffington Post*, updated August 13, 2012, http://www.huffingtonpost.co.uk/2012/08/10/london-2012-david-cameron-david-beckham-bmx-final-olympics_n_1764504.html.

61. Gina Serpe, "David Beckham and Sons Cheer on Misty May-Treanor, Kerri Walsh Jennings to Beach Volleyball Threepeat," *Huffington Post*, August 9, 2012, http://www.huffingtonpost.co.uk/2012/08/09/david-beckham-beach-volleyball_n_1759006.html.

62. Kimberley Dadds, "Gold for Best Spectator! David Beckham Takes to the Olympics with His Boys AGAIN and Goes Wild as Team GB Pick Up More Medals," *Daily Mail*, August 11, 2012, http://www.dailymail.co.uk/tvshowbiz/article-2187179/David-Beckham-takes-Olympics-boys-AGAIN-goes-wild-Mo-Farrah-wins-medal.html#ixzz2dkapfjLE.

63. Dadds, "Gold for Best Spectator!"

64. "2012 London Olympics Day 14: David Beckham," *New York Daily News*, August 10, 2012, http://www.nydailynews.com/sports/2012-london-olympics-day-14-david-beckham-takes-bmx-racing-men-hoops-takes-center-stage-gallery-1.1133758#ixzz2dhYxapno; Ariana Finlayson, "Men's USA Basketball Team Wins Olympic Gold!" *US*, August 12, 2012, http://www.usmagazine.com/celebrity-news/news/mens-usa-basketball-team-wins-olympic-gold-2012128#ixzz2q3cIKK5G.

65. "Victoria Beckham and the Spice Girls Rock the Olympics Closing Ceremony," *In Style.co.uk*, August, 13, 2012, http://www.instyle.co.uk/celebrity/news/victoria-beckham-and-the-spice-girls-rock-the-olympics-closing-ceremony#ORhgaiS5fMqLpyYi.99; "Victoria Beckham wows at Olympic Closing Ceremony," *Belfast Telegraph*, August 13, 2012, http://www.belfasttelegraph.co.uk/woman/fashion-beauty/victoria-beckham-wows-at-olympics-closing-ceremony-28780538.html; Sarah Karmali, "Spice for a Night," *Vogue*, August 13, 2012, http://www.vogue.co.uk/news/2012/08/13/victoria-beckham-talks-overwhelming-spice-girls-closing-ceremony-reunion---dresses-georgia-may-jagger; Tim Nixon, "Girls Spice up the Closing Ceremony," *Sun*, August 13, 2012, http://www.thesun.co.uk/sol/homepage/showbiz/4484895/Spice-Girls-steal-the-show-at-the-London-Olympics-2012-closing-ceremony.html.

66. "Victoria Beckham and the Spice Girls Rock the Olympics Closing Ceremony."

67. Ilya Leybovich, "2012 London Olympics by the Numbers," *Thomasnet*, August 7, 2012, http://news.thomasnet.com/IMT/2012/08/07/2012-london-olympics-by-the-numbers/.

CHAPTER 11

1. Paul Gittings, "Beckham Plays Final Home Match to Tears and Cheers," *CNN*, updated May 20, 2013, http://www.cnn.com/2013/05/18/sport/football/football-psg-beckham-farewell-game/.

2. "David Beckham Joins Paris St-Germain and Will Play for Free," *BBC Sport*, January 31, 2013, http://www.bbc.com/sport/0/football/21281665.

3. "David Beckham Joins PSG, Will Donate Salary to Charity," *Sports Illustrated .com*, January 31, 2013, http://sportsillustrated.cnn.com/soccer/news/20130131/david-beckham-sign-french-club.ap/#ixzz2q0cnN5eb.

4. Simon Kuper, "David Beckham's Career, What Will Happen to Beckham: Our Predictions," *AskMen.com*, http://www.askmen.com/sports/fanatic/david-beckham-s-career.html.

5. Alex Miller, "Beckham's Shirt and Boot Sales Stand at a Staggering £1 Billion . . . and PSG Expect to Bank £15m," *Daily Mail*, February 9, 2013, http://www.dailymail.co.uk/sport/football/article-2276177/David-Beckham-shirt-sales-1billion.html.

6. Brooks Peck, "About 150 Reporters Showed Up to Watch David Beckham's Boring First Training Session with PSG," *Dirty Tackle*, February 13, 2013, http://sports.yahoo.com/blogs/soccer-dirty-tackle/150-reports-showed-watch-david-beckham-boring-first-192828698--sow.html.

7. Gittings, "Beckham Plays Final Home Match to Tears and Cheers."

8. "David Beckham 'Passionate' about Being Club Owner," *CNN.com*, October 30, 2013, http://edition.cnn.com/2013/10/30/sport/football/football-david-beckham-club-owner/.

9. "Bio Beckham DRJ," *England Football Online*, page last updated May 16, 2013, http://www.englandfootballonline.com/TeamPlyrsBios/PlayersB/BioBeckhamDRJ.html.

10. Chris Sherman, "2003's Most Wanted Search Terms," *Search Engine Watch*, January 6, 2004, http://searchenginewatch.com/article/2065650/2003s-Most-Wanted-Search-Terms.

11. Interview, Ellis Cashmore, a professor of culture, media, and sport at Staffordshire University in the United Kingdom, 2013.

12. "#thankyoudavidbeckham," *Twitter*, May 16, 2013, https://twitter.com/search?q=%23ThankYouDavidBeckham&src=typd.

13. Bob Bensch, "David Beckham Says He'll Retire After 21-Year Career," *Bloomberg*, May 16, 2013, http://www.bloomberg.com/news/2013-05-16/beckham-to-retire-from-soccer-after-season-sky-sports-says.html.

14. "Paul Scholes Sad to See Former Manchester United Teammate David Beckham Retire," *Independent*, May, 17, 2013, http://www.independent.co.uk/sport/football/news-and-comment/paul-scholes-sad-to-see-former-manchester-united-teammate-david-beckham-retire-8620441.html.

15. "David Beckham Retires—Thursday 16 May as It Happened," *BBC Sport*, May 16, 2013, http://www.bbc.com/sport/0/22550271.

16. Simon Austin, "Beckham: Football's Global Superstar," *BBC Sport*, May 16, 2013, http://m.bbc.com/sport/football/22559139.

17. "Reaction to David Beckham's Retirement," *Agence France Presse*, May 17, 2013, http://sports.ndtv.com/football/news/207890-reaction-to-david-beckhams-retirement.

18. Patrick Surlis, "Rooney Pays Tribute to David Beckham on Retirement," *Give Me Sport*, May 16, 2013, http://www.givemesport.com/345943-rooney-pays-tribute-to-david-beckham-on-retirement.

19. Austin, "Beckham: Football's Global Superstar."

20. "Paul Scholes Sad to See Former Manchester United Teammate David Beckham Retire."

21. "David Beckham Retires—Thursday 16 May as It Happened"

22. Jenn Selby and Rebecca Cox, "Victoria Beckham Opens Up about David's Retirement Plans," *Glamour*, June 5, 2013, http://www.glamourmagazine.co.uk/news/celebrity/2013/06/05/victoria-beckham-opens-up-david-retirement-plans.

23. Peter Simpson, "Beckham and the Great Wall of Hysteria," *Daily Mail*, June 20, 2013, http://www.dailymail.co.uk/news/article-2345084/Beckham-Great-Wall-Hysteria-Fans-injured-stampede-David-Beckham-met-hysteria-arrives-Chinese-university.html; "Beckham China Visit Causes Stampede," *ESP.NFC.com*, June 20, 2013, http://espnfc.com/news/story/_/id/1480973/david-beckham-visit-causes-stampede-china?cc=5901; "Fans Stampede David Beckham in China, at Least 5 Injured," *UPI*, June 2013; http://www.upi.com/Sports_News/2013/06/20/Fans-stampede-David-Beckham-in-China-at-least-5-injured/UPI-47171371750959/.

24. "Beckham China Visit Causes Stampede."

25. "Chinese Super League," *Asian Football Feast*, http://www.asianfootballfeast.com/?portfolio=chinese-super-league-2.

26. "Beckham Agrees China Deal," *ESPN.com*, March 4, 2013, http://www.espn.co.uk/football/sport/story/195891.html#1gpD5z65jkL4gFBZ.99 http://www.espn.co.uk/football/sport/story/195891.html#8rpISVrScy96tjQx.99.

27. "Beckham China Visit Causes Stampede."

28. Ian McPherson, "IMG's Jeff Slack on David Beckham's Role in China," *Sports Pro*, March 14, 2013, http://www.sportspromedia.com/quick_fire_questions/imgs_jeff_slack_on_david_beckhams_role_in_china/.

29. Zachary Keck, "David Beckham in China as Football Ambassador," *Diplomat*, March 21, 2013, http://thediplomat.com/2013/03/david-beckham-in-china-as-football-ambassador/.

30. "Beckham: I Pick Kids over Knighthood," *Yahoo! Celebrity*, December 28, 2013, http://ph.omg.yahoo.com/news/beckham-pick-kids-over-knighthood-030000333.html.

31. "David Beckham Picks Miami for MLS Franchise," *Sports Illustrated*, October 29, 2013, http://sportsillustrated.cnn.com/soccer/news/20131029/david-beckham-miami-mls-franchise.ap/#ixzz2s2dLhMPH.

32. "David Beckham 'Passionate' about Being Club Owner," *CNN.com*, October 30, 2013, http://edition.cnn.com/2013/10/30/sport/football/football-david-beckham-club-owner/.

33. "LeBron on MLS in Miami: 'We're Working on It,'" *Sports Illustrated*, November 21, 2013, http://sportsillustrated.cnn.com/soccer/news/20131121/lebron-james-mls-miami-beckham.ap/.

34. John D. Halloran, "Examining What a David Beckham-Owned Franchise Would Bring to MLS," *Bleacher Report*, January 2, 2014, http://bleacherreport.com/articles/1908193-examining-what-a-david-beckham-owned-franchise-would-bring-to-mls.

35. "Beckham's Miami Soccer Stadium Search Gets Green Light," *Toronto Sun*, December 17, 2013, http://www.torontosun.com/2013/12/17/beckhams-miami-soccer-stadium-search-gets-green-light; Patricia Mazzei, "David Beckham's Bid to Bring Soccer to S. Fla. and Win Over Fans Is No Easy Task," *Miami Herald*, November 3, 2013, http://www.miamiherald.com/2013/11/03/3727850/david-beckhams-bid-to-bring-soccer.html.

36. Interview, Ellis Cashmore, professor of culture, media, and sport at Staffordshire University in the United Kingdom, 2013.

37. Kevin Palmer, "David Beckham: A National Treasure on and off the Field," *ESPNFC.com*, May, 16, 2013, http://espnfc.com/blog/_/name/espnfcunited/id/5728?cc=5901.

38. "David Beckham Retires—Thursday 16 May as It Happened."

39. Phil McNulty, "David Beckham Retirement: Roll Call of Great Clubs Proves His Quality," *BBC Sport*, May 16, 2013, http://www.bbc.com/sport/0/football/22562501.

40. Jeré Longman and Sam Borden, "Beckham, at 38, Says He'll Bend It No Longer," *New York Times*, May 16, 2013, http://www.nytimes.com/2013/05/17/sports/soccer/david-beckham-announces-retirement-from-soccer.html?pagewanted=1&_r=0.

41. "David Beckham: World's Press Full of Praise for Ex-England Skipper," *BBC Sport*, May 17, 2013, http://www.bbc.com/sport/0/football/22568347.

42. Iain Macintosh, "This David Was a Goliath," *ESPNFC.com*, May 16, 2013, http://espnfc.com/blog/_/name/bootroom/id/302?cc=5901.

43. Jonathan Wilson, "Beckham's Skills with the Ball Were Long Overshadowed by His Celebrity," *Sports Illustrated*, May 16, 2013, http://sportsillustrated.cnn.com/soccer/news/20130516/david-beckham-retiring-psg-column/#ixzz2q12xkj7zhttp://sportsillustrated.cnn.com/soccer/news/20130516/david-beckham-retiring-psg-column/#ixzz2U4VwKzad.

44. "David Beckham: World's Press Full of Praise."

45. Paul Campbell, "David Beckham: Product of Sir Alex Ferguson's School of Hard Graft," *Guardian*, May 17, 2013, http://www.theguardian.com/football/blog/2013/may/17/david-beckham-alex-ferguson-manchester-united.

46. Beckham, David, *David Beckham* (London: Headline), 108.

47. "Beckham Announces Retirement," *ESPNFC.com*, May 16, 2013, http://espnfc.com/news/story/_/id/1449804/david-beckham-announces-retirement?cc=5901.

RECOMMENDED READING

Beckham, David. *David Beckham*. London: Headline, 2013.

Beckham, David, with photography by Dean Freeman. *Beckham: My World*. London: Hodder and Stoughton, 2000.

Beckham, David, with Tom Watt. *Both Feet on the Ground: An Autobiography*. New York: It Books, 2004.

Beckham, Victoria. *Learning to Fly: The Autobiography*. New York: Penguin Global, 2005.

Russell, Gwen. *Arise Sir David Beckham: The Biography of Britain's Greatest Footballer*. London: John Blake, 2007.

Wahl, Grant. *The Beckham Experiment*. New York: Three Rivers Press, 2010.

INDEX

ABOUT THE AUTHOR

Tracey Savell Reavis is a veteran journalist and sports historian who has worked as a reporter at *Sports Illustrated* magazine, press officer for the U.S. Olympic Committee, staff writer at the National Basketball Association, and director of research at Callaway Golf Media Ventures. She is a member of the International Society of Olympic Historians and travels throughout the United States and Europe covering sports events.

In more than fifteen years in the industry, Reavis has also covered the National Football League and NFL Europe, the Professional Golf Association, and the Pan American Games. Based in Washington, D.C., Reavis counts as some of her greatest career moments the thrill of standing on the pitcher's mound at Yankee Stadium, on center court at Madison Square Garden, on the fifty yard line at Giants Stadium, on the pitch at Camp Nou, and attending the opening ceremony of the Atlanta Olympic Games.